INFORMATION BOOKS FOR CHILDREN

INFORMATION BOOKS FOR CHILDREN

Edited by

Keith Barker

Published by
Ashgate Publishing Limited
Gower House
Croft Road
Aldershot
Hants GU11 3HR
England

Ashgate Publishing Co
Old Post Road
Brookfield
Vermont 05036
USA

British Library Cataloguing in Publication Data is available

ISBN 1 85742 023 3

Printed in Great Britain by
Billing & Sons Ltd, Worcester

CONTENTS

◆

CONTENTS

INTRODUCTION

◆

The importance of information

Lip service has always been paid to the importance of children and young people developing and using ways of retrieving information, both in education and the wider context, but it is only recently that this has been endorsed by legislation. Both the Scottish and the Northern Ireland education systems have pronounced the retrieving and utilization of information to be essential while the National Curriculum for England and Wales has declared its importance from the beginning. For example, attainment targets at level 3 in Science state that children should be able to store and retrieve information, while at level 5 in English they would be expected to 'select reference books and other materials in classroom and library collections or held on a computer and use organizational devices (e.g. chapter titles, sub-headings, symbol keys) to find answers to their own questions'.

Books have long been seen as a retrieval system for information and despite the increasing use of computerized systems, it is likely that book formats will retain their supremacy in this area for some time, mainly because of the diverse and attractive ways in which they can present information in comparison with their competitors. As long ago as 1659 the Moravian educator, Comenius, was using pictures and text in his famous encyclopedia, *Orbis pictus*, as a method of introducing young scholars to information. The techniques Comenius used are still the norm for children to absorb information from books despite the modern use of full colour photography and typographical techniques to provide information.

The purpose of this book

With the number of children's books published increasing each year, it is important for those who have the responsibility of selecting material for young people to be given the opportunity to choose only those books which are most suitable and of a high enough standard. Information book publishing accounts for about 40 per cent of the 5000 titles published for children each year. It is difficult for even the most assiduous selectors to keep up to date and even more difficult for them to be totally *au fait* with the subject matter of the books they are considering. That is where this book aims to help.

Nearly 500 current children's information book titles are assessed by a range of reviewers who not only have expertise in the subjects covered but are also fully aware of the needs of young people through their work for the quarterly journal, *The School Librarian*. The majority of the books included here are recommended: where a title is included about which the reviewer has some doubt, it is usually there because no other book exists on that topic. Obviously there will be gaps: new titles are being published at an alarming rate but there are still some subjects not adequately covered by the plethora of information book titles. It is hoped that any future editions of this book will fill any existing gaps or supply better versions of those books which cannot be wholeheartedly recommended.

So how can this book be used? It can be used by teachers looking for titles within their subject area or selecting books for their school library. It can be used by librarians as a selection tool for filling gaps in stock or as a stock list for a new collection. It can be used by parents whose children have a voracious appetite for a particular subject or just as a guide to the wide variety of available material. Or it could be used as an indication of the state of children's information book publishing as we head towards a new century.

Publishing

Information book publishing, whether for adults or children, has always been less glamorous than its fiction counterpart. Media coverage is geared to the blockbuster saga, preferably by a famous actress, while the information book plods on, selling copies steadily but not remarkably. What distinguishes information book publishing for young people from the publishing of picture books and novels? For one thing, an information book is likely to remain in print for a longer period – somewhat surprising in view of the fact that our perception of facts is changing all the time. The book is more likely to be published by a publisher whose main trade is in information books: some publishers have dealt with both fiction and information books but the spread is not as wide as it is with fiction publishing. And of those specialist publishers, two of them will produce over 45 per cent of the titles produced each year.

So where does this leave the subjects covered by these information books? It could be said that with such a restriction on the variety of publishers, there is likely to be a limit to subjects and also to the way information is displayed. It is certainly true that the double page spread is incredibly dominant in information book publishing although in recent years some publishers, most notably Dorling Kindersley, have found new ways of presenting information (or could it be an old way redesigned?). There are gaps also in the subjects covered, if the titles in this book are to be examined (although, of course, it is a selective collection). Animal subjects are prolific; titles on the environment are increasing monthly; and topics like social issues, health and sexual matters are well covered. But where are the writers who can successfully explain politics to young people or the magic and mystery of religion? Why does there appear to be no other period of German history of interest than the Third Reich and why is chemistry less fascinating than physics?

How to find your way around this book

The arrangement of the titles in this book follows the *Dewey Decimal Classification for school libraries* (4th edition, 1986) as it was felt this is the most frequently used method to classify books in school and children's libraries. Therefore all the vagaries of the Dewey system are in force (e.g. flags sandwiched between biography and history). As anyone who has ever tried to classify a book knows, it is often difficult to slot it into only one place. It is hoped that if you do have problems finding particular items, the indexes will be a useful guide.

Each entry follows the same pattern:

Author

Title

Publication and bibliographical details

Review of book

Reviewer's initials

Age range

The age range is approximate, mainly because each child has different needs. However, it was decided to include an age range so that, for instance, teachers would not become too interested in a book which is totally wrong for their pupils. But do treat these age ranges with some liberality.

NOTES ON CONTRIBUTORS

◆

Editor

KEITH BARKER is the author of *In the realms of gold: the story of the Carnegie Medal* (Julia MacRae) and compiler of *Bridging the gap* (Book Trust/British Council) and *The School library selection of recommended books* (Bailey). He is the review editor of *The School Librarian* and editor of *Youth Library Review*. He has written numerous journal articles on children's literature. He is a librarian at Newman/Westhill Colleges, Birmingham.

The Reviewers

JOHN FELTWELL (JF) is director of 'Wildlife Matters', an organization established in 1978 to promote conservation and education. When he is not in Asian rainforests or North American deserts he is busy working from his bases in England and France. He has published 22 books in the last ten years.

ROBIN GREGORY (RG) is tutor librarian for the Litcham Federation of Schools, Norfolk.

PRABHU GUPTARA (PSG) reviews for a number of journals including *Times Literary Supplement* and is the author of *India in the classroom* (Commonwealth Institute) and *Black British literature* (Dangaroo Press).

STUART HANNABUSS (SH) teaches management and statistics at the School of Librarianship and Information Studies at Robert Gordon's Institute of Technology at Aberdeen. He has written and reviewed widely on children's literature and published *Managing children's literature* (MCB University Press).

JOHN HEATON (JH) is a former principal lecturer in physical education at St Paul's College, Cheltenham, and the author of several books on athletics. He is life president of the British Colleges Sports Association.

HILARY MINNS (HM) is an educational consultant and former headteacher. She is the author of *Read it to me now!* (Virago), editor of *English in education* and general editor of *Primary Associations*.

PIPPA RANN (PMR) has reviewed for a number of journals including *British Book News*.

JILL WARREN (JW) is teacher of juniors and school librarian at Richard Pate School, Cheltenham.

FRANK WARREN (WFW) is a retired teacher and university lecturer and is now a freelance writer. He regularly reviews books and concerts for the press.

SUE DAVIS (SD), STEWART SCOTT (SS) and BARBARA SLATER (BS) are teachers at Courthouse Green Primary School, Coventry.

All the contributors review children's books regularly for *The School Librarian*, the quarterly journal of the School Library Association. For more details of this journal contact the School Library Association, Liden Library, Barrington Close, Liden, Swindon, Wiltshire SN3 6HF.

BOOKS AND LIBRARIES

◆

What better way to introduce young people to the importance of using books for information than to show children in books doing just that – and also getting pleasure in the process!

GAWITH, Gwen

LIBRARY ALIVE! PROMOTING READING AND RESEARCH IN THE SCHOOL LIBRARY

Black, 1987, Hdbk, 0–7136–2900–2
Contents list, black and white line drawings

This work first appeared in 1983 under the title *Library Alive!* and has established itself as an imaginative stimulus for librarians wanting to use the library in a lively and enjoyable way. Look at who, what, where, when and how, and that will give you a framework for library promotion. There are some fifty promotion activities, all copyright-free for reproduction. For busy or beginning teachers and librarians working with children 7 to 12, this is an especially useful feature. Some activities are games (make a joke book, design a space-age library), others classic library skills made fresh and new (like designing a Dewey mobile). All are presented with text and witty diagrams (for the author is both writer and illustrator), with a clear practical application: given such advice, anyone can make something similiar, and trust that it will work. Research is also important – retrieval, bibliographical, reading skills: there are helpful pages of advice on what to do, and the underlying structure and rationale for it. It looks like a picture book for children, but it's really for teachers and librarians who work with them. Distinctive books like this are very much for children in terms of what they can help us to achieve.

SH

Age range: For adults (especially librarians) dealing with children (especially 7–12)

GRIFFITHS, Vivien and FAIRCLOUGH, Chris

MY CLASS GOES TO THE LIBRARY

Franklin Watts, 1985, Hdbk, 0–86313–321–5
Series: My Class . . .
Colour photographs

The reader joins a class of primary children visiting the local public library. It is now, in Birmingham, and our special friend is Angela. She and her friends are in most of the large, bold, colourful photographs, so we get to know them well. The setting is instantly recognizable even though readers may live somewhere else. Vivien Griffiths is the experienced Head of Services to Children and Young People at Birmingham Public Libraries, and does two good things with this book. First, she tells it like it is: going through the streets to the library, meeting the librarian, listening to a story, and then borrowing a book. Second, books like this spread values. It's all easy and fun. You don't need to rush. When she is back home, Angela knows that she can go back on her own and choose a book for her small brother. Griffiths gets a lot across without preaching. A good book for parents and teachers who know the value of encouraging the library habit early on.

SH

Age range: 7–9

KNIGHT, Julia

BOOK PUBLISHING

Wayland, 1988, Hdbk, 1–85210–239–X
Series: The Media
Bibliography, contents list, glossary, index, further information, black and white and colour line drawings and photographs.

This series aims to encourage a critical awareness of the impact of the media on society. This work concentrates on issues now and does it very well, although the lively historical introduction does rather over-simplify. On fiction publishing it opens up issues like bestsellers, media tie-ins, and obscenity which are good topics for personal research. Non-fiction publishing gets shrewd coverage, particularly in terms of the control of ideas (from Darwin and Marx to *Spycatcher*). The range of jobs and participants in the contemporary publishing industry, and issues like net prices, the power of conglomerates, and feminist writing is well chosen, stimulating, and topical. Developments in desktop publishing and videodisc are noted. Text is concise and authoritative, full of good ideas and given impact by informative illustrations with telling captions. Imaginative use of the index will enable readers to pursue themes like copyright further than they think. A totally professional product for young people.

SH

Age range: 10–15

THOMSON, Ruth and FAIRCLOUGH, Chris

MAKING A BOOK

Franklin Watts, 1988, Hdbk, 0–86313–539–0
Series: Making . . .
Contents list, index, black and white and colour
line drawing and colour photographs

This is a series which shows how familiar objects like pencils are made. *Making a Book* literally takes a book, *Piggybook* by writer-illustrator Anthony Browne, and follows it through all its stages from the idea to the book for sale in a shop. Each stage is clearly described in untechnical but accurate language, and realized in precise photographs. The reader sees the dummy, the paste-up and the printing. Characters like illustrator, editor, and designer appear regularly for continuity and total credibility. We get a sense of a team of real people at work producing a real book. Their jobs are interesting, one follows on logically from another, and the reader is likely to look at the very book in their hand in a new way. The style of presentation is not new, and there are other works on the subject, but this one has thought of everthing.

SH

Age range: 8–11

RELIGIONS

◆

The earliest children's books were used as a tool to guide children into thinking about religion. Since then writers have tried to avoid a non-didactic approach in discussing religion and have tried to make their readers understand the feelings of various religious faiths throughout the world, an important element in their tolerance of others.

THE BIBLE

TURNER, Philip

THE BIBLE STORY

OUP, 1989, Pbk, 0–19–273160–2
Contents list, colour line drawings

For whom was this book written? Children brought up to enjoy Brian Wildsmith's illustrations from an early age? Certainly, scenes from the Bible lend themselves to his inimitable style and presented no difficulty to his imagination.

Far greater is the difficulty of abridging Bible stories, for some children would expect to find familiar phrases and incidents in the stories they know, only to find that they were cut out during the abridgement.

However, as a reviewer limited to 150 words, I can fully appreciate the problems that Philip Turner has had to face in producing his versions of these Bible stories and I do not need the instruction that the editor of the *Homilist* gave to his reviewers, not to criticize an author for what he has omitted!

In choosing the language for the stories, he has neither lost sight of the Authorized Version completely, nor simplified it to the extent that it can be read easily by a child.

However, it could be read by an adult to a child, who is looking at the illustrations, or by a child that is a competent reader, with prompting help from an adult.

WFW

Age range: 7–11

CHRISTIANITY

BROWN, Alan and PERKINS, Judy

CHRISTIANITY

Batsford, 1988, Hdbk, 0–7134–5319–2
Series: Dictionaries of World Religions
Bibliography, index, list of dates, black and white photographs

This dictionary is an excellent source of information on specific topics related to Christianity that students might be asked to study for G.C.S.E. in R.E. These topics are arranged alphabetically for quick and easy reference; cross references are also given. The dictionary's concise entries, taken together, provide an introduction to Christianity and a clear account of its history from its roots in Judaism to its multidenominational presence throughout the world today.

There are five other dictionaries in this series, each devoted to a world religion. Although it is easy to spot omissions in these dictionaries, they are highly informative, accurate and well presented.
WFW

Age range: 11–16

KILLINGRAY, Margaret

I AM AN ANGLICAN

Franklin Watts, 1986, Hdbk, 0–86313–427–0
Series: My Belief
Contents list, glossary, index, colour photographs

The writer of this attractive book has looked at her faith through the eyes of her daughters – particularly Joanna, a ten-year-old – and expanded this view with explanatory text and background information in a fact and figures section.

Superb photographs, specially taken by Chris Fairclough, some in the Killingrays' home and church in Sevenoaks, show various aspects of their belief so well that there has been little need to use artwork illustration. The book has been checked by their bishop suffragan (the Bishop of Tonbridge) who acted as consultant.

There can be little doubt that this book will be of interest (perhaps, of inspriation!) to other Anglican children, and of value in a multifaith school (the book is one of a series) by giving an intimate view of the Established Church.
WFW

Age range: 8–13

MARTIN, Nancy

THE LIVES OF THE SAINTS

Wayland, 1986, Hdbk, 0–85078–885–4
Series: Religious Stories
Bibliography, contents list, glossary, list of feast days, colour line drawings

This is a story book that tells us briefly about the lives of nine saints. Each story is illustrated by coloured drawings to please the individual reader, but written in such a way that it could be read aloud in the classroom.

The selection of just nine names from the Church Calendar is very much an individual choice. Some names (such as Mukasa) will probably be unfamiliar to most children. The dates given as their feast days are in some cases surprising, too, e.g. for St Francis of Assisi, 6 October, rather than 4 October. (12 July is given for St Veronica, according to the Roman Calendar, rather than 4 February, the date given in many Anglican Books of Saints.)
WFW

Age range: 7–9

MOORE, Inga

PRAYERS FOR CHILDREN

Kingfisher, 1988, Hdbk, 0–86272–310–8
Contents list, colour line drawings

This selection of 58 prayers is set out in six sections, according to different moods and times of day, and beautifully illustrated by Inga Moore.

Besides new prayers, and those from far away, children will find old favourites, familiar to their parents: indeed, their diversity is matched only by the diversity of the illustrations and the moods and sentiments they reflect.

WFW

Age range: 7–11

PETTENUZZO, Brenda

I AM A PENTECOSTAL

Franklin Watts, 1986, Hdbk, 0–86313–428–9
Series: My Belief
Contents list, glossary, index, facts and figures, colour line drawings and photographs

This book looks at belief through the eyes of an 11-year-old Pentecostal child, Josephine Regis, met by the author Brenda Pettenuzzo. The book is well designed, with explanatory text and background information in the facts and figures section, and illustrative artwork (e.g. Josephine's family tree and a map to show its ethnic roots). The superb photographs, taken by Chris Fairclough, show the home life, places of worship and many other aspects of life in a Pentecostal family. The book has been checked by Pastor Io Smith, General Secretary of the N.T. Assemblies (UK), who acted as consultant. To echo the reviewer of another book in this series, 'Since suspicion and distrust are born out of ignorance, this book, like the others in this series, cannot be but welcome.'

WFW

Age range: 9–13

WATSON, Carol

365 CHILDREN'S PRAYERS

Lion, 1989, Hdbk, 0–7459–1454–3
Contents list, index, colour line drawings

This book is aptly subtitled 'Prayers old and new for to-day and every day', for, besides a few well loved and traditional prayers using such time-honoured phrases as 'by Thy providence', 'steadfast love', and 'diligent spirit', there are many new and topical ones, including some written recently by children in their own language. They were compiled by an experienced freelance writer of children's books, formerly a teacher and a Sunday School superintendent, for use at home, in church and at school, and dedicated to her godchildren.

The prayers, mostly Christian (though some could be used by children of other faiths) are arranged by theme – beginning with home, school and everyday experiences, moving out to cover wider issues, the world, other people, and our different feelings. There are also prayers for special occasions such as birthdays and Church festivals. The list of contents and the indexes, by subject and by first phrases, make it easy for parents, teachers and children to find specific prayers.

The book, with its imaginative colour illustrations, is attractive, and would be an appreciated addition to any child's library.

WFW

Age range: 7–11

COMPARATIVE RELIGIONS

MAYLED, Jon

DEATH CUSTOMS

Wayland, 1986, Hdbk, 0–85078–719–X
Series: Religious Topics
Bibliography, contents list, glossary, index,
colour photographs

Great as the instinct for self-preservation is, it is only on the death of a loved one that most healthy individuals give much thought to their own mortality.

Bereavement is often associated with religious experience and all religions have their special death customs. Whether the bereaved mourn the sad event, or celebrate the life that has ended, each religious group honours the dead and comforts the bereaved according to its own beliefs and traditions.

This excellent little book considers briefly the death customs of seven of the principal religions of the world. The sensible text is illustrated by a colour photograph on every page.

WFW

Age range: 9–13

MAYLED, Jon

HOLY BOOKS

Wayland, 1986, Hdbk, 0–85078–770–X
Series: Religious Topics
Bibliography, contents list, glossary, index,
colour photographs

Most religions have a holy book (or holy books) which contain stories and teaching about their God or gods. Here, about four pages are devoted to the holy books of each of six of the principal religions of the world (Buddhism, Christianity, Hinduism, Islam, Judaism and Sikhism).

The book is clearly written and should prove useful to those seeking information about the holy books, history and culture of these religions.

WFW

Age range: 7–11

MAYLED, Jon and PARAÏSO, Aviva

RELIGIOUS FOOD

Wayland, 1987, Hdbk, 1–85210–039–7
Series: Religious Topics
Bibliography, contents list, glossary, index,
colour photographs

Many of the major religions of the world have religious laws that state which foods worshippers can or cannot eat. Some of these rules concern food in everyday life and others relate to the special foods which people prepare for their festivals.

Some explanations of these laws and customs are given, but for many customs the religious significance is largely lost, or would require lengthy explanation that would be unsuitable for a book for Juniors.

This, no doubt, accounts for the fact that no mention is made of the sacramental use of bread and wine by Christians at the Eucharist, nor is the Seder meal at Pesach mentioned in the chapter on Judaism (although the co-author, Aviva Paraïso, has discussed the Seder meal in another Wayland book, *Jewish Food and Drink*), nor is mention made of the common custom in affluent Hindu communities of giving sweets to children as they leave their Hindu temple.

The book is simply written and attractively illustrated.

WFW

Age range: 7–11

OBADIAH and FAIRCLOUGH, Chris

I AM A RASTAFARIAN

Franklin Watts, 1986, Hdbk, 0–86313–260–X
Series: My Belief
Glossary, index, facts and figures, black and white and colour photographs

For a world of mixed and no faith, reliable information about what and why people believe is important, particularly for primary school where prejudices can easily be formed. Attractively presented in colour photos and blocked text, some as if told by 8-year-old Petra, a girl living in Birmingham, the rest more authoritative from Obadiah (the president of the Birmingham branch of the Ethiopian World Federation), this book has an immediacy and desire to inform which will make it very useful for children and teachers and parents dealing with them. Believing that Ras Tafari (or Heile Selassie) is the human form of Jah (or God), and basing their beliefs on the Old Testament, Rastafarians live, eat, dress, and celebrate in ways outsiders may not understand. This introduction will help children understand belief and lifestyle better, and suggest ways round any ideological introversion which informs some areas of British education.

SH

Age range: 6–9

YUAN-MING, Shui and THOMPSON, Stuart

CHINESE STORIES

Wayland, 1986, Hdbk, 0–85078–886–2
Series: Religious Stories
Bibliography, contents list, glossary, colour line drawings

Traditional Chinese religious beliefs seem mysterious to the newcomer. The medium of story is a good way to introduce them to children, particularly when, as here, the language is designed for storytelling and the typography is like handwriting. Confucian, Tao and Buddhist ideas about virtue, living well, and honouring other people easily underpin these five tales, based on early sutras or scriptures. We see the world made, a journey to hell, and the way a woman honours her husband for dying in the building of the Great Wall. Artwork draws on Chinese and Buddhist conventions to provide a colourful and mysterious backdrop to the stories. Both stories and pictures can be enjoyed by children on their own, and used in groups or classroom for a journey of discovery into the field of Chinese folk story and culture. A useful textual note for adults suggests applications.

SH

Age range: 6–9

BUDDHISM

MORGAN, Peggy

BUDDHISM

Batsford, 1987, Hdbk, 0-7134-5203-X
Series: Dictionaries of World Religions
Bibliography, index, black and white line
drawings and photographs

A curious dictionary, this, devoting more space to the minority cult of Soka Gakkai than to the Buddha. Also it has unnecessarily difficult explanations such as: Gautama 'is thought to be the *buddha* to teach this world aeon'. The author appears to be a convert to Buddhism, which need be no bad thing, except that she allows it to show in the book. Otherwise, the book is fairly comprehensive in its coverage.

PMR

Age range: 14–18

HINDUISM

SINGH, Rani and Jugnu and MULLICK, Biman

THE AMAZING ADVENTURES OF HANUMAN

BBC, 1988, Pbk, 0–563–21426–0
Colour line drawings

Tales from the famous Indian classic *The Ramayana* have perennial appeal for their magic, humour and suspense. Hanuman, the monkey-human hero who dies from a thunderbolt after upsetting the sun, and revives with magic powers, sets off to rescue princess Sita, Rama's wife, who has been captured by the ten-headed and armed demon Ravana. His search leads him across the sea, into the belly of the sea-monster, into Ravana's impregnable palace, and escape by fire and ingenuity. The epic magic of the tale, with its battles and matter-of-fact dialogue, is enhanced by the skilful evocative graphics of the pictures, based on traditional designs and full of ingenious shapes of monsters, landscapes, and Hanuman himself smiling in anticipation of victory. The pictures originated with the BBC Schools Radio Programme *Let's Join In*. Good for storytelling in playgroup, infant school and at home, and for personal reading, the paperback option makes it a good present too.

SH

Age range: 5–9

SIKHISM

ARORA, Ranjit

SIKHISM

Wayland, 1986, Hdbk, 0–85078–723–8
Series: Religions of the World
Bibliography, contents list, glossary, index, map,
colour photographs

Sikhism is the youngest of the main world religions – founded in 1469 by Guru Nanak and developed over the following 200 years by ten successive Gurus. Like most religions, Sikhism is a way of life. Sikhs believe in one God and teach that people should work hard and share with the poor. They place great stress on the equality of all human beings and their Gurdwaras (places of worship) are open to everyone.

Most Sikhs live in the Punjab State of Northern India and there is still friction between them and the Government of India over state boundaries. However, approximately a quarter of a million Sikhs live in Britain: this book shows how well they have adapted to life in a western country. Indeed, it is in multicultural schools that this book will be most useful.
JW

Age range: 9–15

KAPOOR, Sukhbir Singh

SIKH FESTIVALS

Wayland, 1985, Hdbk, 0–85078–573–1
Series: Festivals
Bibliography, contents list, glossary, index, date
chart, list of sikh Gurus, colour line drawings and
black and white and colour photographs

This book looks at the religious and seasonal festivals celebrated by followers of the Sikh faith, and shows how events in Sikh history are still remembered today, with cheerful and colourful ceremonies. Apart from Baisakhi, the first day of the Sikh and Hindu New Year, always celebrated on 13 April, the dates of most Sikh festivals depend on a lunar calendar, though the nearest Sunday to the actual date may be chosen, as it is difficult to celebrate a festival (some of the ceremonies are lengthy and boisterous!) on a working day.

The significance of each gurpurb (a festival associated with the life of a guru) and of each of the melas (fairs) that mark other festivals is briefly stated, and on each page there is a photograph (in most cases in full colour). The book should prove useful for religious education in schools – particularly in those towns where there are Sikh communities.
WFW

Age range: 9–13

JUDAISM

HANNIGAN, Lynne

SAM'S PASSOVER

Black, 1985, Hdbk, 0–7136–2646–1
Series: Celebrations
Bibliography, colour photographs

This book is one of a series that looks at special occasions, showing how they are celebrated at home, and shared by children at school.

In this book, Sam relates how he and his family celebrate the Passover, and how his class are told the story of Moses and the Flight from Egypt, and then how they find out more on a visit to a synagogue.

Well illustrated, the book will be of interest to Jewish children. It is suitable for the library of a multifaith school, and even for use in class. Although it is not part of the duty of such a school to induct the pupils into their particular faith (home and synagogue would do that in this case), children do need to be shown in a practical way that their faiths are acceptable, by having them taught in class.

WFW

Age range: 5–9

KORALEK, Jenny

HANUKKAH

Walker, 1989, Hdbk, 0–7445–1261–1
Colour line drawings

The heroic story of the Maccabees freeing Jerusalem from the Syrian yoke is simply told to explain Hanukkah, the Festival of Lights, and superbly illustrated by twelve coloured plates.

Such is the opulence of these illustrations (that look as if they were originally designed for pilastered wall panels) and the high quality of the printing, that this slim well bound attractive hardback will not only be popular as a gift book for presentation to Jewish children, but will have a wider appeal.

WFW

Age range: 7–11

NEUBERGER, Julia

THE STORY OF THE JEWS

CUP, 1986, Hdbk, 0–521–30601–9
Glossary, colour line drawings

This book is a delightful summary of the life of the Jews – within the limitations set by the format of the series (each small book is only 32 pages long). The series should find a place in any multifaith junior school: the value of this particular book will be in supplying simple information on Judaism to gentile children as much as to those from a Jewish background. It touches on many topics (e.g. the Dreyfus affair) in such a way as to arouse the interest of young readers and to encourage them to seek more information either by asking questions or by further reading.

The coloured drawings that illustrate the book are equally interesting.

WFW

Age range: 9–13

SHAMIR, Ilana and SHAVIT, Shlomo

THE YOUNG READER'S ENCYCLOPEDIA OF JEWISH HISTORY

Viking Kestrel, 1987, Hdbk, 0–670–81738–4
Contents list, glossary, index, black and white and colour line drawings and photographs

This book was written by Jews for young Jews, and first published in Israel by the Massada Press, but this new American edition is obviously aimed at readers other than young American Jews. It will (deservedly) find a place as a well illustrated, easy-to-read reference book in many libraries in this country – especially in secondary schools in which Judaism is taught as part of the R.E. course.

It is, however, essentially a history book rather than one on Judaism. It is an attractive, colourful, well bound hardback that will appeal to those aged 12 or over, for its clarity and its many interesting pictures and maps. Perhaps its title could be regarded as a misnomer – although for a history book it is more appropriate for the facts to be arranged as they are, chronologically rather than alphabetically.

It would be easy to criticize the layout and content of p.121 where 'key events' are set out in four columns, but the chronology is conventional (and, quite rightly, no attempt is made to discuss the recent disputes concerning the Sothic dating of events in Egyptian history).

Jewish history is described from a Jewish viewpoint, but the references to Christianity and Islam are brief and factual and cannot give offence to believers of those religions: Jesus is mentioned, by name, only twice, and Muhammad not at all.

Recent events related to Zionism are described, but there is no real discussion of the current problems of Israel, nor of the present conflict in the Middle East.

WFW

Age range: 11–16

WOOD, Jenny

JEWISH

Franklin Watts, 1988, Hdbk, 0–86313–670–2
Series: Our Culture
Glossary, index, summarized facts about Jews, colour photographs

Superb colour photographs are combined with a simple text, in large bold type, in this attractive book for young readers – one of an excellent series, designed to give an intimate view of some of the main cultures of the world today.

The book is ideal for a primary school library, for use as a class reference book in a multifaith school – or as a gift to a Jewish child.

WFW

Age range: 6–10

ISLAM

AL HOAD, Abdul Latif

ISLAM

Wayland, 1986, Hdbk, 0–85078–688–6
Series: Religions of the World
Contents list, glossary, index, black and white
and colour photographs

There are followers of Islam in almost every country of the world, united by their belief in Allah, the one God, whose word was revealed to the Prophet, Muhammad (Peace be upon him) and preserved in the *Qur'an*.

A brief life of the Prophet is given and an easily understandable view of Islam (despite the regrettable divisions) in the world today. Islam is presented not only as a belief but as a way of life.

The book describes the observance of the five 'Arkan' or Pillars of Faith, explains the complicated rituals which are performed by a pilgrim making the Hajj, and shows how Islamic teaching affects everyday life.

JW

Age range: 9–15

DAVIES, Maryam

THE LIFE OF MUHAMMAD

Wayland, 1987, Hdbk, 0–85078–904–4
Series: Religious Stories
Bibliography, contents list, glossary, notes for
teachers (including books to read and useful
addresses), colour line drawings

The total Muslim population of the world is about one thousand million – roughly the same as the number of Christians. Muslims are found in practically every country and they all believe in the same five pillars of Islam: that Allah is the one true God and Muhammad is His prophet; regular worship; giving alms; the Hajj (pilgrimage to Mecca); fasting during the month of Ramadan.

This book is written by a practising Muslim and a qualified primary school teacher who also trained as a journalist. It relates some of the events in the life of the Prophet Muhammad (Peace be upon him) in simple story form, with colourful modern book illustrations. There are also traditional Islamic geometric drawings, many of which contain Arabic calligraphy, quoted from the *Qur'an*. (The meaning of each quotation is given in English.)

JW

Age range: 7–11

THE SOCIAL SCIENCES

♦

A broad area this, covering everything from transport to racism to Christmas to parliament. It is an area which needs careful planning in the way its information is conveyed. Fortunately it is one which appeals to a number of talented writers.

SOCIAL ISSUES

ALLISON, P. J.

LET'S DISCUSS ANIMAL RIGHTS

Wayland, 1986, Hdbk, 0–85078–871–4
Series: Let's Discuss
Contents list, glossary, index, black and white photographs

This reads as a very dull book. It is full of black and white photographs, many of them outdated. The book is probably more useful to teachers for background information, than to students; even the oldest and brightest children would have difficulty reading the text. There is more topical information available than is presented here. However, there are not many books on this subject so it might marginally justify a place in the school library.

Age range: 12–16

JF

BARTON, Miles

ANIMAL RIGHTS

Franklin Watts, 1987, Hdbk, 0–86313–541–2
Series: Survival
Contents list, index, useful addresses, black and white and colour line drawings and photographs

This book is one of a series that looks at wildlife under threat because of human activities. Miles Barton is a radio producer at the BBC's Natural History Unit, Bristol, who has worked as a researcher on animal welfare, in relation to programmes aimed to change attitudes. He points out that while most people consider that we have the right to use animals to meet human needs, some claim that using animals for our own convenience can never be justified. Some extreme groups are even prepared to kill, injure and destroy the property of those involved in what they consider to

be animal abuse, whether in relation to laboratory experiments, factory farming for food or fur, the slaughter of animals, population culls, ill-treatment of pets and animals in zoos or blood sports.

Most of the illustrations in the book are concerned with animal abuse, and the book is partisan in the sense that there is no discussion of the medical advances that have been made as the result of animal experiments, or of the new techniques that have been devised in recent years to replace the use of laboratory animals.

WFW

Age range: 7–13

BENNETT, Olivia and CORMACK, Christopher

OUR NEW HOME

Hamish Hamilton, 1990, Hdbk, 0–241–12569–3
Series: The Way We Live
Colour photographs

There will always be books for children about moving house. Stories tend to emphasize the disorientation and loss of friends. Fact books, at best, can just get down to it without fuss. When the Singhs move in East London, most of the big furniture has preceded them. It's now just the bits and pieces – and the odd feeling of echoing rooms and sleeping among the packing cases. Through unself-conscious photographs and a sympathetic unfussy text, we see the whole affair from the children's viewpoint. What the text doesn't tell us, the pictures do, and both work well and steadily together, building up the storyline. The climax is to get the house blessed, as, surrounded by friends, the Singhs join the holy man in reading the Sikh scriptures. In pacing, tone and mood, this book describes far more than moving house, which is rather like the real event itself.

SH

Age range: 6–9

MAYLED, Jon

RACISM

Wayland, 1986, Hdbk, 0–85078–866–8
Series: Let's Discuss
Bibliography, contents list, glossary, index, black and white line drawings and photographs

It's there even if you have met it only indirectly, say, through the media or books. It's racism, based on prejudiced interpretations of 'race' and stereotypes. Mayled, a teacher in the multicultural and racial equality area, argues that ignorance is to blame, and in this excellent book places the issues squarely before the reader. He provides facts and figures about racism in immigration and employment, suggests that racism becomes institutionalized in churches and class structures, and contends that the very news we hear biases what we should decide. Case studies of Jews in the 1930s or young people in today's schools or at work furnish vivid ways of discussing these matters in school (and they can be reproduced freely). Discussion points are clearly displayed in boxes, and support readings (fact and fiction) are well chosen. His constructive views for what we can do about it leave the challenge in our own hands.

SH

Age range: 11–14

MILLER, Hugh

YOU AND OTHER PEOPLE

Collins, 1989, Pbk, 0–00–190052–8
Series: Viewpoints
Contents list, index, colour line drawings

Psychology is all about trying to understand the things people do. As I read this book, I was reminded of Thackeray's words in *Pendennis* '. . . could we know the man's feelings as well as the author's thoughts – how interesting most books would be!' I found the book unusual – perhaps more puzzling than interesting as I considered its possible roles in a school library:

1. Would it fill a gap in school libraries (that seldom have much on psychology for pupils)? It certainly would not take up much space: indeed, because it is so small, on the open shelves it would tend to get lost!
2. Would it be read only by youngsters interested in psychology or would it stimulate such an interest? Its layout is not all that attractive: its design reminds me of some DHSS leaflets!
3. Would it prove helpful as background reading to lessons on 'health and human relationships'?
4. Could it be considered as a careers book for psychology, social sciences and the caring professions?
5. Would it prove helpful to those who failed to achieve the exam results for the career of their choice, as it touches not only on failure and 'learned helplessness', but also on the author's own unfulfilled childhood ambitions?
6. Was it intended for self-improvement of the personality? . . . .

There are no firm answers in psychology: it is often a case of speculation and argument.

This amusing book is a brief introduction to a few topics in psychology. It discusses how we get on with each other in everyday life, making friends and being influenced by people. There are some simple experiments for the young reader to try out with friends. It gives careers advice and suggestions for further reading.

WFW

Age range: 14–18

NEAL, Philip

HUNTING, SHOOTING AND FISHING

Dryad, 1987, Hdbk, 0–85219–694–6
Series: Considering Conservation
Bibliography, contents list, glossary, index, useful addresses of organizations concerned with field sports and conservation, black and white line drawings and photographs

The editor of this series of books considering conservation (author of this and two other titles) is to be congratulated on the sensible way he has handled what could be regarded as emotive topics. As General Secretary of the Association for Environmental Education, he has set out to be informative, and has given, in a balanced and thought-provoking way, arguments both *for* and *against* hunting, shooting and fishing, pointing out the hypocrisy of certain stances. The book is interesting, and, though not magically persuasive, is more likely to encourage young people to appreciate, protect and strive to improve their environment, than would a more partisan or provocative treatment of the issues. The theme of this series is not so much that we have inherited the Earth (and certain problems!) from our parents, but that we must act (more) responsibly, for we hold it in trust for future generations.

JW

Age range: 10–15

NEWSON, Lesley

ANIMAL RIGHTS AND WRONGS

Black, 1989, Hdbk, 0–7136–2927–4
Black and white line drawings and photographs

Children aged 11 and upwards wanting to do project work will derive a lot of information from this thorough book. The book is completely unbiased and on every issue from foxhunting and factory farming to testing animals for pharmaceuticals and the role of zoos and dolphinaria, it offers views from contrasting sides. Readers are left to formulate their own opinions since all the arguments are nicely teased out into manageable text blocks. The book reads rather like a serious newspaper journal especially with its typeface, black and white illustrations and facts boxes, but this makes it more of an interesting exploration through its pages for children.

JF

Age range: 11–16

PERRY, Sue and WILDMAN, Norma

GRANNIES AND GRANDADS

Black, 1989, Hdbk, 0–7136–3100–7
Series: Friends
Bibliography, things to do, colour photographs

Based on the idea that children and grandparents really have a lot to share, this bright and thoughtfully illustrated book shows how it can be done in a primary school. The children decide to ask their grandparents to visit the school. They come, with memories, old photos, stamp collections, a wish to teach numbers in Gujarati. The children show them their drawings, their computers, and give them tea. Full of incident and ideas, the photos and text will stimulate discussion and reflection on generations and families, and just plain affection, an approach which can be reinforced by using books like John Burningham's *Granpa* which the children are shown reading. In showing interaction and activity, this series will make readers, children and adult, more aware of what can be done and what happens in terms of thoughts and feelings when it does.

SH

Age range: 5–8

SELBY, David

HUMAN RIGHTS

CUP, 1987, Pbk. 0–521–27419–2

Series: Modern World Issues
Bibliography, contents list, index, black and white
line drawings and photographs

Selby considers a wide range of the usual sorts of questions: What are human rights? How do these differ from legal rights and moral rights? What should we do when one set of human rights conflicts with another? What about animal rights? What about the rights of vegetable life and of mineral matter?

Though he is aware of the limits of his approach, Selby answers such questions from the perspective of modern Western liberalism: 'moral rights are based on general principles of fairness and justice; human rights are universal'. This approach has had enormous influence through the Universal Declaration of Human Rights and the International Covenants on Human Rights. But it is in fact very illiberal, because it ignores the different ideas round the world of what constitute moral and human rights, fairness and justice. The simplest example of such a difference is probably given in the first paragraph above, where some of the questions may appear ludicrous to one person, but essential to another. (Selby gives other examples.) So whose ideas of human rights ought to prevail? That is a question which Selby does not answer; liberalism has no answer to that question.

Where do human rights come from, anyway? Selby provides three of the main answers, but leaves out the answer which is traditional: human rights come ultimately from God and from the nature of the universe He has created. This traditional answer is at present unfashionable in Britain, but that is not a reason to withhold the information: Christians, Muslims, Jews, Hindus and many followers of tribal religions would all give that answer even today.

In other respects, Selby's book is sensitive, thoughtful, probing, well structured. Its limitations are actually the limitations of modern liberal thinking on this subject.

PSG

Age range: 14–18

VISRAM, Rozina

INDIANS IN BRITAIN

Batsford, 1987, Hdbk, 0–7134–5481–4
Series: Peoples on the Move
Bibliography, contents list, glossary, index, black
and white line drawing and photographs

An under-researched and under-published subject, on which Visram has produced (considering its size) a remarkably comprehensive introduction, though many interesting stories have been left out – for example, that of Edalji (Conan Doyle aficionados will recollect his role in clearing the man of the charge of malicious injury to animals, after the poor man had spent years and years in prison).

Beginning the story at the end of the eighteenth century, Visram organizes the material according to themes (servants, sailors, students, princes, soldiers, nationalists and politicians, settlers and refugees). A balanced picture emerges of the variety and strength of the Indian presence in Britain, though less so than might have been the case if some of the stories had been followed through: for example, Sake Deen Mahomed, with whom she begins the book, has descendants who naturally still live in Britain, and who numbered among them at least one famous doctor, one inventor, and a clergyman (known, naturally, as the Reverend Mahomed!).

Every one of the stories in this book could be followed up: it is a book which should stimulate much interest and curiosity among readers, which may mean more people helping to unearth fascinating stories which are too largely untold.

PSG

Age range: 13–16

WARNER, Rachel

OUR FLATS

Hamish Hamilton, 1987, Hdbk, 0–241–12096–9
Series: The Way We Live
Colour photographs

A slice of life in the World's End Estate in Chelsea, London, where there are families of English, Asian, Bangladeshi, Caribbean, Chinese, Iranian, Pakistani, Philipino, Spanish, Sri Lankan and Syrian extraction. Each is given more or less a double spread, in which we share the ordinary details of ordinary lives, along with a few exotic touches such as seeing Chinese telephone boxes in London's Chinatown or cooking with spices.

PMR

Age range: 5–7

WHARTON, Mandy

ABORTION

Franklin Watts, 1989, Hdbk, 0–86313–921–3
Series: Understanding Social Issues
Contents list, glossary, index, useful addresses, colour line drawings and black and white and colour photographs

A broader understanding of social issues is important for teenagers both for their public life in school and work and their private life with partners and in the family. Abortion is such a topic. It has medical, psychological and moral dimensions, all of which Mandy Wharton covers with a sympathetic mixture of information and advice. She balances the views of those who say 'protect unborn children' with those who claim a right to decide, and finally comes down in favour of the second. But it is a reasoned case, with evidence on illegal abortions, past attitudes, the pressures of single parenthood, and coping with foetal abnormalities. Case studies (e.g. a young nurse has to stop her course) are well adapted to the intended readership. Thought-provoking remarks from girls and women occur throughout the text, giving it impact and credibility. The final contention that the responsibility is not just a woman's but her partner's and society's at large, is worth considering.

SH

Age range: 12–16

WHITE, Peter

DISABLED PEOPLE

Franklin Watts 1988, Hdbk, 0–86313–796–2
Series: Understanding Social Issues
Contents list, glossary, index, sources of help, colour photographs

Peter White is well known as a radio presenter and his gift for clear presentation and persuasion is demonstrated here. All kinds of disability are mentioned, but, he argues, disability is not the person, disabled people are not necessarily saints, and many problems are invisible. 'What's wrong with you?' attitudes should be replaced with 'What are you interested in?' He is not content with mere description: he presses his viewpoint through, on matters like separate education, getting work, relationships with able-bodied partners, and the institutionalization of people with mental handicap or illness. Case studies back up issues like these, and imaginative teachers and helpers could devise others. Practical help is a real option, but even thinking about issues White raises will increase the reader's understanding and self-knowledge. A plain-speaking book for young adults.

SH

Age range: 12–16

POLITICS

COOK, Janet and KIRBY, Stephen

POLITICS AND GOVERNMENTS

Usborne, 1986, Pbk, 0-7460-0047-2
Series: Usborne Introduction
Contents list, index, black and white and colour line drawings

This is a beginner's guide to the complex world of politics, its terminology, slogans and beliefs. The book sets out to explain simply the meaning of many political terms in common use, and clear instructions are given, at the beginning of the book, how to use the index to find definitions of the terms used. It examines, in a clear and straightforward way, various ideologies (e.g. communism) and political parties, and there are interesting tables towards the end of the book of international organizations and alliances of countries, and of the main political parties, political institutions and leaders of 14 of those countries.

So many changes in world politics have occurred recently that the need for frequent revision of this book is recognized and it was updated in 1990. Mention is made of the changes in communism (resulting from economic failure and general discontent) that have led to less oppression in Eastern Europe; but only by the study of current affairs can any pupil hope to keep informed of recent political change.

JW

Age range: 9–13

ROSS, Stewart

THE HOUSE OF COMMONS

Wayland, 1986, Hdbk, 0-85078-843-9
Series: Politics Today
Bibliography, contents list, glossary, index, black and white and colour line drawings and photographs

The House of Commons is at the heart of the British system of government. This book tells very clearly what the Commons does and how it works. There is little about the political parties (for there are other books in the series that deal with them) but it is a useful book that explains in simple outline British constitutional government. There are many things about Parliament which need explanation. There are familiar phrases such as 'three line whip' and being 'named' by the Speaker: these are made more interesting, used in their correct context and in such a way as to be self-explanatory.

Although the book was written before debates in the House were televised, it should prove helpful in explaining the ritual of parliamentary debate now seen on the TV screen.

JW

Age range: 9–13

INDUSTRY

LINES, Cliff

EXPLORING INDUSTRY

Wayland, 1987, Hdbk, 1–85210–007–9
Series: Exploring the Past
Bibliography, contents list, glossary, index, black and white and colour line drawings and photographs

In this book the origins, development and, in some cases, the decline(!) of certain manufacturing industries are described and their roles, past and present, are considered.

The order of the chapters seems more arbitrary than logical, but it is a well written book by an experienced author of information books for young people, and is one of an excellent activity-based series that by encouraging children to explore the past, through what they can see and find out about their surroundings, can stimulate the active study of history, environmental studies and CDT and lead to a greater appreciation of our rich heritage.

Moreover, in addition to excellent photographs, mostly in full colour, the book is illustrated by drawings by Steve Wheele, who gives useful tips to pupils on how to illustrate their project work. (However, surely it is easier to make rubbings directly from certain *cast*-iron objects rather than from templates, made from card, of wrought iron designs, as suggested on p.22)

WFW

Age range: 7–11

MILITARY ART

LANGLEY, Andrew

THE ROYAL NAVY

Wayland, 1986, Hdbk, 0–85078–883–8
Series: The Armed Forces
Bibliography, contents list, glossary, index,
colour line drawings and photographs

This attractively illustrated book about
our Senior Service, although it reads
rather like a recruiting brochure, is *not*
designed as a careers book for the
secondary school pupil: its appeal would
be for the younger child who has
enthusiasm for the Royal Navy or who,
looking ahead, is thinking of it as a
possible career.

The book has sections about the
various branches of the Service, how to
join and even about the promotion
ladder. It shows ships, submarines, ship-
borne aircraft and their weapons and
describes briefly the work carried out by
the men and women of the Service and
the complex equipment they must use.

JW

Age range: 7–13

PUBLIC SAFETY

COKER, Chris

TERRORISM AND CIVIL STRIFE

Franklin Watts, 1987, Hdbk, 0–86313–607–9
Series: Conflict in the 20th Century
Bibliography, contents list, index, chronology,
personalities, colour line drawings and black and
white and colour photographs

This incisive and thoughtful book is really
an analysis of international conflict and
the imperfect success of the United
Nations in regulating it. Such conflict
arises for many reasons from nationalism
and disputed territory to world debt and
social tension. The north–south, rich–
poor divisions lie at its heart, and
dilemmas about famine and nuclear
weapons arise largely because of them.
Terrorism thrives in this context,
threatening the free society. Coker
lectures at the London School of
Economics, and his work in this field is
respected. This work certainly does not
describe: it discusses, it takes themes and
issues, it asks why terrorists attack
particular targets and raises the reader's
awareness of why social and economic
violence takes place. A mature style, not
dense but demanding good reading skills,
is linked with a televisual style of
illustration and useful charts and maps. Its
claim that 'the modern terrorist is largely
a creation of the mass media' is a
challenging thesis for older readers to
consider.

SH

Age range: 11–15 (especially 11–13)

MAY, Doreen and PEAD, David

VIOLENCE

Wayland, 1986, Hdbk, 0–85078–868–4
Series: Let's Discuss
Bibliography, contents list, glossary, index,
helping agencies, black and white photographs

Violence is not a subject we can be
neutral about. So books for young
secondary readers need to be thought-
provoking and topical. This one, by two
journalists with *Police Review*, is just that.
War throws up issues about justifiable
violence, terrorism issues about whether
the media enhances it, vandalism if
people are naturally destructive or if
poverty makes them so. At times, the
authors' views are clear – on rape,
violence in the home, and vigilantes – but
no bad thing. Unavoidable arguments are
presented, viewpoints to be weighed up,
not side-stepped. Immediacy is another
characteristic: football violence and
mugging happen every day: we live with
them. Four case studies, fictional but
realistic, with discussion points, can be
copied freely for classroom use. The wide
intended age group presents difficulties:
some text is complex and abstract, some
simple. Yet as a sourcebook and stimulus,
it is always compelling.

SH

Age range: 12–16

EDUCATION

**PRAGOFF, Fiona and
HEASLIP, Peter**

STARTING SCHOOL

Methuen, 1986, Hdbk, 0–416–95470–7
Colour photographs

From getting up to going to bed again,
this is Lucy's first day at primary school.
She knows nursery school, but wonders
what the 'big school' will be like. It will
be new, but, authors and parents know,
accounts of it need to be reassuring. This
one is: her mum goes with her, her dad
picks her up, she makes friends, chooses
her own pudding, and writes her own
name. Un-stagey colour photographs
show all this, and tell their own extended
visual story for young readers to examine
and talk about with caring adults. Lucy
isn't treated as special, just as herself, as
she does things with other children and
then on her own, noisy and then quiet
things. The storyline is matter-of-fact and
interesting, free from an earnest look-
and-say reiterative overlayering of
language which sometimes kills a book
stone dead.

SH

Age range: 4–6

JOBS

BENTLEY, Diana and WOODCOCK, Tim

THE ROAD SAFETY OFFICER

Wayland, 1987, Hdbk, 1–85210–033–8
Series: My School
Bibliography, contents list, glossary, index,
colour photographs

Several adults work at your primary school to make it a safe and enjoyable place, and Mrs Hurst, the road safety officer, is one of them. A group of nine-ten-year-olds are being tested by her. Colour photographs give total realism to it as they cycle about, slowing down, turning left and right, and coping with heavy traffic. Easy-reader text, in large letters, is provided along with smaller text on each double page. Exposition takes three forms: Mrs Hurst talking to the reader, a narrative of what Mark and Caroline are doing, and instructions on how to ride your bike properly. Both text and pictures take the same approach as the Highway Code, which serious young cyclists need to know to pass the test. This small book will spur them on to take the test and enjoy safer riding. Passing the test is 'only the start'.

SH

Age range: 5–9

COOPER, Alison and BENTLEY, Diana

AMBULANCE CREW

Wayland, 1990, Hdbk, 1–85210–851–7
Series: People Who Help Us
Bibliography, contents list, glossary, index,
colour photographs

'Ron and Sharon work on an ambulance. They help people who are hurt'. In this direct and unpatronizing tone we are shown their working day. Each page is a colour photograph against a contrasting ground. Text is bold and simple (playing a role as both side-headings and easier language for slower readers), as well as more complex for better readers. Underlined words are given in a glossary. Realistic and not looking posed, photographs give credible day-to-day feeling to the events. They help a pregnant mum to get to hospital, and then rush out to Gary who was working in a garage when a machine fell on him. None of the technical skill or sympathy the crew have is lost – or exaggerated – in what they do. It's an interesting and responsible job, done well, and that's the message presented to the reader. For younger readers, getting to know what happens, and for older ones, getting to know still more detail (and good for discussion).

SH

Age range: 6–9

COOPER, Alison and BENTLEY, Diana

NURSE

Wayland 1990, Hdbk, 1–85210–849–5
Series: People Who Help Us
Contents list, glossary, index, colour photographs

One of the attractions of this book is that the nurse Tony is male. At last an example of equal opportunities in a reference book aimed at young children! Tony, the charge nurse, is introduced in his place of work, the Casualty Department of a hospital. His patient, Alex, has an accident on her bicycle and then is taken by an ambulance to hospital. Here she is cared for by Tony. The photographs, supported by a clear text, shows how Tony cares for Alex, showing how the doctor and radiographer all have a special role to play. There is a list of contents and the pages are clearly numbered. Words considered to be important are underlined in the text and included in a glossary. Children will easily identify with Alex, and the book would be a useful aid in dispelling children's fears about a visit to a hospital.

BS

Age range: 5–9

STEWART, Anne

THE HEALTH VISITOR

Hamish Hamilton, 1988, Hdbk, 0–241–12217–1
Series: Cherrystones
Index, colour line drawings and photographs

This book introduces the child to Emma Begg, the health visitor, and takes us through a typical day in her life. This puts her in context, and tells us something of the range of activities involved. Relevant matters are explained as we come across them (what is a tummy button, why do we have it, does it hurt mother or child when it is cut?). Though Emma mainly looks after young children, some health visitors look after the elderly, and this too is explained. However, the photographs are workaday and some of the language is suitable for an older child, or needs an older person to explain – what, for example, is a speech therapist?

PMR

Age range: 5–7

STEWART, Anne and FAIRCLOUGH, Chris

THE PARK WARDEN

Hamish Hamilton 1988, Hdbk, 0–241–12218–X
Series: Cherrystones
Index, colour line drawings and photographs

What are other people's jobs really like to do? They can tell you and show you, and this is what this series does – for bus drivers and chefs, hairdressers and vets.

Sam Roberts is Park Warden in Snowdonia National Park where you can go and see his work for yourself. Total credibility comes from a series of colour photographs showing his work. The text is wholly functional, drawing on a familiar vocabulary which can be demonstrated by looking at the pictures. He helps walkers and checks walkways, rescues sheep and teaches first aid. There are routines and high spots. He makes lots of friends and has lots of responsibility. It is a real job, made understandable for younger readers. You want to go there and meet him!

SH

Age range: 6–8

WOOD, Tim

DOCTOR

Franklin Watts, 1989, Hdbk, 0–86313–821–7
Series: My Job
Glossary, index, colour photographs

Lovely photographs, intended to be warm and unthreatening, arranged round a day in the life of a doctor, designed to remove any fear a child may have about doctors. This is supplemented by an exceptionally well written page of facts about doctors, such as how long it takes to train to be one. Very good indeed.

PMR

Age range: 4–7

WOOD, Tim

POSTWOMAN

Franklin Watts, 1989, Hdbk, 0–86313–819–5
Series: My Job
Glossary, index, facts section, colour photographs

In this 'age of equal opportunity' it seems very fitting that, in this book, it is a lady who tells us about her work for the Post Office. Her busy day, starting at 5.30 am in the sorting office and then delivering the letters to the shops and houses on her walk, is shown through a series of large photographs, each with a single sentence in bold type.

It is an attractive book for young children to read and there is a useful glossary, together with a facts section that the teacher may find helpful in answering their questions.

JW

Age range: 5–7

WOOD, Tim and FAIRCLOUGH, Chris

DENTIST

Franklin Watts, 1988, Hdbk, 0–86313–648–6
Series: People and Places
Glossary, index, facts about teeth, colour photographs

This is a visual visit to the dentist. She looks after people's teeth, and we are shown how. The tone is that it simply makes sense, and it's quite normal, to go when you need to. Colour photographs (originally from the *People* series intended for older readers) have been married with very bold simple text for very young readers. Information and attitude are both embedded in the storyline as text and picture help each other along. We see an injection, an X-ray, get advice on brushing teeth. A glossary helps with difficult words; the index in this case is superfluous. A book to share with young children, particularly when they have expressed interest in dentists, or worry about what they do.

SH

Age range: 5–7

WOOD, Tim and FAIRCLOUGH, Chris

TRUCK DRIVER

Franlkin Watts, 1989, Hdbk, 0–86313–822–5
Series: My Job
Glossary, index, colour photographs

The *My Job* series presents books about people seen on most days in the community by children. They illustrate a working day in the life of, for example, a milkman, a baker and a truck driver. The photographs are excellent and will provide many discussion topics for young children. The covers are presented in bright colours with good clear print with an inset photograph of the person the book is about. Each book has a glossary and an index. The 'facts' section provides more information possibly for an adult or a more experienced reader. The books are written in the first person, which makes each one a personal account of a day's work. The truck driver sets off to collect a cargo of yoghurt from Belgium. The illustrations show in detail the inside of his cab, a variety of road signs, the driver checking his engine for oil, loading the truck with yoghurt and driving his truck onto the ferry – finally reaching the factory in England.

BS

Age range: 5–7

TRANSPORT

GREY, Michael

SHIPS AND SUBMARINES

Franklin Watts 1986, Hdbk, 0–86313–424–6
Series: Modern Technology
Contents list, glossary, index, colour line
drawings and black and white and colour
photographs

An attractive, well written book which
outlines, in not too much technical detail,
the great advances in maritime
technology which have occurred in the
past 20 years. Computer-aided design
and new building techniques are dealt
with first. Following chapters describe
improved methods of ship propulsion,
navigation and communication, as well as
modernized port facilities which have
greatly increased cargo handling
efficiency. We are shown how container
ships, ro-ro ferries and today's giant gas
and oil tankers work. Modern designs for
specific weapon systems and electronic
warfare are highlighted in the chapters on
warships and submarines. We are also
given a brief look at some futuristic
designs for cruise and merchant vessels.
The information in each double-spread
chapter is conveyed very clearly through
one or two subheaded paragraphs of
easy-to-read main text. This information
is linked to and supplemented by the
extended captions which accompany the
excellent colour diagrams and
photographs. Recommended.

RG

Age range: 9–14

JACOBS, Anne

PASSENGER SHIP

Hamish Hamilton, 1987, Hdbk, 0–241–11880–8
Contents list, index, colour photographs

Unusual book, offering an insight into life
aboard the most famous luxury liner in
the world, the Queen Elizabeth II. There
is a brief history of the pleasure cruise
business before the description of the
complex organization required for each
of the ship's many cruises. In loving
detail, we share the initial planning of the
route. We have behind-the-scenes visits
to the bridge, the engine room, the radio
room, to the kitchens and storerooms.
We sample the entertainments on offer to
passengers. When the tour is over several
days later, and the passengers depart, we
almost feel as if we had shared the
journey with them.

PMR

Age range: 9–13

ANON

THE PICTURE WORLD OF HELICOPTERS

Franklin Watts, 1989, Hdbk, 0–86313–849–7
Series: Picture World
Contents list, glossary, index, colour photographs

Flying a helicopter, types of helicopters,
carrying and lifting by them, special
operations such as fire-fighting, rescue
and police work done by helicopters, and
fighting helicopters are all covered in this
highly visual book, though its
photographs are not of the highest
quality. The text is simple and bold, and
this is the sort of book that any child
would enjoy looking through.

PMR

Age range: 5–9

WILLIAMS, Betty

THE RAILWAY INDUSTRY

Batsford, 1987, Hdbk, 0–7134–5539–X
Series: Working Lives

Bibliography, contents list, glossary, index, black and white photographs

The development of the British Railway Industry, from the first steam locomotives to today's advanced technology, is traced through the lives and experiences of generations of railway workers. In 1850, 60 000 people worked for the railways, doing jobs as diverse as station master to lamp boy. These 'railway servants' were expected to dedicate their lives to their jobs, although conditions and discipline were harsh. The story of the formation of the first Railway Trade Union, the important part the industry played in both world wars, nationalization, the effects of the 'Beeching Axe' and present-day changes are all brought to life by extracts from personal accounts given by railway employees. These anecdotes, often amusing, often sad, are linked to a full supporting text with interesting black and white well captioned photographs. This book, with its in-depth interpretative appoach, will be useful for G.C.S.E. pupils doing history and sociology projects.

RG

Age range: 14–adult

YOUNG, Caroline et al.

SHIPS, SAILORS AND THE SEA

Usborne, 1988, Pbk, 0–7460–0286–6
Series: Beginner's Knowledge
Contents list, glossary, index, colour line drawings

This is a story of ships from Ancient Egypt to nuclear submarines and hydrofoils. The authors use a variety of methods to inform and amuse the reader, one to show in intricate diagrammatic detail what ships like men-of-war and steamships are like, another to people such drawings with busy sailors firing guns or consulting charts, climbing rigging or filling the hold with cargo. Colin King's illustrations use colour and line wittily, and the colour register is exact. Text and pictures work in interesting and busy layouts on the page without being cluttered, even though young readers will take time to take in everything there. There is history (Vikings, Columbus) and principles (navigation, radar, propellers), recreated or demonstrated in organized panels within the page. Useful general information which can be put into context when a project or a hobby is being developed.

SH

Age range: 7–10

COSTUME

HERBERT, Helen

THE CLOTHES THEY WORE: 19TH AND 20TH CENTURIES

CUP, 1986, Pbk, 0–521–31326–0
Places to visit, colour line drawings

Writer-illustrator Herbert follows her similar work on the seventeenth and eighteenth centuries with this slim, Dinosaur-style, paperback. Witty fluent description of fashions through the nineteenth century picks out the era of corsets and tiny waists, and the flamboyance of hooped crinolines and bustles, with Victorian respectability in between. Some fashions, she thinks, were intended to keep women still or make them look merely decorative. Later influences were world wars, which made things practical (like utility wear), and popular culture and music (Elvis, teddy boys, beatniks, mini-skirts, hippies, and Laura Ashley). All these have brightly coloured line drawings, easy to copy and trace for projects, accurately researched, without caricature. Places to visit will suggest ideas for seeing originals. A quick tour of the subject, suited to any situation, from classroom use to casual chat in the car.

SH

Age range: 7–12

MOSS, Miriam

TRADITIONAL COSTUME

Wayland, 1988, Hdbk, 1–85210–101–6
Series: Costumes and Clothes
Bibliography, contents list, glossary, index, colour photographs

People dress in all kinds of ways for many reasons, work and play, herding cattle, going to weddings. Their clothes are often made from materials found locally (skins, lace, llama wool, calico). This simple book never loses sight of that deeper explanatory level, and therefore does not merely describe. Neither is it simply a catalogue of costumes: it is organized around clearly sequenced geographical areas of the world, fully documented with technical terms (sari, keffiyeh, parka, mantilla) all explained or translated in the text. Bright, relevant colour photographs illustrate the costumes, and captions and text work well with them, getting young readers to think carefully about what they are looking at. A useful work for projects in primary and lower secondary, although, at the higher level, much more information would have to be independently sought out, and by then the text would be too simple.

SH

Age range: 9–13

CHRISTMAS

ANON

THE CHRISTMAS HOLIDAY FUN BOOK

Lion, 1989, Pbk, 0–7459–1720–8
Black and white line drawings

Recognizing and accepting reality, Lion Publishing has now built obsolescence into this book. The child is advised to get a grown-up to help detach the stiff cover of this A4-sized book: the cover then becomes a Christmas calendar.

This publication is well worth the money. Every page is packed: there are jokes, puzzles, games, and a scattering of fascinating facts on every page (London has had only seven white Christmases this century; they were much more common in the nineteenth century, though no one knows why). There's also rather more pertinent information, scattered around in digestible chunks: Christmas round the world, the first Christmas, the legend of the real Father Christmas. An excellent way to brighten a child's Christmas while painlessly increasing their knowledge about a range of related matters.

PMR

Age range: 8–12

LUDLOW, Angela

THE FUN AT CHRISTMAS BOOK

Lion, 1990, Pbk, 0–7459–1877–8
Black and white and colour line drawings

By using different colours on different pages, the publishers are able to provide quite a colourful book for minimal outlay, with multicolour printing reserved only for the do-it-yourself centre page nativity scene in tough paperboard. The back cover, in similar paperboard, can be turned into a Christmas calendar. More oriented to fun activities than *The Christmas Holiday Fun Book*, with less information, but the same sort of principle. Excellent buy.

PMR

Age range: 6–8

THOMSON, Ruth

MY CLASS AT CHRISTMAS

Franklin Watts, 1986, Hdbk, 0–86313–446–7
Series: My Class
Colour photographs

As a series, all of *My Class* books invite the reader to share the experiences of a class of children on a visit or celebrating a festival at their school. Most children will enjoy sharing the activities of Christmas with Lola Almudeval and her class in this book. I am not sure whether I would describe it as a 'true' reference book, but there is some interesting information in its content – how for example to make a pomander. The photographs are excellent throughout the book, showing the children working in their classrooms and their completed work on display. The book is full of ideas for adults and children and would have been even more effective if there had been an index at the back and numbered pages throughout.

BS

Age range: 5–8

DICTIONARIES

◆

Writers of dictionaries for young people have often resorted to gimmickry in the past to try to interest children in a seemingly dull subject. Fortunately the newer breed of dictionary makers are more concerned with clarity than with trickery.

BELLAMY, John

KINGFISHER ILLUSTRATED THESAURUS

Kingfisher, 1987, Hdbk, 0–86272–244–6
Black and white line drawings

'Over six thousand words' is the official claim, and there is a good variety of words, all examined from the perspective of young people ('alien' has the usual meaning of foreigner associated with it, but also a Martian figure in a good line drawing). There is at least one illustration on every double page, and some have four.

The entries provide the synonyms of course, but also the antonyms. But this is not merely a thesaurus; it is also a speller: homonyms are therefore provided in small capitals at the end of each entry.

So: 'raze', for example, is associated with the synonym 'destruction' in ordinary type, followed by the antonyms 'restore', 'rebuild' in bold italics, followed by the homonym 'raise' in ordinary capitals. That homonym can of course be looked up in the usual alphabetical order.

Excellent. However, I have one difficulty with thesauri for young children: it is difficult enough to explain to them the differences of nuance between similar words (say, 'instruct', 'train', and 'drill') without thesauri coming along and suggesting that they mean roughly the same. And of course, it is far better to learn it right the first time round; far more difficult to unlearn something and then relearn it aright.

So what I think is needed for children (publishers please note) is not thesauri but a 'word-book' which not only lists synonyms, antonyms and homonyms, but also explains the distinctions between the synonyms.

At the very least, the introduction to a thesaurus ought to alert children to such differences of nuance. And should it not explain what a thesaurus is?

PSG

Age range: 8–12

GOLDSMITH, Evelyn and DANN, Penny

COLLINS FIRST DICTIONARY

Collins, 1989, Pbk, 0–00–190055–2
Colour line drawings

This dictionary defines 'dictionary' as a book which tells you what words mean and helps you to check the spelling. It is intended for use by children from seven up, and imaginatively contains words they use, are coming to use, or might be expected to meet in reading and talking. Some 2700 words are cited, many of them with examples in the form of full sentences giving usage. Definitions and usages are both targeted well within the lexicon of young readers: 'fury: if you are in a fury you are very angry'; 'stranger: a person you do not know or have never met before'. Conceptual and social experience are also borne in mind in choice and definitions of terms like 'diary', 'stamp', 'love', and 'jealous'. Many words have several meanings, and these are disentangled clearly: 'raise', 'low', 'mind', 'drop'. Comparative and superlative forms are given where needed, as are simple guides to pronouncing difficult words (no phonetic cryptograms!). Background information is provided for words like 'dig', 'windmill', or 'tiger', and going round in circles with one definition defining another is carefully guarded against. The format is tough, and the text decorated by a profusion of witty, helpful line drawings by Penny Dann.

SH

Age range: 7–10

GRISEWOOD, John

KINGFISHER ILLUSTRATED DICTIONARY

Kingfisher, 1989, Hdbk, 0–86272–386–8
Colour line drawings

This is a revised, re-illustrated and reformatted version of the *Kingfisher Pocket Dictionary* first published in 1984. There are 8000 words in it, words which young readers are likely to need, use, find, say and spell. Grisewood is head of the reference division at Kingfisher Books. Care has been taken not to make nouns incestuous ('exhaustive' is thorough and complete, but thorough and complete are defined using other words and concepts). Related terms are provided: analysis to analyse, madden to mad, recession to recede. Parts of speech are indicated, plurals given, past tenses sometimes placed in sequence, differences to emphasis and meaning shown (increase as noun and verb). The many meanings of terms like 'deep' and 'nick' and 'port' are given, and usage suggested (e.g. 'promote', 'indigenous') in full sentences which often gloss the meaning too. Few colloquial, naughty, or dialect words appear, and some newcomers (like 'greenbelt') are well established. Colour coding helps locate letters. Pictures can be very useful for terms like 'joint', 'ear', and 'pulley', giving extra information in the style of an encyclopaedia. Different typefaces are used to discriminate between parts of speech. A practical and cost-conscious addition to a school/library or personal collection.

SH

Age range: 9–13

LANE, Dianne and PEEL, Elizabeth

COLLINS PICTURE DICTIONARY

Collins, 1989, Hdbk, 0–00–190054–4
Index, colour line drawings and photographs

Arranged by topic are over a thousand words, with fascinating colour illustrations to feast the eye on. The list of included words, at the end of the book, provides a gentle introduction to indexes as well as to dictionaries proper. However, some of the explanations are more difficult than the word whose meaning a child might seek. For example, bones 'are the hard parts you can feel inside your body'. So far, so good. Then comes the problem sentence. Bones 'are joined together to make your skeleton'. This is inaccurate in the context of the previous sentence and is it likely that a child will not know what a bone is if he/she does not know what a skeleton is: there is no explanation of this word in the book! Such odd oversights apart, this is a book which many children will enjoy looking through, so it will provide a welcome introduction to the intriguing world of words.

PMR

Age range: 5–8

PURE SCIENCES

◆

This is possibly the area which requires the most skilled information book writer, the expert who is fully versed in scientific knowledge and who has to impart that knowledge in a way which will be fully understood by a novice.

ALLISON, Linda and KATZ, David

THINKING SCIENCE

CUP, 1987, Hdbk, 0–521–34267–8
Series: 'Off Beat' Books
Contents list, black and white line drawings

Though this edition has English spellings, it has not lost its original American flavour. This off-beat book is *not* a conventional science book: indeed, it sets out to show in a most unconventional way that the correct approach to science needs intellectual curiosity, well designed experiments, and untrammelled imagination – for things are not always as they seem. (The book is dedicated to Gallileo!)

With the help of comic cartoons, featuring Dr Bumble, the Great Wizard ('Gee Wiz' for short) and the know-it-all kid (Smart Art), various fun activities are suggested – experiments to carry out, toys to make and tricks to try out. These, it is hoped, will stimulate interest in science: children, perhaps with occasional promptings from an adult, should find them of educational value. (Answers are, in fact, given to most of the puzzle questions in the book!)

Teachers will enjoy dipping into this book where they will find interesting (memorable) analogies to enliven their teaching patter.

WFW

Age range: 7–13

CRAIG, Annabel and ROSNEY, Cliff

THE USBORNE SCIENCE ENCYCLOPEDIA

Usborne, 1988, Hdbk, 0–7460–0192–4
Contents list, glossary, index, and charts and tables, colour line drawings

This colourful well illustrated encyclopedia is arranged thematically, but the alphabetical glossary and index, and the many charts and lists, make it an easy-to-use reference book for young children. It is most informative, although there is only a very short paragraph of text for each illustration. The hundreds of drawings (both realistic and cartoon illustrations) are sure to appeal, for they show that science is linked to everyday life – and can be fun.

WFW

Age range: 8–13

HISTORY OF SCIENCE

CLARKE, Brenda

WOMEN AND SCIENCE

Wayland, 1989, Hdbk, 1–85210–390–6
Series: Women in History
Bibliography, contents list, glossary, index, black and white photographs

'We know of few female scientists today because only recently did anyone think of looking for them'. Clarke's study of women's involvement in science through the ages helps set the record straight without strident feminism. The women she describes had battles to be taken seriously. There was Mary Somerville who taught herself because there was no formal education for women. Medicine finally admitted women like Elizabeth Garrett in this century, while women's contribution to science was still being underplayed in the 1960s in the Watson/Crick DNA affair. These are not merely inspiring examples: they are presented as determined talented women who got the recognition and self-esteem they deserved. The factual and narrative elements work well together, make their spirit of inquiry infectious, and confirm that girls can do it if they really want to. Projects and research ideas for classroom and library abound here.

SH

Age range: 11–14

DINEEN, Jacqueline

TWENTY INVENTORS

Wayland, 1988, Hdbk, 1–85210–138–5
Series: Twenty Names
Bibliography, contents list, glossary, index, colour line drawings and black and white photographs

This is a deliberately non-technical biographical gallery of mostly nineteenth and early twentieth-century inventors. Although the aim is to portray inventors whose works have significantly changed our lives (i.e. the Wright brothers, Marconi and Stephenson) more prosaic names, such as Biro, are included. Women in those times, as the book points out, had few opportunities in engineering and inventing and so are only represented three times. Of these, arguably only Caresse Crosby with the brassiere has a real claim as an inventor. Marie Curie and Rosalind Franklin ought to be in a book devoted to great scientists. Each entry is confined to a double-page spread which hardly does justice to a man like Edison with 1300 patents to his name. However, I do not quarrel with the overall selection and the language is simple. There are handy panels which record the main events in each inventor's life.

RG

Age range: 8–13

MATHEMATICAL CONCEPTS

PLUCKROSE, Henry

CAPACITY

Franklin Watts, 1988, Hdbk, 0–86313–652–4
Series: Knowabout
Colour photographs

This is a book of large, attractive, coloured photographs of a variety of containers, with a simple text, designed to encourage discussion about capacity. It will certainly inspire plenty of practical work, to answer the questions posed by the text, and this will help the child arrive at an understanding of some of the basic concepts of capacity. It could be used as part of a class maths project, or it could provide a good activity for a rainy day at home: the time spent would be educational as well as fun.

I though it a pity that many of the familiar containers photographed had their labels written in French, as this could puzzle an observant child.

JW

Age range: 4–7

PLUCKROSE, Henry

NUMBERS

Franklin Watts, 1988, Hdbk, 0–86313–507–2
Series: Knowabout
Colour photographs

A book full of beautiful photographs, each illustrating a different use of numbers; for example – on buses, house numbers, shoe sizes, clocks. Many of the pages have questions on them, encouraging further discussion. Other pages have simple text to support the photos. The photos themselves cover many of the situations a young child would meet.

When I presented this book to a group of five-year-olds it kept them chatting happily for some time and the discussion that emerged was of a high standard.

I do have reservations over the illustrations of an American car and the use of the word elevator on the photo of a lift; but otherwise an excellent book worthy of a place in any playgroup, home or early years classroom.

SD

Age range: 4–7

ASTRONOMY AND ALLIED SCIENCES

COUPER, Heather and HENBEST, Nigel

GALAXIES AND QUASARS

Franklin Watts, 1986, Hdbk, 0–86313–473–4
Series: Space Scientist
Contents list, glossary, index, colour line
drawings and photographs

This prize-winning book is for anyone who needs help pondering the big cosmological questions: How did the universe begin? How big is it? What does it look like? Starting with the size and workings of our own Milky Way and working outwards to speculate eventually about quasars, the most violent and remote of all the galaxies, we are given excellent help with the answers. The skill of the two expert authors is in their ability to draw analogies, which convert potentially mind-boggling facts into images which young and old minds can easily encompass. Coupled with this clear and perceptive text is an excellent set of illustrations, which also help bring the enormous scope and scale of space into manageable proportions. The diagram on pages 16 and 17 could hardly be bettered for explaining the size, make-up and beauty of the universe. Highly recommended.

RG

Age range: 10 and upwards

JONES, Brian

THE PRACTICAL ASTRONOMER

Facts on File, 1990, Hdbk, 0–8160–2362–X
Contents list, glossary, index, black and white
and colour line drawings and photographs

The author's intention with this very comprehensive astronomical handbook is quite clear. He wants to encourage practically minded youngsters, who already have more than a passing knowledge and enthusiasm for the heavens, to becoming fully-fledged astronomers. To whet their appetites and put amateur observation into context, the beginning reference section provides up-to-date information on the solar system and surrounding galaxies. It also gives glimpses of the historical background which led up to the current theories of the universe. The second section, which is the real strength of the book, gives sound advice on such things as how to choose or build a first telescope and then how to move on to build a back garden observatory! Specializations such as observing meteors and basic astrophotography are also covered. The final section contains the traditional monthly starcharts and a catalogue of significant astronomical objects the young observer ought to work his or her way through.

RG

Age range: 11–adult

WHITLOCK, Ralph

SUMMER

Wayland, 1986, Hdbk, 0–85078–840–4
Contents list, glossary, index, colour line
drawings and photographs

The national curriculum requires that children know all about the seasons, so this series is well suited to current legislation. After a brief introduction to the earth's orbits, which five-year-olds will understand, the book moves on to portray different types of summers worldwide (or lack of them in equitorial areas), from Europe, Africa, Asia and Australia. Summer is typified by spreads of colourful flowers, insects and birds, crops being harvested, various ethnic festivals and summer sports. 'Summer in art and literature' is particularly sensitive and well done. There is a section on things to look for in summer for young naturalists.

JF

Age range: 8–12

WHYMAN, Kathryn

SOLAR SYSTEM

Franklin Watts, 1990, Hdbk, 0–86313–438–6
Pbk 0–7496–0388–7
Series: Simply Science
Contents list, glossary, index, colour line
drawings and photographs

This book is one of a colourful series that aims to give a brief introduction to the first principles of science, and to be used as a resource for Key Stages 2 and 3 of the National Curriculum.

The quality of some of the photographs and artwork in this book is, perhaps, not quite so high as in others in this series but the difficulties of getting good, attractive photographs from space probes is great. Nevertheless, the text is clear – straightforward, informative and well set out.

WFW

Age range: 7–10

VBROVA, Zuza

SPACE AND ASTRONOMY

Franklin Watts, 1989, Hdbk, 0–86313–757–1
Series: Today's World
Contents list, glossary, index, colour drawings
and photographs

Although very detailed and factual the explanations in this book about such things as the 'Big Bang' theory, the birth and death of stars, our solar systems and the space probes which have explored it, etc., are straightforward and accessible. The double spreads in each section follow a consistent layout. There are, for example, in the two chapters on the giant planets, simple introductory paragraphs followed by more in-depth information in blocks, with similar subheadings. Furthermore, easy-to-compare facts about Jupiter and Saturn, such as their magnitude (brightness) and density are also carried in quick reference panels. The real strength of the book, however, is its many excellent diagrams which are integral to the text but at the same time make everything inviting and convey much additional visual information about the size, distance and beauty of space.

RG

Age range: 10–adult

PHYSICS

BAILEY, Jill and SEDDON, Tony

GUIDE TO THE PHYSICAL WORLD

OUP, 1987, Hdbk, 0–19–918222–1
Series: The Young Scientist Investigates
Bibliography, contents list, glossary, index, black and white and colour line drawings and photographs

This is an attractive reference book for browsing and dipping into, for it is packed with fascinating facts and bits of interesting information about the physical history of our planet, and the geography, geology and landscape of the world.

There are seven main sections, but each double page contains a dozen or so snippets of information under one heading, with colour photographs or drawings, and often a quiz or 'Do You Know?' box. Although the information is presented in this piecemeal fashion, there is a lot of it, set out in an easily assimilated form.

JW

Age range: 8–13

CASH, Terry and TAYLOR Barbara

SOUND

Kingfisher, 1989, Pbk 0–86272–429–5
Series: Fun With Science
Contents list, glossary, index, colour line drawings, and photographs

This colourful book enables children to investigate topics such as how sound is made and heard, echoes, acoustics, pitch, music from strings, pipes and percussion, the speed of sound, and how animals (and man) communicate by sound. The book is designed as a series of well illustrated double-page spreads, each under its own heading. Like other books in this series, it suggests activities,

for, by carrying out experiments, making toys and trying out tricks, children can discover how things work and why things happen and come to understand the underlying scientific principles.

WFW

Age range: 9–14

CATHERALL, Ed

EXPLORING SOUND

Wayland, 1989, Hdbk, 1–85210–704–9
Series: Exploring Science
Contents list, glossary, index, colour line drawings and photographs

The *Exploring Science* Series is designed to meet the Attainment Targets in the National Science Curriculum, levels 3 to 6. The topics are divided into knowledge and understanding sections followed by exploration. Carefully planned questions (Test Yourself) at the end of each topic help to ensure that the pupil has mastered the appropriate level of attainment specified in the Curriculum.

How do sounds travel? What can cause deafness? How does your voice work? These and many other questions are answered in this colourful book.

The interesting and informative text and suggested activities will be most useful for children working with the new Science Curriculum.

JW

Age range: 7–11

DAVIES, Kay and OLDFIELD, Wendy

MY BOAT

Black, 1990, Hdbk, 0–7136–3201–1
Series: Simple Science (Through Play)
Colour line drawings and photographs

This little book is one of a series which uses familiar play objects to introduce children to ideas at an early stage in their development of scientific concepts.

The text that accompanies the attractive colour photographs is simple and brief, but at the back of the book are some notes for adults to help them explain and enlarge on the scientific discoveries the children should make in the course of the activities suggested: constructing boats of various shapes and materials; making them float and move; using them for carrying cargo; studying the problem of keeping them afloat on an even keel and the circumstances under which they sink. Such 'practical work' is fun, and interests children of different ages throughout the junior school.

JW

Age range: 4–7

JENNINGS, Terry

FLOATING AND SINKING

OUP, 1988, Hdbk, 0–19–918257–4
Series: Into Science
Colour line drawings

The National Curriculum requires that children should know about contrasting things such as hot and cold, night and day, and, in this case, floating and sinking. The book has been well planned to be used by teachers for infants, with bright colours, easy instructions (which can be read out loud) about how to experiment with various things such as corks, bottles, plasticine, cans and balls, which float or sink and to change their weights and shapes. Experimentation, manipulation and participation are encouraged. There are also drawings of ferries and container ships, with and without loads, about which important questions can be asked of the children.

JF

Age range: 5–8

JENNINGS, Terry

SLIDING AND ROLLING

OUP, 1989, Hdbk, 0–19–918272–8
Series: Into Science
Glossary, index, colour line drawings

Oxford's *Into Science* series is a set of simple picture-cum-information books produced to help teach Key Stage 1 National Curriculum science. In this title children are seen ice and roller skating as well as rolling and sliding objects down gradients and over rough or smooth surfaces. The easy-to-read text is designed to introduce the language and concepts associated with friction, pushing and pulling as well as sliding and rolling. In addition, several simple experiments and activities are described, including how to make old-fashioned cotton reel tanks powered by elastic bands. Guidance notes for parents and teachers, as well as an index and glossary, are also included. Unfortunately, in my opinion, a perfectly good text is let down by the quality of the colour illustrations, which are not nearly as attractive as the glossy colour photographs of real children which other similar, admittedly more expensive, series have.

RG

Age range: 7–11

LAFFERTY, Peter

ENERGY AND LIGHT

Franklin Watts, 1989, Hdbk, 0–86313–758–X
Series: Today's World
Contents list, glossary, index, colour line drawings and photographs

For children with the barest interest in science, this book will provide an excellent introduction to energy and light. It does not pretend to arouse the interest of those who are at present uninterested.

Terms such as mass and weight, surface tension and lasers, optical fibres and endoscopes, are explained simply and concisely, with homely examples.

The explanations are adequately full without going on too long, and the text is broken up by typeface and colourful illustrations.

A good reference book, this certainly deserves a place in any children's library.

PMR

Age range: 11–13

WALPOLE, Brenda

LIGHT

Kingfisher, 1987, Pbk, 0–86272–288–8
Series: Fun With Science
Contents list, index, colour line drawings and
photographs

This colourful book encourages children to investigate topics related to light. The main themes it deals with are light and shadow, reflection, refraction, light and sight, light and colour, light for life, and laser light, but it is set out as a series of well illustrated double-page spreads, each under its own heading. Like other books in this series, it suggests activities, for, by carrying out experiments, making toys and trying out tricks (and optical illusions), children can discover how things work and why things happen, and perhaps come to understand the underlying scientific principles. However, to arrive at a full explanation in some instances would require considerable help from a science teacher. In a reading, any lengthy explanation would be out of place.

WFW

Age range: 9–13

WALPOLE, Brenda

MOVING

Kingfisher, 1987, Pbk, 0–86272–289–6
Series: Fun With Science
Contents list, index, colour line drawings and
photographs

This colourful book is one of a series,

designed to encourage children to have fun, finding out how things work and why things happen as they do in the world around them.

It suggests experiments to do, toys to make and tricks to try out – activities by which children can investigate topics such as gravity, balancing, inertia, friction and movement on slopes, wheels, pulleys, levers and pendulums, and study different types of machines and movement.

The illustrations are most attractive. Young readers turn the pages eagerly: turning the page reveals, in most instances, a completely new topic and always new things to do.

WFW

Age range: 7–11

WARD, Alan

EXPERIMENTING WITH SOUND

Dryad Press, 1987, Hdbk, 0–8521–9662–8
Series: Experimenting With . . . .
Contents list, index, black and white line
drawings

This lively book, designed for top juniors (and middle schools) is one of a series, each book of which provides over 50 ideas for safe science experiments that can be done at home or that can be demonstrated in school, using ordinary inexpensive materials found around the house. The text is short, simple, and brim full of ideas, attractively illustrated by line drawings (at least three on each double-page spread) and is both educationally sound and fun.

The author, formerly a lecturer on science in primary schools, is an experienced writer and child entertainer.

WFW

Age range: 8–11

WEBB, Angela

REFLECTIONS

Franklin Watts, 1988, Hdbk, 0–86313–552–8
Series: Talkabout
Colour photographs

Chris Fairclough, the photographer involved with the *Talkabout* series, has played an integral part in the success of the layout and design of these books. They have all been accessible for their intended infant audience and visually very attractive. This particular title, because of the nature of its subject matter, provides him with a special opportunity to demonstrate his imagination and skills as a photographer. The result is a book which is still right for its audience – fun to look at but not over-sophisticated with visual trickery. There are some beautiful pictures of buildings reflected in water etc., as well as some cleverly staged shots including a distorted self-portrait of Chris in a fairground hall of mirrors. The book positively invites children to try the simple experiments with mirrors for themselves. One page, about simple shapes, is only designed to work interactively with a mirror. Recommended.

RG

Age range: 4–7

WEBB, Angela

SOUND

Franklin Watts, 1988, Hdbk, 0–86313–564–1
Series: Talkabout
Colour photographs

This is a book with large bright pictures and simple text which aims to increase young children's awareness of the sounds around them. It suggests various activities and experiments, which use a wide range of familiar objects, and many of which can be carried out without adult help. By these fun activities in a playgroup, school or at home, youngsters can explore basic scientific themes concerning sound and the generation, movement and properties of sound waves.

JW

Age range: 5–9

WHYMAN, Kathryn

SPARKS TO POWER STATIONS

Franklin Watts, 1989, Hdbk, 0–86313–931–0
Series: Hands on Science
Contents list, glossary, index, colour line drawings and photographs

This title, in the *Hands on Science* series, is written for children with teachers in mind, in order to support, in a practical way, the teaching of National Curriculum Science in junior schools. Many such titles have appeared recently, all intended as basic introductions to the theory, natural occurrences, generation and practical applications of electricity in our daily lives. Although the scope of the book is wide, covering lightning, batteries, conductors and insulators, heating and lighting, simple circuits, electromagnets, electrolysis, electric motors and power stations, there is nothing particularly outstanding about the approach. The explanations are done reasonably well with the aid of colour photographs and diagrams. The text is sparing and some of the diagrams, if anything, are oversimplified. The experiments, rather grandly called projects, could do with better introductions and there is hardly any mention of the hazards of playing with wires and sockets, etc. at home.

RG

Age range: 9+

CHEMISTRY

COBB, Vicky

STICKY AND SLIMY

Black, 1988, Hdbk, 0–7136–2990–8
Series: Science Safari
Contents list, index, colour line drawings

Based on the text of a book first
published in New York under the title
Gobs of Goo, this is a well written book
on syrups, mucopolysaccharides,
proteins, lipids, waxes, plastics,
elastomers, adhesives, resists and
detergents, in language that is simple
enough for children to understand and
enjoy.

Examples, drawn mostly from their
own experience, are used in this well
illustrated introduction to the science of
gooey materials. The emphasis is on
suggesting their biological roles, rather
than explaining their chemical and
physical properties, as that would require
scientific concepts and terminology not
suited to their age. (No mention of
colloids, viscosity and intermolecular
forces here!)

A few simple experiments are
sugested, and some questions posed.
                                    WFW
Age range: 5–9

WERTHEIM, Jane et al.

THE USBORNE ILLUSTRATED
DICTIONARY OF CHEMISTRY

Usborne, 1986, Pbk, 0–86020–821–4
Series: Dictionary
Contents list, glossary, indexes, famous chemists,
units, colour line drawings

Many young school children feel
overwhelmed by the welter of factual
details and new concepts that a chemistry
course can present. This little colourfully
illustrated dictionary which defines terms
concisely, and in which explanations are
supported by thumbnail sketches and
diagrams, and facts set out in compact
charts and tables, should prove useful for
quick reference and as an aid to
understanding.

It is so informative, and such fun, that
some pupils will use it as a *vade mecum*,
while others may well use it as an aid to
revision, just before exams.
                                    WFW

Age range: 11–14

EARTH SCIENCES

BARRETT, Norman

HURRICANES AND TORNADOES

Franklin Watts, 1989, Hdbk, 0–86313–881–0
Series: Picture Library
Contents list, glossary, index, colour line
drawings and photographs

In the tradition of the *Picture Library*
series, this title covers a subject which is
likely to appeal to most junior and older
children, of all abilities, and provides
them with a short leisure read. There are
plenty of easily accessible facts and
figures as well as visual evidence of the
tremendous destructive power of
hurricanes and tornadoes. In addition,
the excellent satellite and aerial
photographs compare and contrast the
opposite size, scale and yet symmetrical
beauty of these two sets of low pressure
wind systems. It is, however, in the
combination of these pictures and the
large type text, which is quite simple and
pacey, where the book is mindful of the
needs of less willing and less able readers.
Although not comprehensive, this book is
admirably suited for topic or assignment
work and will find a readership across a
wide age and ability range.

RG

Age range: 7–14

BENDER, Lionel

GLACIER

Franklin Watts, 1988, Hdbk, 0–86313–738–5
Series: The Story of the Earth
Contents list, glossary, index, facts about glaciers,
colour line drawings and photographs

The series is intended to introduce young
readers to the ways in which physical
geography works and landscape is
formed. Complex ideas are carefully
adapted in simple explanations: how

snow becomes ice, how ice gets heavy
and travels downhill as a glacier.
Throughout colour photographs
complement text, providing not just
information but atmosphere, but never
just aiming to look good on the page. A
vivid idea of 'glacier' comes across, yet so
too do specifics – the moraines, rocky
remains like eskers and drumlins,
landscape like Swiss valleys and
Norwegian fjords. Sectional diagrams in
colour make clear how the processes
work. Considering how often books like
this are glorified travelogues, this work
has an integrity and selectivity which
makes it an exciting introduction for the
junior reader.

SH

Age range: 8–11

BENDER, Lionel

VOLCANO

Franklin Watts, 1988, Hdbk, 0–86313–704–0
Series: The Story of the Earth
Contents list, glossary, index, facts on volcanoes,
colour line drawings and colour photographs

A sleeping volcano, quiet and calm, can
suddenly erupt, throwing out a mixture of
gases and rocks, causing considerable
devastation, before it finally becomes
quiet again.
   In this colourful book, the story of a
typical volcano is told in ten stages.
Although the ten drawings depict an
imaginary volcano, there are numerous
colour photographs from all over the
world to illustrate the real thing.
   The text is clear and straightforward
and the graphic pictures highlight the
dangers of living in volcanic regions.

JW

Age range: 7–11

BRAMWELL, Martyn

MOUNTAINS

Franklin Watts, 1986, Hdbk, 0–86313–451–3
Series: Earth Science Library
Contents list, glossary, index, colour line
drawings and photographs

This book, one of a full-colour series which explores the world of physical geography, explains the forces that have shaped mountains and describes the landscapes and features that have been created. Explanatory diagrams illustrate the theory of plate tectonics, and the great collisions that have formed our greatest mountain ranges. There are also important sections on the people and animals that live in mountainous areas. The text is clear and factual, with plenty of coloured photographs.

A useful resource book for the junior school library.

JW

Age range: 8–13

BRAMWELL, Martyn

VOLCANOES AND EARTHQUAKES

Franklin Watts, 1986, Hdbk, 0–86313–409–2
Series: Earth Science Library
Contents list, glossary, index, colour line
drawings and photographs

The mysteries of earthquakes and volcanoes are explained in an interesting and straightforward way in this title in the *Earth Science Library* series. Each two-page chapter has a single column of text and is very well populated with colour photographs and simple, cut-away diagrams. The eye-catching 'inside a volcano' diagram on pages 6–7 is particularly useful and large enough to be copied straight into a topic book. Apart from the basic chapters which look at the formation and eruption of volcanoes, the aftermath of an eruption, tremors and earthquakes, etc., there is plenty of additional information. For example, one chapter details the discovery by archaeologists in 1970 of footprints in beds of volcanic ash in Africa, proving that humans crossed the landscape three-and-a-half million years ago! The small format, easy text and abundance of excellent illustrations make this a very accessible and useful book for a school library.

RG

Age range: 9+

BRAMWELL, Martyn

WEATHER

Franklin Watts, 1987, Hdbk, 0–86313–526–9
Series: Earth Science Library
Contents list, glossary, index, colour line
drawings and photographs

The British people have always taken an interest in the weather, but in these days of increased media interest in our changing weather patterns, it is important that we understand what really causes our weather changes.

This book is concisely written, and deals with the causes and effects of our common weather patterns. The text is clear, supported by explanatory diagrams and well chosen photographs and set out in double-page spreads.

Weather forecasting has benefited enormously from our improved telecommunications and the development of computers, but we are still only able to report and, to some extent, forecast the weather; we have little control over it. However, we can intentionally induce thunderstorms by seeding clouds on a small scale, and there is now some evidence of slight (accidental) global warming, by the 'greenhouse effect', due to the combustion of fossil fuels and destruction of forests and by the creation of windows in the ozone layer by polluting the atmosphere.

JW

Age range: 8–13

BRESLER, Lynn and GIBSON, Tony

EARTH FACTS

Usborne, 1986, Pbk, 0–7460–0023–5
Series: The Usborne Book of . . .
Contents list, index, colour line drawings

At a bargain price this is a mini-encyclopedia to earth and its natural habitats. The whole book is organized with short text blocks and boxes containing nuggets of interesting information. There are numerous colour diagrams and tables which cover the pages, making it a fascinating digest for children from eight upwards. Most of the book is organized habitat by habitat, for instance mountains, tundra, and different types of forest, grasslands, deserts and so on. The environment generally is well covered under 'atmosphere', 'natural resources' and 'geology' headings and there is much more to discover.

JF

Age range: 8–12

JENNINGS, Terry

VOLCANOES AND EARTHQUAKES

OUP, 1988, Hdbk, 0–19–917092–4 and Pbk, 0–19–917086–X
Series: The Young Geographer Investigates
Contents list, glossary, index, quiz, colour line drawings and photographs

This attractive book deals with aspects of the geography syllabus that are popular with the pupils, and of particular interest in this age of media reporting, when earthquakes and eruptions are headline news.

A clear and detailed account of the reasons for our earth's restless behaviour is given, and some important examples of volcanic eruption are described, and there are numerous colour illustrations (maps, drawings, diagrams and photographs). Each page deals with its own topic under a separate heading. There are also 'Things to Do' and 'Things to Find Out' with problems posed and questions to answer.

An excellent resource book for library-based project work.

JW

Age range: 7–11

LAMBERT, David

SEAS AND OCEANS

Wayland, 1987, Hdbk, 0–85078–877–3
Series: Our World
Bibliography, contents list, glossary, index, colour line drawings and photographs

This is a multi-purpose book, covering a wide variety of related topics, aimed at a wide age and interest range, and useful for curricular and personal reading. Any one of some twenty openings contains a subject likely to be of relevance to some enthusiasm or project. Key issues like waves and tides, currents and islands are presented in concise, simply constructed prose, with diagrams and well captioned photographs alongside. Lambert emphasizes that seas and oceans came into being under certain conditions, and they keep on changing. They are a source of wealth (fish, oil) but also vulnerable to abuse and pollution. Many pictures can be used as research material in their own right, although some appear to have gone in to look nice. Because it covers so much, issues at depth will need other books and the context of discovery and discussion.

SH

Age range: 10–14

LYE, Keith

MOUNTAINS

Wayland, 1986, Hdbk, 0–85078–873–0
Series: Our World
Bibliography, contents list, glossary, index, colour line drawings and photographs

This handsome book is one of the titles

in Wayland's well produced *Our World* geography series. The thoroughly readable text, from a recognized expert, is supported by an extremely effective combination of colour photographs and clear diagrams. It covers all the aspects of mountains that 10–14-year-olds need to know about, including the physical and human geography as well as the natural history of the world's mountains and volcanoes. It also goes on to emphasize the need for conservation measures now that recreation and tourism on mountains is increasing and, at the same time, mountain resources, both timber and minerals, are being exploited at an ever-increasing rate. Whatever the author describes, whether it is plate tectonics, erosion by glaciation of hydroelectric power stations, there are super photographic examples of the real thing and large, often cut-away diagrams to make understanding clear. Highly recommended.

RG

Age range: 10–14

PETTIGREW, Mark

WEATHER

Franklin Watts, 1990, Hdbk, 0–86313–463–7 and Pbk, 0–7496–0387–9
Series: Simply Science
Contents list, glossary, index, colour line drawings and photographs

This book is one of a series that aims to provide a simple introduction to the first principles of science, and to be used as a resource for Key Stages 2 and 3 of the National Curriculum.

By means of attractive colour photographs, we are reminded of the importance of the weather in our daily lives, and, by clear text and coloured diagrams, several topics relating to weather are briefly explained. Each topic is well set out as a double-page spread

under a clear heading. The sentences are short and fairly easy to read.

WFW

Age range: 7–10

ROWLAND-ENTWISTLE, Theodore

RIVERS AND LAKES

Wayland, 1986, Hdbk, 0–85078–872–2
Series: Our World
Contents list, glossary, index, colour line drawings, and photographs

Rivers and Lakes is another title from Wayland's excellent *Our World* series. The nine chapters span the geology, biology and human use and misuse of the world's rivers and lakes. How are rivers and lakes formed? What is the hydrological cycle? What is the highest navigable lake in the world? What is acid rain? This book answers these questions and many others. The large format befits the magnificent photographs and carefully chosen colour diagrams and artwork. The medium sized print, in double columns, is well spaced and easy to read. Although the book has an extensive glossary, most of the geological and technical terms used are explained very effectively in the text. A very attractive presentation, which treats the subject in a thoroughly cross-curricular way. Recommended.

RG

Age range: 10–14

SYMES, R. F.

ROCK & MINERAL

Dorling Kindersley, 1988, Hdbk, 0–86318–273–9
Series: Eyewitness Guides
Contents list, index, black and white and colour line drawings and colour photographs

Because of the quality of the photographs and number of specimens and artefacts in this title, it is hard to see how this introduction to rocks and minerals could be bettered. It dispels the idea that geology is a dry academic subject. If anything, it resembles an expanded catalogue to a wealthy private collection. As well as explaining the origin and types of rocks there are fascinating spreads about seashore pebbles, the story of coal and the production of pigments from minerals. Poring over the chapters on crystals, gems and precious metals is like glimpsing a treasure trove. You do feel you could almost pick the objects up off the page. My only complaint is that, owing to the format and the almost exclusive use of photographs, there are few diagrams and no maps to show how ores and minerals are mined or where they are distributed around our planet.

RG

Age range: 9–adult

WALPOLE, Brenda

AIR

Kingfisher, 1987, Pbk, 0–86272–287–X
Series: Fun With Science
Contents list, index, colour line drawings and
photographs

This colourful book encourages children to investigate topics related to air. It is in six sections: where and what is air? (its properties, especially volume and weight); warm air (convection and insulation); air pressure; moving and compressed air (and a look at flight); wind and weather; and air all around (to support combustion and life and to carry sound). These sections are set out as a series of double-page spreads, each under its own heading. Like other books in this series, it suggests activities, for, by carrying out experiments, making toys and trying out tricks, children can discover how things work and why things happen and come to understand the underlying scientific principles. Although so attractively presented, it is, in places,

positively misleading, on account of omissions or misrepresentations. For instance, a water *barometer* cannot be made from a plastic bottle; it requires a tube over 32 ft long. (The apparatus shown would be far more susceptible to changes in saturated water vapour pressure with fluctuations of temperature than to changes in atmospheric pressure!)

WFW

Age range: 9–13

WALPOLE, Brenda

WATER

Black, 1988, Hdbk, 0–7136–3050–7
Series: Threads
Contents list, index, colour line drawings and
photographs

Water, as a topic for lower and middle junior children, has tremendous potential for broad cross-curricular investigations and activities, from the study of hydroelectric power to the identification of pond life. However, this title in the *Threads* series deliberately concentrates almost entirely on the experiences children have of water in their everyday lives. There are chapters on the origins, supply, treatment and use of domestic tap water. The book is written for children with teachers in mind, and the emphasis is on learning through doing easy, practical experiments, with ideas for taking measurements and collecting data. The language is kept simple and links well with the colour photographs. These extend the text and, for example, make clear what happens at a water treatment works and then show a child using a class-made filter to clean muddy water. Recommended.

RG

Age range: 7–12

WEBB, Angela

AIR

Franklin Watts, 1986, Hdbk, 0–86313–475–0
Series: Talkabout
Colour photographs

Comprehending the existence of something we cannot see is difficult! The book's colourful photographs, taken on a windy day, serve to remind us that we can feel air moving, while a few deep breaths remind us of its importance to life. The brief text suggests simple experiments to show that air fills space and has weight and buoyancy.

It is a book to promote enjoyable talk and thought about important scientific concepts.

JW

Age range: 4–7

PREHISTORIC LIFE

BENTON, Michael

DINOSAURS: AN A–Z GUIDE

Kingfisher, 1989, Pbk, 0–86272–480–5
Contents list, glossary, index, black and white
and colour line drawings

It is good to have an up-to-date guide to the mysterious world of dinosaurs, even though most of the 140 species mentioned in this book have unpronounceable names. Help and explanation is at hand and the world of dinosaurs becomes much more alive in the hands of such a capable expert who researches these 'terrible lizards'. There are sections on dinosaur evolution, classification, the geological time scale and dinosaur collectors – and all this will enthrall the novice who has perhaps become interested from the model dinosaurs which fall out of cereal packets.

JF

Age range: 8–12

BENTON, Michael

ON THE TRAIL OF DINOSAURS

Kingfisher, 1989, Hdbk, 0–86272–498–8
Contents list, glossary, index, colour line
drawings and photographs

Older children will derive a great deal of information from this serious book – just about every aspect of dinosaurs has been thoroughly discussed, from their early history, evolution, to their biology and behaviour. The lifestyle of dinosaurs is brilliantly executed in vivid detail with marvellous colour illustrations of imagined countryside scenes, of fossils, of individual dinosaurs as we assume they might have looked, and of diagrams which depict bone articulation and identification features. This is clearly a

magnus opus on the subject at higher secondary level.

JF

Age range: 12–16

BENTON, Michael

PREHISTORIC ANIMALS: AN A–Z GUIDE

Kingfisher, 1989, Hdbk, 0–86272–458–9
Contents list, glossary, index, black and white
and colour line drawings and colour photographs

Dinosaur enthusiasts will enjoy this sequel to *Dinosaurs: An A–Z Guide*, for it covers 170 other prehistoric animals which lived before, during and after the age of the dinosaurs. The alphabetical arrangement of these prehistoric names works well because of the simple format. Seventy species have been illustrated in colour and there are charts which provide additional information on time scale, size in relation to man, and pronunciation. Short introductions to, for instance, life on earth, geological history and the process of fossilization make this a very worthwhile book for school libraries.

JF

Age range: 8–12

NORMAN, David and MILNER, Angela

DINOSAUR

Dorling Kindersley, 1989, Hdbk,
0–86318–369–7
Series: Eyewitness Guides
Contents list, glossary, index, black and white
and colour line drawings and photographs

Dinosaurs are enjoying something of a revival, and there are a number of books to choose from. This one, which is part of a very good series, is extremely good value for money. It is prepared by staff at The Natural History Museum and is lavishly illustrated in colour and black and white. Each double page of the book explores a different aspect of the dinosaurs, their sizes, their necks, their defences, their diet and so on. Each page is a mass of illustration with short notes, all very relevant, absorbing and the kind of book one can browse without really reading from cover to cover. Excellent as a source of information and stimulation.

JF

Age range: 8–14

LIFE SCIENCES

ATTENBOROUGH, David

DISCOVERING LIFE ON EARTH

Collins, 1982, Pbk, 0–00–195148–3
Contents list, index, colour line drawings

Following the successful book and
television series *Life on Earth* by the same
author, this title was especially written for
children to make it much clearer and
simpler to read. It is such an amazing
value book for the school library that
everyone should have at least one copy.
No other natural history text is in the
same league with this classic book. It is a
feast of colour and fascinating detail on
every page, with a well planned
evolutionary text covering the main
animal groups. A mine of information and
a mini-encyclopedia.

Age range: 8–14

JF

CHIMERY, Michael

COUNTRYSIDE HANDBOOK

Kingfisher, 1990, Hdbk, 0–86272–420–1
Contents list, index, colour line drawings and
photographs

This is a book packed with colour on
every page, mostly line drawings,
interspersed with colour photographs.
Nine different habitats are dealt with from
coniferous wood forest to man's
environment. Only the commonest
species are described and it is relevant for
anywhere in Western Europe. Children
will probably find this a good read and a
source of inspiration, and for going on
holiday to the continent, a delight. It is
written by one of the leading natural
history writers in Britain.

Age range: 8–12

JF

COLDREY, Jennifer and GOLDIE-MORRISON, Karen

DANGER COLOURS

André Deutsch, 1986, Hdbk, 0–233–97928–X
Colour photographs

The world of colour in animals is always
fascinating, especially for the uninitiated,
with a gay variety of species from which
to choose. This book takes as a central
theme the disguises, shams, bluffs and
mimicry of animals, blending form and
colour into an interesting insight into
animals' defences. Curiously, some
animals without dangerous colours are
included, such as ants and their mimics,
and a spread on truly green-camouflaged
animals (a snake and a caterpillar) which
never have danger colours even when in
danger. This book has missed many
educational opportunities by not
complementing the fine photographs
with explanatory information on topics
like camouflage, mimicry and crypsis.

JF

Age range: 7–12

LILLY, Kenneth and COLE, Joanna

DAYTIME ANIMALS AS LARGE AS LIFE

Walker, 1985, Hdbk, 0–7445–0239–X
Natural history notes, black and white and colour
line drawings

This book is large format because it sets
out to show ten small creatures as large
as life. It is a companion volume to *Night
Time Animals*. It shows that, close and
large, small creatures are as real as they
are at the zoo, or in a TV close-up. You
can almost feel the squirrel monkey's fur,
almost believe that the tree frog, poised
on a leafy twig to catch a ladybird, will

jump away when it sees you watching. Kenneth Lilly's striking illustrations reveal their detailed closeness without becoming sentimental, and Joanna Cole's matter-of-fact 'natural history notes' (neatly gathered together at the back) give the plain facts. Her 30-word opening-by-opening text is concise and witty: Lilly's bee humming-bird weighs less than half a teaspoon of sugar! Foliage, tree-trunk and terrain are credibly real, showing that these creatures really live and are not just portraits. An eye-opener for young children.

SH

Age range: 5–7

LILLY, Kenneth and COLE, Joanna

NIGHT TIME ANIMALS AS LARGE AS LIFE

Walker, 1985, Hdbk, 0–7445–0240–3
Natural history notes, colour illustrations

This delightful book of attractive illustrations, painted in full colour by Kenneth Lilly, shows ten night time animals large as life. They have been painted so life-like and in such detail that, at first glance, they could be mistaken for enlarged colour photographs. A few well chosen words accompany each of the paintings, but there are fuller Natural History Notes, at the back of the book, on each of the animals shown. This book is certain to give great pleasure to young readers.

WFW

Age range: 5–10

MACQUITTY, Miranda

SIDE BY SIDE

André Deutsch, 1988, Hdbk, 0–233–98291–4
Facts pages, colour photographs

As a basic introduction to the world of parasites and symbiotic relationships in plants and animals, this book does well. It provides many interesting colour photographs (all of a high standard one now expects from Oxford Scientific Films) and covers the familiar associations such as hermit crab and sea anemone, cuckoo and mistletoe. Considering the subject is relevant from Attainment Target 2 in the National Curriculum, the book could have gone considerably further in explanations and a glossary. Lots of good ideas are presented but totally uncoordinated for teaching. Children will find this of passing interest, with not much gritty information.

JF

Age range: 7–12

PLUCKROSE, Henry

GROWING

Franklin Watts, 1988, Hdbk, 0–86313–505–6
Series: Talkabout
Colour photographs

The close collaboration, shared understanding and common aims of the author, photographer and the publisher's production team is very obvious in this title. The result is an extremely attractive and visually well produced book which deals with a subject that young children often ponder and naturally want to discuss. The themes explored include: how growing things increase in size and weight, look different when fully grown, need food and water, and become old. The book is designed with great flair to stimulate questioning, deepen understanding and provide ideas for further investigation. It is, just as importantly, fun to look at and share with a grown-up. The cognitive links between sheep and lambs, sunflowers and seeds, and blossom and apples, etc. are established by an excellent combination of apt phraseology and superb matching colour photographs. The simple text

59

flows along with, and often literally fits into, the pictures. Highly recommended.

RG

Age range: 4–8

PORTER, Keith

HOW ANIMALS BEHAVE

CUP 1987, Hdbk, 0–521–33242–7
Series: Science World
Contents list, glossary, index, colour line drawings and photographs

This book provides more information on how animals function than on how animals behave. The mix of subjects is good and will interest children from eight and nine years old. A few spreads link animals and where they are found, such as 'trees and animals', 'life in the air', and 'nests and dens'. Other topics include social insects, animal families and animals at work. There is a section at the back on how to study animals, animals in zoos and how to care for them.

JF

Age range: 8–12

PORTER, Keith

LOOKING AT ANIMALS

CUP, 1987, Hdbk, 0–521–33241–9
Series: Science World
Contents list, glossary, index, colour line drawings and photographs

The main animal groups – insects, reptiles, birds, fish and mammals – are the 'meat' of this book. With such a wide choice to make from animals worldwide, the commonest and most publicized animals are included, sometimes in their habitats; butterflies and moths, 'animals about the home' and 'animals of the seashore'. 'Technology and science' are the themes of the series to which this book belongs but there is little technological information – using infra-red binoculars might have been more

useful than 'how birds fly', and underwater photography better then how gill slits work. The book seems to lack direction and purpose.

JF

Age range: 8–12

SEDDON, Tony and BAILEY, Jill

THE YOUNG SCIENTIST'S GUIDE TO THE LIVING WORLD

OUP, 1986, Hdbk, 0–19–918220–5
Series: The Young Scientist
Contents list, glossary, index, colour line drawings and black and white and colour photographs

This has the feel of a Guinness Records book, with facts and figures and 'Did you Know?' boxes everywhere. It is a mine of information for inquisitive children and will keep them occupied for a long time. It is a book to dip into, or to use as an encylopedia, and certainly needs to be in the school library, perhaps as a restricted reference work. Line illustrations are everywhere interspersed with colour photographs and boxes of information on mini-topics. Access to information is either via the index or through the 65 or so subjects which make the whole book. Once on the relevant page, there are pointers to other pages in the book which have other useful information.

JF

Age range: 8–12

STOCKLEY, Corinne

THE USBORNE ILLUSTRATED DICTIONARY OF BIOLOGY

Usborne, 1986, Pbk, 0–86020–707–2
Contents list, index, black and white and colour line drawings

Dictionary of Human *Biology* might have been a more appropriate title for this book, as a significant part is taken up with the workings of the human body. Three of the items on the front cover (frog, butterfly and earthworm – staple laboratory animals) are not included in the index, so the content is a little strange. However, what is in the book is accurate, and rather concentrated, in the manner of revision notes. It is probably useful to have in the library but it does not live up to its title.

JF

Age range: 11–16

WILKINSON, Phil et al. (eds)

EARLY PEOPLE

Dorling Kindersley, 1989, Hdbk, 0–86318–342–5
Series: Eyewitness Guides
Contents list, index, black and white and colour line drawings and photographs

The 'eyewitness' characteristic of this book is to show implements, clothing, jewellery, weapons, skulls, and other artefacts as touchably real as if they were exhibits in a museum display case. Colour photographs of flints and farm tools, mummified parts and Iron Age swords are certainly stunning, and superb as a pictorial aid for classroom and library research. Young readers will probably be uncritical because this pragmatic use is so obvious. Teachers will have some doubts about the snapshot knowledge which implies order through mere juxtaposition, context-less profusion of illustrations of many types (Victorian engravings and the lot), the inclusion of anything anthropological when the truly ancient runs short, pictures of anything at all (almonds? wheat?), and facetious captions. Discovery for sure, but see it for what it is.

SH

Age range: 9–12

ECOLOGY

BENDER, Lionel

MOUNTAIN

Franklin Watts, 1988, Hdbk, 0–86313–737–7
Series: The Story of the Earth
Contents list, glossary, index, colour line
drawings and photographs

The idea of the passage of time, in a geological sense, and the fact that the topography of our earth is continuously changing are both difficult concepts for young minds to accommodate. This title, in the *Story of the Earth* series, conveys these ideas very well. It is designed very carefully to help juniors appreciate that certain geological processes cause mountains to form and rise and that others eventually break them down and wear them away. The concise introduction outlines the geological lifetime of a mountain and explains how the book is organized. Ten double-spread chapters follow and each provides a time-lapse 'snapshot' of an imaginary mountain, from its birth to its eradication. Each of these chapters contains a straightforward paragraph or two of explanation and good photographic examples of the real thing from somewhere around the world. The excellent cut-away diagrams also help to make what is going on underground very clear. Recommended.

RG

Age range: 8–13

BRAMWELL, Martyn

DESERTS

Franklin Watts, 1987, Hdbk, 0–86313–525–0
Series: Earth Science Library
Contents list, glossary, index, colour line
drawings and photographs

Deserts are places with less than 25 cm of rain a year. Each year an area as big as Belgium becomes desert. These statements characterize this fascinating book on deserts: it is full of interesting and important information, and it stresses how deserts come into being and are always changing. As an introduction to physical geography for junior readers, such books are outstanding. Expository prose is simple, integrating technical vocabulary easily (e.g. loess, inselberg) with the support of a glossary, and using a variety of typefaces for different levels and motivations of reader. Diagrams imaginatively represent processes like erosion by wind or the movement of sand dunes. Strange rock formations and the ingenious adaptations of desert fauna are exciting and memorable. Picture research shows apt examples from round the world. The final message about caring for deserts (e.g. by not overgrazing or exploitation) is not moralistic.

SH

Age range: 9–11

FITZGERALD, Janet

WINTER IN THE WOOD

Hamish Hamilton, 1987, Hdbk, 0–241–12092–6
Series: Science Through the Seasons
Colour photographs

Children are encouraged in this book to make observations and do practical work around the theme of the wood in winter. Making bark rubbings, listening to the wind blowing by blowing through straws, looking for animal signs and interpreting animal marks in the snow are just some of the ideas. At the end of the book further suggestions are made for teachers and parents. The series has four titles to correspond with each season.

JF

Age range: 5–8

KING-SMITH, Dick

WATER WATCH

Penguin, 1988, Pbk, 0–14–032341–4
Black and white line drawings

Older children who want to read their first ecology book might consider this little title; it is in larger type for first-time readers who want to do some serious reading. The line drawings help to break up the text. This ecological title is all about life in different habitats such as rivers, seas, wetlands and ponds and is written by the country-living author who has published other books on the environment at this level (as well as his novels). The book is a great success since it introduces ecology without ever mentioning it.

JF

Age range: 7–12

LUCHT, Irmgard

FOREST CALENDAR

Black, 1988, Hdbk, 0–7136–3024–8
Contents list, index, colour photographs

This is a delightful book, and an inspiration to all children who leaf through its pages. The illustrations which evoke the heart of European forests (e.g. the Black Forest) are thought-provoking, lively and interesting, and carry the reader through the year. The flora and fauna are slotted in sympathetically and accurately and one certainly has a sense of place – of actually being in the wood, or forest. The illustrations are excellent and evocative.

JF

Age range: 5–8

LYE, Keith

DESERTS

Wayland, 1987, Hdbk, 0–85078–875–7
Series: Our World

Contents list, glossary, index, black and white and colour photographs

This is a very informative book on deserts. It covers the worldwide distribution of the different types of desert, availability of water, oases and erosion. The plants and animals of deserts and their adaptations to this dry environment are dealt with, including the blooming of deserts after rainfall. Children will be interested in the life of desert nomads and indigenous people, about expeditions across famous deserts and survival in them. The processes of desertification, reclamation and exploitation of mineral resources brings this book well up to date, certainly making it a recommended book on the subject for all school libraries.

JF

Age range: 10–16

ROWLAND-ENTWISTLE, Theodore

JUNGLES AND RAINFORESTS

Wayland, 1987, Hdbk, 0–85078–874–9
Series: Our World
Contents list, glossary, index, colour line drawings and photographs

Jungles *per se* are not included in this book which is a pity, and the true distinction between jungles and rainforests is not properly attended to. Rainforest coverage is good, with details on distribution, structure, flora and fauna, pollination and death and decay. Mangrove swamps, as coastal rainforest, are also included, as is the interaction of man and forest with details of fruits of the forest and agriculture. There are some irritating omissions and mistakes; some of the line drawings have no captions or explanations; others do not show what is labelled and there is one caption which doesn't make sense.

JF

Age range: 10–16

THE ENVIRONMENT

◆

This looks to be the growth area in children's publishing for the 1990s. But publishers beware: where are all those computer books which sprang up a decade ago? As Wendy Cope said in a recent review, 'These days a lot of trees are being pulped so that bad writing about environmental problems can be published'.

BAINES, John

ACID RAIN

Wayland, 1989, Hdbk, 1–85210–694–8
Series: Conserving Our World
Bibliography, contents list, glossary, index, useful
addresses, colour line drawings and photographs

Our planet is threatened by pollution in many forms, one of which is acid rain. Baines is Director of the Council for Environmental Education, and uses powerful, clear arguments to pin down the extent of the problem, and then, optimistically, to suggest how individual and international action can combat the problem. His persona is friendly and responsible, coming through an authoritative and well structured text which really has been written with the illustrations in mind. Information and persuasion are used in fair ways to encourage young readers to take a more informed and active interest. Fact boxes, insets with telling comments from concerned people round the world, and numerous practical exercises (like testing soil samples) make this a versatile addition to a personal or school library. The range of follow-up readings and addresses implies help from a teacher.

SH

Age range: 11–15

BECKLAKE, John

THE CLIMATE CRISIS: THE GREENHOUSE EFFECT AND OZONE LAYER

Franklin Watts, 1989, Hdbk, 0–86313–946–9
Series: Issues
Contents list, index, colour line drawings and
photographs

That global warming, resulting from changes in the earth's atmosphere brought about by man, could cause a climate crisis is certainly a topic worthy of consideration in a book, in a series designed to discuss some of the important issues on earth today.

However this colourful book, as an information book for young children, is rather disappointing, for it assumes not only that they have been made aware of the issue by newspapers and TV programmes, but that they have understood the terms being used. (It would be nice to think they had!)

Thus we find the phrase 'greenhouse effect' used several times before an attempt is made on p.8 to explain it. (The ozone hole is discussed on p.18!) Little explanation is to be found in the labelling and titles that accompany the colour photographs and other illustrations. The text contains a few typographical errors, and a few misleading phrases – as some ill-chosen words have crept in. Many facts are given but, from an educational point of view, they are in places rather poorly presented: there is insufficient scientific discussion.

WFW

Age range: 10–14

BRIGHT, Michael

POLLUTION AND WILDLIFE

Franklin Watts, 1987, Hdbk, 0–86313–542–0
Series: Survival
Contents list, index, useful addresses, black and
white and colour line drawings and photographs

This book looks at wildlife under threat because of our failure to protect the environment from pollution. Various types of pollution (of land, the sea, fresh water and the atmosphere) are considered – pollution due to ignorance, carelessness and money-saving malpractice: man-made litter; industrial, agricultural and domestic waste; oil slicks; the products of combustion of fuels; the toxic waste such as heavy metal compounds and cyanides from the metal extraction and plating industries; nuclear waste; sewage, and effluents from industry, agriculture and land-fill; airborne sprays of herbicides and pesticides, that can accumulate in food chains; pollutants of the atmosphere, especially by CFCs, PBCs and those gases causing acid rain, or threatening the ozone layer.

A wide variety of wildlife under threat is considered, and beautifully illustrated: sea birds and marine mammals, fish, reptiles, amphibia and land mammals, large raptors, colourful insects such as butterflies, and various plants, especially trees.

WFW

Age range: 8–13

JAMES, Barbara

WASTE AND RECYCLING

Wayland, 1989, Hdbk, 1–85210–697–2
Series: Conserving Our World
Bibliography, contents list, glossary, index, colour line drawings and photographs

The subject of waste and recycling is an increasingly big one, and greater attention is likely to be focused on it for educational purposes in the future. This book is superb. It is up to date with pollution disasters, gives an impartial overview of the subject, is easy to work through, and is well illustrated. Plenty of facts are produced, hypotheses offered, basic problems (e.g. population growth) stressed and solutions suggested. Altogether a tremendous treatment, but be forewarned about the lines of bodies waiting to be burnt at Bhopal, which elicits curious comments from five-year-olds.

JF

Age range: 10–16

LAMBERT, Mark

POLLUTION

Wayland, 1988, Hdbk, 1–85210–110–5
Series: Let's Discuss
Contents list, glossary, index, black and white photographs

This is a book to stimulate active thought and discussion. The pictures throughout

are in black and white (some well dated), and cover the main issues that face mankind, particularly pollution of the air, sea and water, though noise pollution seems to have been missed out. There is a big section on radioactivity with details about Chernobyl. Of great interest to children will be the case stories of individuals whose lives are caught up in one sort of pollution or another. Different views are explained and children asked which ones they agree with. A very thought-provoking book which must be on every school library shelf.

JF

Age range: 12–16

MARKHAM, Adam

THE ENVIRONMENT

Wayland, 1988, Hdbk, 1–85210–141–5
Bibliography, glossary, index, black and white and colour photographs

Written by an expert from the Friends of the Earth, this is a reasonable account of the state of the environment up to 1988. Bophal, Chernobyl, the polluted North Sea, the Rhine – they are all here. For a first introduction to children this is certainly an eye-opener, and certainly makes them ask questions like exactly how many whales were killed, for instance, when they look at pictures of dead whales. Acid rain, ozone layer, greenhouse effect – the basic facts are all here, albeit dating rapidly. Advanced children will be champing for more.

JF

Age range: 12–16

MIDDLETON, Nick

ATLAS OF ENVIRONMENTAL ISSUES

OUP, 1988, Hdbk, 0–19–831674–7
Contents list, index, colour line drawings and photographs

It is rare amongst nature conservation

books to find one which shines above all others and has a great deal to offer the educational establishment. This is it. Go out and buy one or two copies for the school library, for what it portrays is infinitely more useful than its outlay. There is hardly a subject not covered, from acid rain and Antarctica to desertification and deforestation. Richly embroidered in full colour throughout, making for easy interpretation by children, it is a mini-encyclopedia.

JF

Age range: 12–16

NEAL, Phillip

THE URBAN SCENE

Dryad, 1987, Hdbk, 0–85219–685–7
Series: Considering Conservation
Contents list, glossary, index, black and white line drawings and photographs

This is a mine of information on the urban environment, full of illustrations. Almost too much is packed in, but this is not a bad thing for the older child who will hardly exhaust the material presented. It is a good book for browsing through, simply for tit-bits of information. Children are encouraged through the book to interpret what they see and to be inquisitive – from the embellishments on buildings to waste disposal and

infrastructure. Many of the photographs were taken in the West Midlands and Eastborne, as contrasting sites, and a small amount of material is relevant to the USA.

JF

Age range: 12–16

PENNY, Malcolm

PROTECTING WILDLIFE

Wayland, 1989, Hdbk, 1–85210–698–0
Contents list, glossary, index, colour photographs

Overall this is a very good book, and should be bought for all school libraries. The range of subjects described is excellent and up to date, and the supporting photographs are explicit and well thought-out. The problems arising from man are stressed, especially habitat destruction, and many examples are given of increasing the populations of endangered animals by captive breeding. There could have been more on definitions of, for instance, 'threatened', 'vulnerable' and 'endangered', and the story of the extinction of the large blue butterfly could have been tightened up on accuracy – otherwise a book to be recommended.

JF

Age range: 10–16

BOTANICAL SCIENCES

BAILEY, Jill

DISCOVERING TREES

Wayland, 1988, Hdbk, 1–85210–064–8
Series: Discovering Nature
Bibliography, contents list, glossary, index,
colour line drawings and photographs

Since this book was published, we have all become aware of the vitally important part trees play in our environment. The continuing destruction of the rainforest and the subsequent speeding up of the greenhouse effect has become a major world environmental concern.
Discovering Trees provides children with a much broader understanding of the economic value and beauty of trees, besides detailing their very important role as absorbers of carbon dioxide. The introductory chapters describe and distinguish, in simple language, broadleaf from coniferous trees and go on to outline tree biology, i.e. photosynthesis, growth, reproduction and fruit and seed dispersal, etc. As with other titles in this series, there are excellent photographs and a useful glossary. The final chapters describe tree products we all take for granted and how, in both life and death, trees provide homes and food for thousands of other plants and animals. Recommended.

RG

Age range: 7–11

BURNIE, David

PLANT

Dorling Kindersley, 1989, Hdbk, 0–86318–368–9
Series: Eyewitness Guides
Contents list, index, black and white line
drawings and colour photographs

As part of a series of thoroughly good books, this one is quite simply of equally high standard and to be recommended.

After considering what actually is a plant, it goes on to look at the different parts of the plant, stem, leaves, flower and fruits, often using an interesting and sometime colourful means of expressing the change in form of each. Thus the flower is shown as a small bud, developing larger, opening, flourishing and falling apart then revealing different stages of the developing fruit. Forms of reproduction (sexual and asexual), forms of defence, carnivorous and parasitic plants are well treated. There are also sections on the different environments in which plants live and a potted history of plant collectors.

JF

Age range: 8–14

COLDREY, Jennifer and BERNARD, George

HYACINTH

Black, 1989, Hdbk, 0–7136–3095–7
Series: Stopwatch
Index, black and white line drawings and colour
photographs

Stopwatch books are an exciting set of information books which could be used by a variety of age groups in a primary school. They invite the reader to pick them up by the beautiful photographs on the front cover. All the books follow the same format, good real-life photographs supported by a simple but informative text. Children with very little reading experience would be able to extract information solely by looking at the photographs which follow a natural progression throughout the books. The pages are clearly numbered and the first sentence on each page is in larger letters than the rest, which again would help to hold the interest of a younger reader. At the end of each book is an index and a series of small photographs providing a summary of the contents of the book. This set of books would be an excellent introduction to non-fiction books for young children. *Hyacinth* held the interest of my own class of 5–6-year-olds last year while they observed a pot of hyacinth bulbs growing in the classroom. As the bulbs grew so the appropriate page was displayed next to it. It was almost possible to smell the scent of the hyacinth from one of the excellent photographs.

BS

Age range: 5–8

KILBRACKEN, John

TREE RECOGNITION

Kingfisher, 1983, Pbk, 0–86272–398–1
Series: The Easy Way to
Index, colour line drawings and photographs

The whole of this book is taken up with a key to trees, some 172 questions and answers, to help identify 114 tree species, regarded as being the commonest in Britain and Ireland. Children of about eight and above will be able to handle this book. The format is quite simple and effective; questions are asked about the nature of the tree being investigated. Any difficult words concerning identification are explained, just before details are given as to where to go next in the key; thus there is no need for a glossary. The text is generously interspersed with colour diagrams and line drawings showing key identification items. This is a good companion book to birds in the same series.

JF

Age range: 8+

REDFERN, Margaret

INSECTS AND THISTLES

CUP/Richmond, 1983, Pbk, 0–521–29933–0
Series: Naturalists' Handbooks
Contents list, glossary, index, black and white and colour line drawings and colour photographs

All titles in this series represent the most amazing value for money. Sixth formers and those without university training are the targeted audience and much field work is encouraged. Most of this book is made up of a comprehensive biological key for identifying organisms from thistles. There are numerous illustrations for assistance. The first section of the book goes into great detail about the structure of communities, stem-borers and leaf-miners and effects of herbivores in biological control of thistles. The book is written by experts and supported by worthy scientific bodies. There is much here to stimulate students' interest.

JF

Age range: 16+

WATTS, Barrie

APPLE TREE

Black, 1989, Hdbk, 0–7136–2818–9
Series: Stopwatch
Index, black and white line drawings and colour photographs

This is a picture book of superb colour photographs for the youngest children. It describes the development of the apple, through the stages of flowers, pollination by insects and fruit formation. There is also information on seasonal changes by line drawings which explain what can be seen in the pictures, though three labels spread between five drawings is not very helpful. There is a useful revision section at the back.

JF

Age range: 5–10

ZOOLOGY

ALTHEA

ANIMALS AT NIGHT

Dinosaur, 1987, Pbk, 0–85122–666–3
Colour line drawings

For children who are aged five or more
this is a picture story book which they can
manage with assistance. The illustrations
are large and interesting and describe
creatures that children are likely to see,
such as frogs, toads and snails. The story
is also told of living things that come out
well after children have gone to bed –
badgers, foxes, wood mice and owls.

JF

Age range: 5–8

BAILEY, Jill

MIMICRY AND CAMOUFLAGE

Hodder and Stoughton, 1988, Hdbk,
0–340–42660–8
Series: The Young Naturalist
Bibliography, contents list, glossary, index,
colour line drawings and photographs

This book is full of fascinating detail of the
animal world and pages of discovery.
Over 100 colour photographs depict
scenes which pose mysteries and deceits
enabling the amateur naturalist to unravel
stories. There are so many mimicry
stories to tell and this author has collected
together a veritable assembly. Some of
the classic camouflage stories such as
peppered moth are retold; others of, for
instance, butterfly mimicry in the simplest
terms are not. Altogether this is a
worthwhile book for school libraries.

JF

Age range: 7–14

BRAMWELL, Martin and PARKER, Steve

THE SMALL PLANT-EATERS

Facts on File, 1988, Hdbk, 0–948894–27–X
Series: Encyclopedia of the Animal World
Bibliography, contents list, glossary, index, black
and white and colour line drawings and
photographs

This book is one of the most enjoyable of
this series for children, perhaps because
they can associate with so many
mammals as pets, compared with reptiles
or insects. The colour photographs and
the colour artwork in this book are
particularly excellent and enthralling to
children with many a life-like scene
captured on the page. The information is
all very good, with a strong and useful
section on evolution at the start. This
book is thoroughly recommended.

JF

Age range: 12–16

PENNY, Malcolm

ANIMAL MIGRATION

Wayland, 1987, Hdbk, 0–85078–965–6
Series: The Animal Kingdom
Contents list, glossary, index, colour line
drawings and photographs

Migration is a big subject and is
adequately tackled in this book. It will
make a good project book for older
primary school children who will be able
to glean notes. The range of species is
drawn from insects (butterflies), birds
(swallows, swans, cranes, humming-
birds, seabirds), mammals (caribou,
wildebeest, sea mammals) and fish.
There are only five colour photographs in
the book, the remaining line illustrations,
all colour, are artistic and rather pleasant,
ideal for a younger audience.

JF

Age range: 8–12

PLUCKROSE, Henry

LOOK AT FUR AND FEATHERS

Franklin Watts, 1989, Hdbk, 0–86313–831–4
Series: Look at
Index, practical section, colour line drawings and
photographs

This is an innovative title likely to attract readers. It covers mammals and birds pretty evenly and starts from the standpoint of children's hair, then through the birth of animals and the hatching of birds with fur and feathers respectively. The use of fur for animal colouration is covered a little more thoroughly than bird colouration but the pictures throughout the book are of excellent quality. A section about the use of animals' fur and feathers by man is a good introduction to conservation and there is interesting detail on how to make a quill pen.

JF

Age range: 5–8

RUFFAULT, Charlotte

ANIMALS UNDERGROUND

Moonlight, 1987, Hdbk, 1–85103–026–3
Series: Pocket Worlds
Index, colour line drawings and photographs

This is a delightful little book (4 1/2 × 7in) and a must for the school library. The illustrations are exquisite and full of interest. Some of the scenes such as the badgers, moles and insects underground are very endearing, and scientifically accurate too. Animals chosen represent those in Europe and the Americas, but this makes for a more encylopedic and

educational book. A small book couldn't be better.

JF

Age range: 6–12

STIDWORTHY, John

SIMPLE ANIMALS

Facts on File, 1990, Hdbk, 0–8160–1968–1
Series: Encyclopedia of the Animal World
Bibliography, contents list, glossary, index,
colour line drawings and photographs

Simple Animals takes a very impressive look at invertebrate life forms, ranging from the familiar pond-dwelling amoeba through marine jellyfish, octopuses and crabs to landforms such as earthworms and snails. Although detailed and factual, the information is made accessible and inviting, for a middle school audience, by the straightforward non-patronizing language and the numerous top quality colour photographs and illustrations. The articles are mostly on double-page spreads and begin with a simple 'scene-setting' paragraph that puts each group of animals into context with their environment. The descriptions which follow outline habitats, physical traits and feeding and breeding habits. Furthermore, these are accompanied by useful fact panels which itemize such things as world distribution, diet and the conservation status of the animals. Good use is made of bold sub-headings throughout which lead the eye to the salient facts at the beginning of each paragraph and there is a thorough index and glossary.

RG

Age range: 8–13

MOLLUSCS AND OTHER RELATED ANIMALS

ARTHUR, Alex

SHELL

Dorling Kindersley, 1989, Hdbk, 0–86318–341–7
Series: Eyewitness Guides
Contents list, index, black and white line
drawings and colour photographs

This title is number nine in the extremely successful *Eyewitness Guides* series from Dorling Kindersley. For the purpose of this book the definition boundaries of the term 'shell' are extended well beyond merely snails and sea-shells. As well as the world of molluscs, we are invited to view a wide variety of other invertebrates such as crabs, lobsters and sea urchins as being 'shelled'. Obvious vertebrates such as turtles, tortoises and terrapins are also covered. Spread by spread the detailed morphology and life-styles of these often intricate and beautiful creatures are dealt with by superb sets of colour photographs and crisp, extended captions. The 'exploded' lobster illustration on pages 22 and 23 is an excellent example of the high technical quality of this book. An authoritative picture caption encyclopedia which is both stimulating and very informative. Highly recommended.

RG

Age range: 7–adult

BAILEY, Jill

DISCOVERING CRABS AND LOBSTERS

Wayland, 1987, Hdbk, 0–85078–819–6
Series: Discovering
Contents list, glossary, index, colour line
drawings and photographs

The intimate world of these crustaceans is unravelled through a series of good colour photographs and line drawings.

Important educational themes are played on with the inclusion of details on locomotion, migration, feeding and predators. Land, sea and fresh water crabs are explained and illustrated. The association of crustacean and mollusc is exemplified by the hermit crab. There are some interesting details on courtship and communication as well as how to study these animals.

JF

Age range: 7–12

COLDREY, Jennifer

DISCOVERING SLUGS AND SNAILS

Wayland, 1987, Hdbk, 0–85078–817–X
Series: Discovering
Bibliography, contents list, glossary, index,
colour photographs

Slugs and snails are dealt with in a most comprehensive and professional way in this book. The photographs are of high quality and stunning in the amount of information they impart. The book first deals with form and function, range of habitats used by slugs and snails, feeding, reproduction and predator–prey relationships. The impact of man on the group panders to curriculum requirements, so too do the recommended practical guidelines on how to look after slugs and snails. An excellent educational book.

JF

Age range: 7–12

HENWOOD, Chris

SNAILS AND SLUGS

Franklin Watts, 1988, Hdbk, 0–86313–691–5
Series: Keeping Minibeasts
Contents list, index, colour photographs

A series of wonderful close-up photographs show this group of animals in a new light, and worthy of keeping at home or in the classroom. The complete process of where to find slugs and snails, how to make a tank, caring for them, their special needs, hibernation and how to breed and release them back into the wild are all covered. A great book for a young audience.

JF

Age range: 6–8

OLESEN, Jens

SNAIL

Black, 1985, Hdbk, 0–7136–2708–5
Series: Stopwatch
Index, black and white line drawings and colour photographs

This book provides a very simplistic introduction to snails. It does not show their place in nature, or explain their great variety; it simply shows a few of their features and biology, such as how they move, how they mate (including love-darts), how the eggs develop and how snails eat and sample the environment. The line drawings and the electromicrograph which complement the colour photographs could have been improved with labels.

JF

Age range: 6–10

INSECTS

BARRETT, Norman

SPIDERS

Franklin Watts, 1989, Hdbk, 0–86313–813–6
Series: Picture Library
Contents list, glossary, index, black and white
and colour line drawings and colour photographs

Several of the photographs in this book
have been printed the wrong way up, for
spiders normally hang downwards on
their webs, but apart from this gaffe, the
colour pictures are revealing, informative
and will be a source of inspiration to
children. There are wolf spiders,
tarantulas, raft spiders and crab spiders
illustrated in threatening close-up with all
their brilliant colours, fangs and palps
displayed. How silk webs are fashioned,
how they are employed for capturing
prey and how spiders reproduce are all
covered.

JF

Age range: 7–12

BENDER, Lionel

POISONOUS INSECTS

Franklin Watts, 1988, Hdbk, 0–86313–764–4
Series: First Sight
Contents list, index, colour line drawings and
photographs

By the use of full page colour
photographs, and a large format book,
the publishers have brought together a
story about poisonous insects. The
poisonous nature of the insects chosen is
mostly in reference to other unsuspecting
invertebrates rather than man, with the
exception of the fleas, lice, bugs and flies.
There is great emphasis on predators and
insect vectors and less on poisonous
brightly coloured insects. For the most
part the photographs are quite stunning,
but one feels that much more information

could have been packed into the book
and the aim more clearly defined.

JF

Age range: 7–12

FORSYTHE, J. G.

COMMON GROUND BEETLES

Richmond, 1987, Pbk, 0–85546–263–9
Series: Naturalists' Handbooks
Contents list, glossary, index, black and white
and colour line drawings and colour photographs

Written by one of the leading
carabidologists in the country, this is a
long awaited book. Good books on
beetles are scarce and this one dealing
with the carabids, of which 342 species
occur in Britain, is most welcome,
especially with its fine collection of colour
illustrations of a selection of common
carabids. There are many black and white
illustrations too, and these support the
biological keys which will keep
coleopterists busy for a long time. The
natural history section is particularly
thorough and interesting and there is
plenty of information about how to
collect specimens, where to look for them
and how to collate data. This book, like
others in the series, will be an essential
item for all field studies.

JF

Age range: 16+

LOSITO, Linda

DAMSELFLIES AND DRAGONFLIES

Wayland, 1987, Hdbk, 1–85210–061–3
Series: Discovering
Contents list, glossary, index, colour line
drawings and photographs

Young pond-dippers will enjoy this book,
for it will link up their field observations

with what these carnivorous insects are all about. In fact a child leafing through this book would understand much about the way of life of damselflies and dragonflies without going on a field visit. The differences between these two groups of aquatic insect are explained, their evolutionary (fossil) history is expounded, how they fly, hunt and are hunted are admirably touched on. Reproduction is well done too. It will be good to have this set of photographs in the school library for reference, though the colours are not particularly stunning.

JF

Age range: 7–12

McGAVIN, George

BUGS

Wayland, 1988, Hdbk, 1–85210–065–6
Series: Discovering
Contents list, glossary, index, colour line
drawings and photographs

This is an important book on true bugs, that is hemipterous ones, rather than all sorts of unrelated insects which the layperson calls 'bugs'. It takes on the world of bugs in all their magnificent colour, form and diversity and describes all their antics and deceits in a way that children will enjoy. The colour photographs and drawings are excellent, introducing children to life cycles and defence as well as a section on how to study them.

JF

Age range: 7–12

OLESEN, Jens

BUMBLEBEE

Black, 1988, Hdbk, 0–7136–2976–2
Series: Stopwatch
Index, black and white line drawings and colour
photographs

This title in the *Stopwatch* series is a good

example of a 'first fact' picture book for very young readers. It would be an ideal resource for any infant/lower junior mini-beast project. The eleven excellent, whole-page, colour photographs give us intimate knowledge of a year's goings on in a bumblebee's nest. There are many clear line drawings which further explain the bumblebee's life cycle and are very good for inexpert artists to copy into their topic books. The text which explains each stage is simple and has a bold heading for very young children. The slightly more detailed information relating to the photographs is intended for more advanced readers. This arrangement is admirably suited for a shared reading session with a parent or teacher. These endearing furry creatures are extremely photogenic and their industrious, short lives are captured beautifully in this super book. Recommended.

RG

Age range: 5–9

O'TOOLE, Christopher

DISCOVERING ANTS

Wayland, 1986, Hdbk, 0–85078–737–8
Series: Discovering Nature
Bibliography, contents list, glossary, index,
colour line drawings and photographs

Frequently primary school libraries have an over-abundance of old Nature Study books. This is partly because young children have always been naturally interested in wildlife and also because, over the years, teachers have used mini-beast projects as an easy way of tapping into this enthusiasm. If, in the course of stock editing, a new title on ants is deemed necessary, then *Discovering Ants* is a title which should prove hard to resist. There is an excellent set of well captioned colour photographs, from Oxford Scientific Films, which are extremely well integrated into the easy-to-read text. The medium-sized print, with bold-type words explained in the glossary, is arranged in two columns. This, together with good use of sub-headings and wide margins, makes each page seem non-intimidatory and renders the information contained there easily accessible to young, reasonably fluent readers. Highly recommended.

RG

Age range: 7–11

O'TOOLE, Christopher

DISCOVERING FLIES

Wayland, 1986, Hdbk, 0–85078–814–5
Series: Discovering
Contents list, glossary, index, colour line drawings and photographs

It is very unusual to have a new subject offered on the natural history market for children. This is one, since flies have never been dealt with in such a manner before. Teachers might be squeamish of the images, but it is a world of discovery for children (and for teachers too) since the world is the limit for this big order of insects. The regulars are covered, such as the mosquito, housefly and hoverfly but there are tropical African flies to impress or to be wary of, as well as beneficial and pest flies. This books excels in its portrayal of flies, which might otherwise be neglected.

JF

Age range: 7–12

PENNY, Malcolm

SPIDERS

Wayland, 1989, Hdbk, 1–85210–735–9
Series: Nature Study
Contents list, glossary, index, colour line drawings and photographs

By matching a superb collection of colour photographs with an excellent set of short, simple captions, Wayland has the right formula for a first fact book on spiders that top infants and juniors can

read and enjoy. The text, all in large type, is supported by chapter and sub-headings and a concise glossary. Most importantly, the captions are rarely more than four sentences long. The photographs, from Oxford Scientific Films, show clearly the wide variety of habitats and life-styles spiders have adopted. One chapter describes the multifarious ways different species use webs as traps, tunnels, nets and even as bolas to catch their prey. The chapter on reproduction describes the risks male spiders have at mating time and goes on to show the various ways eggs and offspring are given aftercare. There are also chapters on poisonous spiders and those that don't use webs at all. Highly recommended.

RG

Age range: 7–11

PRESTON-MAFHAM, Ken

CENTIPEDES AND MILLIPEDES

Wayland, 1989, Hdbk, 1–85210–386–8
Series: Discovering
Contents list, glossary, index, colour photographs

Preston-Mafham's stunning close-up photographs are brought together here in a rare book, for centipedes and millipedes have hardly ever had a photographic book devoted to them. This book opens the lid on the familiar millipede and centipede of the garden, to a world of beautiful, sometimes poisonous exotica that people, let alone children, probably did not realize exist. The photographer has also written the text and has been to many continents to see these creatures at first hand and to speak from personal experience with them. This is a thoroughly good book, benefiting all libraries, on a much neglected subject.

JF

Age range: 7–12

WATTS, Barrie

BEETLES

Franklin Watts, 1989, Hdbk, 0–86313–854–4
Series: Keeping Minibeasts
Contents list, index, colour photographs

Pets are of all kinds but mini-beasts are not pets. This series, about slugs and snails and spiders and the rest, shows young readers how to collect, house, feed and observe creatures which ultimately should be returned to their original habit (unless they are pests!). Beetles can be big or small, fly or not, feed on aphids or dung or worms or even meat, pupate from larvae and lay eggs which can be watched in their various stages of growth. Information about beetles is coupled with advice about handling them, from catching them with a pitfall trap to making sure beetles of different types don't share accommodation and eat each other. Excellent colour photos help a concise text to make all these features clear, and conceptual levels and stylistic tone are just right to make the hobby interesting, without smirking about its being gruesome or pretending to be coy. Taken seriously, this is a fascinating area of knowledge discovery for young children.

SH

Age range: 5–8

WATTS, Barrie

BUTTERFLY AND CATERPILLAR

Black, 1985, Hdbk, 0–7136–2709–3
Series: Stopwatch
Index, black and white line drawings and colour photographs

This book, which is designed for Juniors, shows by excellent colour photographs the stages in the life cycle of the cabbage white butterfly, which are explained in simple language, with bold headings for very young children and more detailed information for the slightly more competent readers.

There are also some clear black and white drawings. These lack the detailed labelling required for biological drawings for secondary school pupils, but even they would appreciate the superb colour photographs and simple account in this book.

Strangely, the damage caused to the leaves of cabbage plants by feeding caterpillars is not shown.

JW

Age range: 5–9

WATTS, Barrie

CATERPILLARS

Franklin Watts, 1989, Hdbk, 0–86313–844–6
Series: Keeping Minibeasts
Contents list, index, colour photographs

This is a story book for youngsters, as well as a simple practical guide to rearing techniques. There is plenty of background information on colour, habitats of caterpillars and life cycle explained from egg to adult of the cabbage white, and one is left feeling that perhaps a little more space might have been devoted to the diverse world of caterpillars and how to look after them. There are, though, some useful practical tips, and the large type is suited for children to enjoy.

JF

Age range: 5–8

WATTS, Barrie

DRAGONFLY

Black, 1988, Hdbk, 0–7136–3053–1
Series: Stopwatch
Index, black and white line drawings and colour photographs

Nature programmes on TV are ideal for showing whole sequences, but they go at their own speed. This book gives key stages in fast-freeze still photographs, skilfully sequenced so as to be easy for younger readers to understand. Text works on two levels, simple bold headings for slow readers, fuller text for better ones. Close links between text, diagrams and photographs is imaginatively maintained so that at all stages the reader is looking hard, learning, and never lost. The photographs are as good as any TV, and commentary simple without distortion. The overall narrative structure is easy to comprehend: from mating and birth, through nymph ('it is now as big as a match') and emergence from the old skin, to adult. At the end the readers are invited to tell the story for themselves, helped by a small series of key pictures. A useful addition to the infant/primary library.

SH

Age range: 5–9

WATTS, Barrie

EARWIG

Black, 1989, Hdbk, 0–7136–3094–9
Series: Stopwatch
Index, black and white line drawings and colour photographs

The close-up quality of the 23 colour photographs used in the production of this book, including those on the eye-catching cover, make this a book for all ages to enjoy. The excellent line drawings are used to good effect to bring in the scale of things, such as the tiny size of the earwig nymphs at birth. There is a really good feature at the end of the book, common to all the series, where a set of photographs is used to summarize all the stages of the earwig life cycle. This offers the chance for young readers to recall these events in their own words. The text is clear and, again, written with good educational aims in mind. There are bold headings which young readers can attempt. These encapsulate the main idea of each page and the rest of the text, intended for better readers, gives

supporting detail to the accompanying large photograph on the opposite page. Recommended.

RG

Age range: 5–9

WATTS, Barrie

LADYBIRD

Black, 1987, Hdbk, 0–7136–2856–1
Series: Stopwatch
Index, black and white line drawings and colour photographs

This book simply depicts the life cycle of the ladybird in excellent close-up colour. There are some line drawings on opposite pages to some of the photographs which seem to explain what is shown – however, with only three labels between seven diagrams an opportunity has been missed and no explanations are given. The text is very basic and contains no scientific information; and as such it is only suitable for the lowest age group as a picture book which they will enjoy.

JF

Age range: 6–10

WHALLEY, Paul

BUTTERFLY AND MOTH

Dorling Kindersley, 1988, Hdbk, 0–86318–319–0
Series: Eyewitness Guides
Contents list, glossary, index, black and white and colour line drawings and photographs

Written by a stalwart of the butterfly world formerly based at The Natural History Museum, this volume complements well this series. The book seeks to sort butterflies and moths out from each other, even though they are so closely related. The first half is about the diverse world of butterflies; the second half is about the even more diverse world of moths. Life cycles from eggs to adults via caterpillars and pupae are explained, and the wonderful world of colour, mimicry and general exotica are all well presented. Overall a thorough, well balanced and good treatment of the subject and a book to be recommended.

JF

Age range: 7–14

YEO, P. F. and CORBET, S. A.

SOLITARY WASPS

CUP/Richmond, 1983, Pbk, 0–521–23387–9
Series: Naturalists' Handbooks
Contents list, glossary, index, black and white and colour line drawings and colour photographs

The study of solitary wasps is a specialized one but here for the first time is a practical book especially for sixth-form students and those without any university training. It is ideal for students engaged on field work, making observations, using hand lenses and working with binocular microscopes. A section at the back recommends ways to study solitary wasps and to find out much more on the subject. The numerous illustrations support the substantial biological key which makes up most of the book. Students will find interesting the section at the beginning of the book on the natural history of solitary wasps.

JF

Age range: 16+

FISHES

BREWSTER, Bernice

FRESHWATER FISH

Wayland, 1989, Hdbk, 1–85210–062–1
Series: Discovering
Contents list, glossary, index, colour line
drawings and photographs

This is about freshwater fish the world over, not just the UK. So there are pictures of familiar aquarium fishes like neon tetras, scissor fish, angel fish, guppies and sucking loaches. Most are photographs taken in aquaria, not taken in freshwater in the wild. Items relevant to the curriculum include details on how to look after fish and how they are bred in captivity. There are good sections on courtship, nest building in the stickleback, food feeding and predators. Goldfish and koi carp are described. This is quite an interesting book, a bit jumbled, but good.

JF

Age range: 7–12

CLARK, Elizabeth

FISH

Wayland, 1989, Hdbk, 1–85210–255–1
Series: Food
Bibliography, contents list, glossary, index,
colour line drawings and photographs

Those wanting to know where fish come from will find it in this digest of information. Freshwater and seawater fish are given separate sections and there are spreads on fish farming, netting at sea and simple angling. The importance of clean water is stressed through a spread on effects of pollution on fish stocks, and all the processes to get fish from the water to the table are explained. A number of fish recipes are provided at the end of the book.

JF

Age range: 7–11

COUPE, Sheena and Robert

SHARKS

Facts on File, 1990, Hdbk, 0–8160–2270–4
Series: Great Creatures of the World
Contents list, glossary, index, colour line
drawings and photographs

Facts on File has published this book about sharks with an eye to the market. This, along with other titles in the series, describes the physical characteristics and habitats of a wild animal that, for one reason or another, fascinates adults and children alike. Any idea, however, that this title has been produced only to capitalize on the gruesome reputation sharks have as man-eating monsters should be dropped immediately. This is a comprehensive, thoroughly recommendable, authoritative production. It is written in a straighforward narrative style with double-spread chapters on shark evolution, feeding habits and shark products, etc. Inevitably longer chapters describe shark attacks and how we deal with this problem. The production highlights are, however, the many superb colour photographs, obviously taken by brave and accomplished professionals which, along with the colour drawings and diagrams, really suit the large format and augment the very informative text.

RG

Age range: 5–adult

PATTERSON, Geoffrey

FISH FROM THE SEA

André Deutsch, 1989, Hdbk, 0–233–98272–8
Colour line drawings

This is a fish book with a difference. It is composed of evocative artwork on each double-page spread and a neat and concise text which can either be read out by teacher or parent, or worked through by a child of seven and older. The appeal is very much in the illustrations, so the reading to the child would make this book most effective. The illustrations show the disposition of fish in the sea, in midwater, on the bottom and in shoals. Identification of fish is dealt with; so too is the important impact of man on fish, how they are caught, processed and taken to the fishmonger. A unique way to look at fish, and a fine fish book.

JF

Age range: 6–10

POPE, Joyce

FISH

Franklin Watts, 1990, Hdbk, 0–86313–416–5
Series: Taking Care of your Pet
Contents list, index, checklist, black and white line drawings and colour photographs

The what and how of books like this are crucial. Young readers want reliable and easy-to-understand instructions and advice on keeping pets, and no unnecessary verbiage and indulgence. Joyce Pope's experience as a lecturer at the British Museum of Natural History shows through in this book. It is a model of common sense and practical wisdom expressed in crystal-clear words with relevant well positioned photographs and illustrations. Fish aren't toys but living creatures; they get sick, they need thought. Some are aggressive and there are times when they get frightened. Pictures of the most popular kinds, and of children doing tasks like cleaning out and adding new arrivals to a tank, are just what readers want and expect to see. Lots of good ideas are provided by the photographs, and advice on plants and fish food. A checklist and question and answer slot are good features. With a book like this, it would be your fault if the fish died.

SH

Age range: 8–10 (and younger with adult help)

WATTS, Barrie

STICKLEBACK

Black, 1988, Hdbk, 0–7136–2977–0
Series: Stopwatch
Index, black and white line drawings and colour photographs

In very simple terms for infants, this book gives an excellent account of the life history of the familiar stickleback. The photographs are excellent, particularly those in close-up and they reveal details which are difficult to perceive with the naked eye. Courtship, nest building, egg laying, parental care and development of the eggs through to the adult are described and illustrated. In this series, line drawings help to clarify features and there is a useful photographic summary at the end.

JF

Age range: 6–10

WHEELER, Alwyne

DISCOVERING SALTWATER FISH

Wayland, 1987, Hdbk, 1–85210–066–4
Series: Discovering Nature
Bibliography, contents list, glossary, index, colour line drawings and photographs

There are, according to this title, 1300 different kinds of fish living in our seas, many of which we rarely see and know very little about. This book gives a reliable and attractively presented overview of this enormous and often highly photogenic group of animals. Following the introductory chapter, which describes and distinguishes the bony fish from the sharks and rays, further chapters include information on the importance of fish food chains and also how fish are at risk from pollution and over-fishing. Both these are points which today's environmentally conscious children, who frequently do projects on the sea, need to know and understand. Once again, as with other titles in this series, the excellent photographs from Oxford Scientific Films help make this a book whose pages youngsters will want to keep turning.

RG

Age range: 9–13

WHEELER, Alwyne

SHARKS

Franklin Watts, 1987, Hdbk, 0–86313–585–4
Series: First Sight

Contents list, index, colour line drawings and photographs

This is a popular book for children from late primary upwards. It is quite big, with large pictures of sharks often doing scary things and coming too close for comfort. Teeth are very much in evidence and the colour diagrams show the disposition of fins and functioning of the gills. Different types of sharks and where in the world they can be found is explained. A symbol indicates which shark species are currently being researched by scientists. Reproduction, diet and sharks' enemies are also covered.

JF

Age range: 7–11

AMPHIBIANS

HENWOOD, Chris and WATTS, Barrie

FROGS

Franklin Watts, 1988, Hdbk, 0–86313–693–1
Series: Keeping Minibeasts
Contents list, index, colour photographs

Mini-beasts include beetles and spiders, caterpillars and slugs. This work deals with frogs. They are likely to be kept for a short period, during which young children get to know them and learn how to look after 'pets'. Close-up colour photographs identify the frogs vividly, and show young readers what is required for frogs to live safely (tanks, small ponds, vivaria). Advice will certainly be needed on what plants to use, because, though they are shown, they are not named and sources of supply not given. Diet, too, is clearly defined, but adult support will be required to get items like crickets and mealworms. Information about breeding and watching frog spawn develop is useful, though more could be provided on safety when getting it from ponds. Concepts like amphibian and cold-blooded appear to hit the reader too soon, when the excellent photographs are working on a simpler, more direct level. Uneven but makes you want to take it up.

SH

Age range: 5–8

SMITH, Anne

FROGS AND TOADS

Wayland, 1986, Hdbk, 1–85210–765–0
Series: Nature Study
Contents list, glossary, index, colour photographs

Apart from eight blank pages in this book,

it is a bright and colourful account of these two important groups of amphibians. The series of photographs depict differences between frogs and toads, the range of species, camouflage and advertisement, poisonous species, stages in life cycles and hibernation. These are just some of the subjects covered. The text is easy enough for a bright six-year-old to work through and stimulating enough for them to get involved with these animals.

JF

Age range: 5–10

WATTS, Barrie

NEWT

Black, 1989, Hdbk, 0–7136–3123–6
Series: Stopwatch
Index, black and white line drawings and colour photographs

The newt has become much less common these days, so the colour photographs in this book may provide many children's first glimpse of this amphibian. A brief, simply worded account of the life history of the newt is illustrated, chiefly by the superb colour photographs.

Biology pupils in a higher age group than that for which this book is intended, who require, as a rule, fully labelled diagrams, may still find these colour photographs helpful.

Even very young children could cope with the simple language of the headings. Because the text is so easy and the pictures so attractive, this book would also be suitable for a sick child to read in hospital or at home.

JW

Age range: 5–9

REPTILES

BARRETT, Norman

SNAKES

Franklin Watts, 1989, Hdbk, 0–86313–812–8
Series: Picture Library
Contents list, glossary, index, colour line
drawings and photographs

Snakes is another title which is likely to be as popular as its predecessors in the *Picture Library* series. It has an eyecatching cover and over half the space inside is given over to detailed, good quality colour photographs of these fascinating and yet frightening creatures. The pictures which show snake camouflage work particularly well. The text, being economical, relatively simple and in large type, is not too intimidating. This book is for picking up and flicking through. Children will be attracted enough to learn almost coincidentally as they scan the captions and relevant text accompanying the photographs. It is not intended for infants or as a comprehensive topic book. The brief chapters follow the usual series pattern, including Introduction, Looking at . . . (physical attributes), Life of . . . (egg laying, skin shedding, etc.), The story of . . . (isolated historical facts) and Facts and records. It is a pity, however, that there is no bibliography.

RG

Age range: 7–13

McCARTHY, Colin

POISONOUS SNAKES

Franklin Watts, 1987, Hdbk, 0–86313–591–9
Series: First Sight
Contents list, index, colour line drawings and
photographs

Snakes and snake biology are explained in this book which portrays snakes in very threatening postures. The photographs are excellent and will excite younger readers. Children will be able to understand the 'instincts' of snakes, how they find their prey, how they are camouflaged or are dressed in warning colours, how they bite, how their fangs work and venom is produced. Information is drawn from cobras, vipers, rattlesnakes and sea snakes including tales of sea snakes. At the back of the book there is a section on exhibition of snakes at zoos and a chart to help in snake identification.

JF

Age range: 7–11

STIDWORTHY, John

REPTILES AND AMPHIBIANS

Facts on File, 1989, Hdbk, 0–8160–1965–7
Series: Encyclopedia of the Animal World
Contents list, glossary, index, black and white
and colour line drawings and colour photographs

Reptiles and amphibians are currently basking in a surfeit of books written on them after years of oblivion; naturalists have penetrated many a lush jungle or rainforest and have come home with spectacular pictures of these brilliantly coloured creatures. This book is most instructive, educational and a joy to read. It is full of information on evolution, identification and affinities, and sets the scene in the wild where these reptiles and amphibians live. Children will enjoy the comprehensive treatment of frogs and toads and of snakes swallowing all sorts of creatures. All major groups of reptiles and amphibians are covered and there are symbols to help interpret more about the animals' life-style and habitats. Thoroughly recommended.

JF

Age range: 11–16

BIRDS

BAILEY, Jill and PARKER, Steve

THE PLANT- AND SEED-EATERS

Facts on File, 1989, Hdbk, 0–8160–1958–4
Series: Encyclopedia of the Animal World
Bibliography, contents list, glossary, index, black
and white and colour line drawing and
photographs

There are over 3000 species of plant- and seed-eating birds that can be divided into several distinct groups (of orders): there are the ratites (flightless birds such as the ostrich, the emu and the rheas); the game birds and domestic fowls (which are valued in human diet); many types of passerine (or perching) birds – including some of Britain's commonest garden birds.

This beautifully illustrated book is highly informative and, because of the special emphasis it places on behaviour, ecology, conservation and taxonomy, it is a useful introduction for the would-be ornithologist, while the inclusion of the Linnean names will appeal to those learning Latin.

Such is their quality and their popularity with young people that, despite their cost, I regard the books in this series as among the 'best buys' for the junior school library.

JW

Age range: 9–16

BRAMWELL, Martyn

BIRDS: THE AERIAL HUNTERS

Facts on File, 1989, Hdbk, 0–8160–1963–0
Series: Encyclopedia of the Animal World
Bibliography, contents list, glossary, index, black
and white and colour line drawings and
photographs

This attractive book is part of a series which surveys the main groups of animals alive today. Four books are devoted to mammals and three to birds. This volume includes not only entries for raptors such as owls, but also the gentler insect-eating birds of the garden. Each article is about an individual species, and the text starts with a short scene-setting story that highlights one of the bird's unique features before dealing with details of physical appearance, diet and general life-style, etc. A fact panel includes a map that shows where the bird lives in the world, while all the illustrations have a clear indication of scale. The beautiful artwork and colour photographs, together with the concise text, make this a good book for the non-specialist bird lover.

JW

Age range: 9–16

BURNIE, David

BIRD

Dorling Kindersley, 1989, Hdbk, 0–86318–270–4
Series: Eyewitness Guides
Contents list, index, colour photographs

A cornucopia of information, a digest of facts is found on every page. A great deal of planning obviously went into this volume, photographs especially taken to reveal the minutiae of bird make-up. There is little to fault this book, except perhaps to give more on where to find birds to complement the 'how to study them' section. The double-page spreads on the fine details of the skeleton, feathers, eggs, nests and chicks are quite exquisite – these publishers are clearly masterly purveyors of natural history facts and figures.

JF

Age range: 8–14

BURTON, Robert

DISCOVERING OWLS

Wayland, 1989, Hdbk, 1–85210–385–X
Series: Discovering
Contents list, glossary, index, colour line
drawings and photographs

The colour photographs of owls in this book are stunning and numerous. The text is very comprehensive and the subject matter exhaustive for the level intended. Children studying by themselves can get a great deal of information from this book. The range of owls in the world and their lifestyles are presented well. By implication their habitats are covered with descriptions of different types of bird. How they feed, move around in the dark, their environmental problems and how to look and listen for owls are dealt with too.

JF

Age range: 7–12

GOODERS, John

THE PRACTICAL ORNITHOLOGIST

Facts on File, 1990, Hdbk, 0–8160–2363–8
Contents list, glossary, index, black and white
and colour line drawings and photographs

This is a welcome addition to the library of an amateur naturalist; but it is more than this – it bridges the gap between amateur and professional without being scientific and laborious. Written by an expert ornithologist who is equally at home either side of the Atlantic, this is a comprehensive account of birds in all their facets. The book is in three sections. There are two shorter sections on how birds work and behave, and on the practical side of being an ornithologist, then slightly more than half the book is about birds in their different habitats, brilliantly executed habitat by habitat. A thoroughly recommended encylopedic work.

JF

Age range: 10–16

HANSEN, Elvig

BIRTH OF BUDGERIGARS

Dent, 1986, Hdbk, 0–460–06236–0
Colour photographs

This book describes the breeding of budgerigars in captivity, from mating through egg laying, incubation, parental care of the young to juvenile birds. The fine series of colour photographs captures each stage from a peep-hole position inside a specially arranged nest box. The private life of the budgerigar is exposed, for instance how the female constantly attends the eggs and young while the male keeps her fed. Much useful and quantitative information is worked into the text, such as the time between egg laying or time taken for incubation, while differences between sexes are explained – this latter point a curriculum requirement. The familiar 'budgie' is put in context as a drought-tolerant species of Australia, now rarer in the wild than captivity. The text is fine for the age range, though a glossary would have been useful.

JF

Age range: 7–12

KERROD, Robin

THE WATERBIRDS

Facts on File, 1989, Hdbk, 0–8160–1962–2
Series: Encyclopedia of the Animal World
Contents list, glossary, index, black and white
and colour line drawings and photographs

Waterbirds gives a kalaeidoscopic account of the great variety of birds on earth – some 8805 species – all broken down into their natural groups and dealt with in a very professional way, in a style which is easy to access and informative to children from aged eleven up. There are plenty of explanatory diagrams, colour illustrations interspersed with marvellous colour photographs depicting characteristics of each group. World distribution of each group is given; so too are the Latin names of all species mentioned for the more serious enthusiast. As usual for this series this is a sound investment for the school library.

JF

Age range: 11–16

KILBRACKEN, John

THE EASY WAY TO BIRD RECOGNITION

Kingfisher, 1989, Pbk, 0–86272–397–3
Index, black and white line drawings and colour photographs

Originally published in 1982, this book relies on a simple biological key for the identification of 184 common birds in Britain. Throughout the book are a set of questions to help identification, 290 in total, and a range of possible answers. The pupil starts at the beginning and is led through to identification, aided by good colour illustrations. There is a supplementary key for some 38 rarer birds, a checklist and a few blank pages for notes; a useful book for young twitchers to work at.

JF

Age range: 12–16

PETTY, Kate

BIRDS OF PREY

Franklin Watts, 1987, Hdbk, 0–86313–584–6
Series: First Sight
Contents list, index, Spotters' Guide, colour line drawings and photographs

Many creatures are now at risk in the world, and this series aims to tell young readers about this problem and get them involved, if they aren't already. Many birds of prey are endangered, like the peregrine falcon and the osprey, hunted, poisoned, their habitats invaded by man. Without preaching, letting the photos and information work objectively on their behalf, Kate Petty describes main birds of prey in bold displays of picture and text across two-page displays, not holding back on technical words but keeping syntax simple and the message always sincere and direct. Line drawings allow readers to examine, compare wings and beaks and silhouettes, and copy for their own classwork or poster design. A useful study resouce book in a competitive field.

SH

Age range: 8–11

ROGL, Manfred and EPPLE, Wolfgang

A FAMILY OF OWLS

Black, 1988, Hdbk, 0–7136–3124–4
Series: Animal Families
Contents list, index, colour photographs

A splendid introduction invites the reader to follow the authors inside the nest home of a pair of barn owls to watch them breeding and rearing their chicks. It's the way these authors do it that's so good. Rogl and Epple have that quality all good bird-watchers – and all good writers of non-fiction – seem to possess: a desire to share the excitement and knowledge of their subject in a way that shows us how to observe animal behaviour. There is the feeling of putting oneself in the hands of experts and listening as they share their secrets. The authors use a narrative framework to tell their story, and have the confidence to use value judgements and metaphor. The photographs are magnificent; each shows an aspect of owl behaviour, and they work together with the text to form a whole. Highly recommended for all primary children.

HM

Age range: 7–11

WHARTON, Anthony

SEA BIRDS

Wayland, 1987, Hdbk, 0–85078–820–X

Series: Discovering
Contents list, glossary, index, colour line
drawings and photographs

A comprehensive account of seabirds worldwide is presented here, although a few photographs of seabirds in school grounds would have been useful too. The text is a little 'thin' and economical with the facts, even inaccurate in parts and the photographs are not up to a high standard. More could have been told in the text in the same amount of space.

JF

Age range: 7–12

MAMMALS

BANKS, Martin

DISCOVERING BADGERS

Wayland, 1988, Hdbk, 1–85210–427–9
Series: Discovering Nature
Bibliography, contents list, glossary, index,
colour line drawings and photographs

Discovering Badgers is another title in
Wayland's *Discovering Nature* series
which gets this reviewer's seal of
approval. Considerable care has been
taken with page layout and the match
between pictures and text. There is
enough attractively presented
information in the 46 pages to form an
ideal core reference for any child, of
middle school age, who is doing a project
on badgers. Having said that, the book
does provide an extensive further reading
list for those who are keen to find out
more. The contents and order of the
seven chapters follow the usual
convention for the series. The first
chapter deals with the physical
description of the genus and its world
distribution. Following chapters describe
habitats, how and where badgers forage,
their dietary and eating habits,
reproduction, enemies and survival –
including their relationship with man –
and, finally, there is a useful chapter on
how to go badger watching.

RG

Age range: 8–13

BANKS, Martin

DISCOVERING OTTERS

Wayland, 1988, Hdbk, 0–85078–821–8
Series: Discovering
Contents list, glossary, index, colour line
drawings and photographs

The European otter is not the only otter
dealt with here; South American, Asian
and sea otters among others are included.

The range of information covered is
excellent, and one feels that much of the
natural history of otters generally has
been imparted with the details in the
photographs and the text. Children will
learn about otters living in the sea,
around the coast or along streams and
rivers, and how they move in and out of
water, how they construct their holts,
how they scent-mark the bankside and
what they eat. The impact of man on
otter is explained and there is a section
on how to look for otter signs in snow and
mud.

JF

Age range: 7–12

BARRETT, Norman

DOLPHINS

Franklin Watts, 1989, Hdbk, 0–86313–817–9
Series: Picture Library
Contents list, glossary, index, colour photographs

Any book on dolphins would be
appealing since they are endearing,
intelligent and relatively helpless in man's
world. Rather too many dolphins (and all
their allies) are photographed in zoos and
dolphinaria here, instead of being
photographed 'in the wild'; this is a pity
in these days of conservation
enlightenment. However, there is much
interesting dolphin biology and ecology
expressed through the pages and the
book will be a useful addition for primary
schools.

JF

Age range: 7–12

BRIGHT, Michael

GIANT PANDA

Franklin Watts, 1988, Hdbk, 0–86313–793–8

Series: Project Wildlife
Contents list, index, colour line drawings and photographs

Many species are in danger of extinction, and giant pandas are one of them. Through TV and the activity of WWF (World Wide Fund for Nature), these creatures are a focus of concern. They are in danger because of poachers and because their habitat (and bamboo) is being destroyed. Bright makes his own position clear in his statement: 'soon the only Giant Pandas left will be seen behind bars'. Yet captive breeding, and the scientific conservation activity associated with it, can work, as the few panda cubs testify. Information and opinion mix well in a mature unpatronizing way, while pictures extend the storyline, and don't merely look decorative. The efforts to save pandas are given special attention. Panda Fact Files at the end provide a deeper level of information. Interest and responsibility shine from this book.

SH

Age range: 9–12

BRIGHT, Michael

HUMPBACK WHALE

Franklin Watts, 1989, Hdbk, 0–7496–0069–1
Series: Project Wildlife
Contents list, index, whale fact files, black and white and colour line drawings and photographs

The humpback whale is most famous for its beautiful melancholic song, which has become the symbolic voice for all endangered whales. Almost hunted to extinction, the humpback was saved, just in time, by the 1986 moratorium on commercial whaling – though its future is by no means secure while many countries still kill them for 'scientific' purposes. The book's pictures show clearly the great beauty of these creatures as well as the brutality of whaling. It ends with three informative fact files on features of its anatomy, life history, diet

and behaviour. An excellent book – one of a series for the young conservationist.

JW

Age range: 7–13

BRIGHT, Michael

TIGER

Franklin Watts, 1988, Hdbk, 0–86313–792–X
Series: Project Wildlife
Contents list, index, facts file, colour line drawings and photographs

At last a book with a strong conservation thread throughout, rather than a page devoted to conservation at the back of the book. This is not just about tigers per se; the series could be called 'Protect Wildlife' instead of 'Project Wildlife'. The book is divided into two parts; the decline of the tiger, and saving the tiger. Historical accounts show the folly of shooting parties, and draw attention to the extinction of the Balinese tiger. The success of Project Tiger in India, started in 1973, is an introduction to reserves for tigers and current research on tiger ecology, especially using radio-tagging. The future of tigers and their role in zoos and captive breeding are also dealt with.

JF

Age range: 10–14

CHIVERS, David

GORILLAS AND CHIMPANZEES

Franklin Watts, 1987, Hdbk, 0–86313–613–3
Series: First Sight
Contents list, glossary, index, colour line drawings and photographs

The similarity to man is stressed throughout this book, from interpreting facial expressions, to the limited use of tools in captive and in wild animals and in the general similarity of hands and feet and skeleton, as well as intelligence. Children will derive much important and comparative information from this book, and there are tempting boxes of facts on every page of text. Conservation of these animals is stressed and at the end of the book is a test-chart and details of how to make a chimpanzee mask.

JF

Age range: 7–12

FISCHER-NAGEL, Heiderose

A FAMILY OF DONKEYS

Black, 1988, Hdbk, 0–7136–3125–2
Glossary, index, colour photographs

This is the story of a pet donkey called Griselda who is mated and produces a foal. How the foal is born and brought up is told through the photographs until it is a year old. A great deal of donkey biology and behaviour underlies the text and it is skilfully wound in. There are pages which describe donkey moods, donkeys playing and donkeys enjoying dust baths. There is a brief description of other related animals at the back. Children should learn wider implications about looking after pets from this story of a donkey.

JF

Age range: 7–12

GOODALL, Jane

THE CHIMPANZEE FAMILY BOOK

Picture Book Studio, 1989, Hdbk,
0–88708–090–1
Colour photographs

This is an absolutely delightful story book, written by the expert in her subject who has spent her life studying the intimate life of chimps. The everyday life of chimpanzees is followed through members of different family groups and their interactions with other groups of chimpanzees and other animals of the Gombe National Park in East Africa. The pictures are revealing and emotive, and generate sympathy for these social mammals which are not too dissimilar to

man. It is easy to admire the work of dedicated enthusiasts such as the author, and from an educational point of view there is much that budding naturalists can glean from these pages.

JF

Age range: 5–12

GOODALL, Jane

CHIMPS

Collins, 1990, Pbk, 0–00–184719–8
Contents list, colour photographs

Written by one who has studied chimps the whole of her life, this text is imbued with her enthusiasm and experiences in the wild. The book will be suitable for children to flick through and look at the pictures (which have generally good compositions but are not the best chimp pictures available), or to read through. The evolution and allies of the chimp are dealt with, so too their communities, how they move and communicate, and their everyday life is described. A section on captivity and conservation concludes the book.

JF

Age range: 8–12

GOODALL, Jane

HIPPOS

Collins, 1990, Pbk, 0–00–184718–X
Series: Jane Goodall's Animal World
Contents list, colour photographs

The vegetarian life of the hippopotamus is well explained in this book. Almost half of Africa has hippos according to the distribution map provided, and details are given of the life history with particular attention devoted to endearing baby hippos. The colour photographs are very good, and show families of hippos enjoying their natural habitat *en masse*, sometimes wallowing in mud, and walking underwater. Other pictures are amusing, highlighting the peculiar form of the hippo and what he gets up to. Their place in nature, their senses and 'hippos in zoos' are all attended to.

JF

Age range: 8–12

GOODALL, Jane

LIONS

Collins, 1990, Pbk, 0–00–184721–X
Series: Jane Goodall's Animal World
Contents list, colour photographs

Lions is beautifully done, with an easy text for children of eight and older, and suitable for parents reading to their children. There are sections on the evolutionary tree of lions, where exactly they live in Africa, family groups and ties, communication, hunting and lions in captivity. The colour pictures are excellent and children will learn a great deal from them. The book is thoroughly recommended.

JF

Age range: 8–12

GOODALL, Jane

PANDAS

Collins, 1990, Pbk, 0–00–184720–X
Series: Jane Goodall's Animal World
Contents list, colour line drawings and photographs

At half the price, this book on pandas tells not only the life history of the panda, but the evolution of pandas and all their allies, compared to the Simon and Xuqi book, *The Giant Panda*, reviewed below. The quality of the colour photographs is superior in *Pandas*. Jane Goodall is the noted mammalogist who has worked extensively in Africa.

JF

Age range: 8–12

HANSEN, Elvig

A FAMILY OF GUINEA PIGS

Black, 1988, Hdbk, 0–7136–3126–0
Contents list, index, black and white line drawings and colour photographs

Young children will really enjoy this book, whether or not they have guinea pigs as pets. It is an informative text woven around a truly impressive spread of colourful pictures. The life cycle, behaviour and biology of the guinea pig is covered in intimate detail and the different breeds of guinea pigs included at the back is a useful addition. The book will excite, stimulate and educate and is a definite must for the school library.

JF

Age range: 7–12

KALAS, Sybille and Klaus

THE BEAVER FAMILY BOOK

Picture Book Studio, 1987, Hdbk, 0–88708–050–2
Colour photographs

Beavers are interesting rodents that we can never get really close to in their semi-aquatic environment. This book helps us interpret more of the secret world of beavers, since the authors looked after three baby beavers and took photographs of them over a two-year period. The animals were originally from Sweden, but were reared in the Austrian mountains for release. The photographs give not only a good idea of the life-style of the beaver, its habitat, its gnawing and its dam building, but a close-up introduction to the biology of beavers.

JF

Age range: 7–12

O'TOOLE, Christopher and STIDWORTHY, John

THE HUNTERS

Facts on File, 1988, Hdbk, 0–948894–28–8
Series: Encyclopedia of the Animal World
Bibliography, contents list, glossary, index, black
and white and colour line drawings and
photographs

The Hunters is the second volume in the extremely well produced *Encyclopedia of the Animal World* set. Nearly 400 mammalian carnivores are featured, including the big cats, wolves, bears, otters, seals, dolphins and whales. The chapters follow a convention with superb colour photographs and illustrations, which are integral, taking up around half the available large format space. The text is both clear and interesting. Most chapters are double-page spreads beginning with a simple scene-setting paragraph which introduces the hunting animal in its natural environment. There are quick reference panels which give facts about diet, habitats, world distribution and also indicate if the species is endangered. The page design is excellent with clear type and good use of sub-headings. The accompanying glossary and index are thorough and well set out. This book would be useful on its own or as part of the set.

RG

Age range: 8–13

PARKER, Steve

MAMMAL

Dorling Kindersley, 1989, Hdbk, 0–86318–340–9
Series: Eyewitness Guides
Contents list, index, black and white line
drawings and black and white and colour
photographs

Exceptionally well produced, this book has enormous wealth of detail. Perhaps too much so for most children, though those who are already interested in natural history may find it absorbing.

Certainly, most children would be interested in finding out about the uses of tails, how bush babies see in the dark, why elephants have such big feet and exactly how hedgehogs roll up when in danger. And using the life-cycle of a mammal to structure the book is a clever idea. However, it is doubtful if anything is added by the speculative material on how mammals may relate to each other in an evolutionary way.

PMR

Age range: 12–14

PETTY, Kate

CATS

Franklin Watts, 1988, Hdbk, 0–86313–798–9
Series: First Pets
Contents list, glossary, index, colour line
drawings and photographs

This is a book made around a set of full-page images of cats doing familiar things: stalking, pouncing, jumping, meowing, sleeping, hissing, and picking up kittens, even looking hungrily at a goldfish in a bowl. The short text on the page opposite each picture gives a little introduction to the subject. The book is suitable to be read aloud by teacher or parent, while showing the images to the children. A child of six could work his/her way through the book with ease. There is a double page which shows different types of cats.

JF

Age range: 6–11

PFEFFER, Pierre

THE LONG LIFE AND GENTLE WAYS OF THE ELEPHANT

Moonlight, 1987, Hdbk, 1–85103–023–9
Series: Pocket Worlds
Index, colour line drawings and photographs

This is simply a delightful little book about elephants. The book is planned round a series of questions such as where do elephants come from, what do they do with their tusks, what is the function of the trunk? The illustrations are vivid, most evocative and full of information. The text is rich and educational and at the end there is a true or false question section to test the reader's skill; a recommended book for the school library.

JF

Age range: 7–11

POPE, Joyce

GERBILS

Franklin Watts, 1987, Hdbk, 0–86313–414–9
Series: Taking Care of
Contents list, index, black and white line
drawings and colour photographs

This falls directly into the sphere of National Curriculum requirements which demand that children know how to care for animals. The book is about as complete a compendium on gerbils in the school and at home that one could wish and the colour photographs cover all aspects including feeding, health and hygiene in both those environments. If you want to start keeping gerbils it is all explained here. There is a question and answer section at the back on finding out more about gerbils – an excellent and exciting production.

JF

Age range: 8–12

POPE, Joyce

RABBIT

Franklin Watts, 1987, Hdbk, 0–86313–413–0
Series: Taking Care of
Contents list, index, colour photographs

Caring for animals is a requirement of the National Curriculum and is well expressed here. The rabbit has long been a typical animal of the classroom and the book will be useful for infants and a

useful prompt for teachers. There are pictures of different types of rabbit, making a hutch, looking after the rabbit at school and at home, maintaining good hygiene, providing the right food and so on. There is a checklist of things to do daily, weekly and monthly and a revision section at the back.

JF

Age range: 8–12

SIMON, Noel and XUQU, Jin

THE GIANT PANDA

Dent, 1986, Hdbk, 0–460–06249–2
Colour photographs

Very few naturalists have the insight into the private life of the mysterious panda, but this book tells the story, as far as is known, based on the translated works of two researchers who have spent time in China's twelve panda reserves. Conservation is put in true perspective, so too the fragile link between panda and its environment, especially with the die-off experienced by bamboo after flowering. The book is full of colour photographs which depict many aspects of the life of the panda, many scenes not seen in the West, with a special section on giving birth and looking after the young. Altogether this is a pleasant book with a good narrative.

JF

Age range: 8–14

SPROULE, Anna

HAMSTERS

Wayland, 1988, Hdbk, 1–85210–379–5
Series: Know Your Pet
Contents list, glossary, index, colour line
drawings and photographs

Hamsters have hardly had a more thorough treatment than presented here. This is essential reading on the subject for all schools, particularly those who wish to have hamsters, or already have hamsters in the classroom, or those who want them at home. The text is historically interesting, starting from the discovery of hamsters in the wild to their use as pets. There is a section of different types of hamster, but the core of the book is devoted to choosing the right hamster, making its accommodation, feeding, breeding, cleaning, hygiene and generally keeping it in good health. There is also a section on showing.

JF

Age range: 10–14

STEWART, John
ELEPHANT

Black, 1986, Hdbk, 0–7136–2814–6
Colour photographs

This is simply a very pleasant and endearing book about the working life of Asian elephants. It follows two young trainers and how they train elephants to work in the forests. It is set in a 'young elephant training centre' in Northern Thailand and the beautiful pictures show how baby elephants are taught to wear their harnesses and carry and pull timber, how they are washed in the river and given dust baths. Born in captivity, these elephants are not overworked and are retired to the forest with their trainers when they are 60 years old.

JF

Age range: 6–11

TECHNOLOGY

◆

This is the area most often read for pleasure by those young people who spurn fiction as too fanciful. Not only do the books have to be attractive and readable but the information has to be totally accurate.

REID, Struan

INVENTION AND DISCOVERY

Usborne, 1986, Pbk, 0–86020–956–3
Series: Usborne Illustrated Handbooks
Contents list, glossary, index, colour line
drawings

With an excellent combination of succinct explanations and clear colour illustrations, this cleverly designed and well organized handbook, containing hundreds of entries, catalogues the history of technology. There are nine colour-coded main sections which include, for example, energy, transport and warfare. The entries are organized chronologically and thematically in sub-sections which cover topics such as nuclear power, aircraft and weapons, etc. Each entry has the date of the invention or discovery, the name of the person responsible, the country he or she came from and the invention or discovery itself. At a glance, the sub-sections show how discoveries have been developed and how original inventions have been refined and improved on over time. There is also a useful list of key inventions and discoveries as well as a brief biographical dictionary of famous inventors at the back of the book. Recommended for both primary and G.C.S.E. projects on the development of science and technology.

RG

Age range: 9–16

HUMAN PHYSIOLOGY

BALDWIN, Dorothy and LISTER, Claire

YOUR SENSES

Wayland, 1983, Hdbk, 0–85078–304–6
Series: You and Your Body
Contents list, glossary, index, colour line
drawings and photographs

Most of the time we are unaware of our senses at work. This book tells us how our senses constantly gather information about what is happening in the body and what is going on in the outside world. There is a chapter devoted to each of the main senses. The text is clear and, though the vocabulary is quite demanding, there is a comprehensive glossary. The book is well illustrated. The instructions for the practical activities are integrated into the general text: perhaps it would have been better if they had been inset separately.

JW

Age range: 7–11

BENDER, Lionel

ATOMS AND CELLS

Franklin Watts, 1989, Hdbk, 0–86313–951–5
Series: Through the Microscope
Contents list, glossary, index, colour line
drawings and photographs

Although early infants are taught the concept of atoms, this book is for all those who start to do microscopy work. The book is all-colour throughout, and comprises photomicrographs and explanatory colour diagrams. Each of the photomicrographs carries a symbol denoting whether it was photographed down a microscope or down an electron microscope, which is useful since many readers have no idea what they are looking at unless it is explained; sizes and scales are given. The world of bacteria,

viruses and single-celled plants and animals is explored, so too are spores, elements and molecules. It's a worthy book for the school library and full of interest.

JF

Age range: 8–12

BROWN, Fern G.

CHILDBIRTH

Franklin Watts, 1988, Hdbk, 0–86313–791–1
Series: Teen Guide
Contents list, glossary, index, colour line
drawings and photographs

Facts, feelings, and tone are crucial in books like this and others in the series (e.g. on birth control and safe sex). In a friendly and direct style, Fern Brown takes the reader through hospital and home births, preparing for childbirth through exercise, early signs of labour, the process of birth, and after-effects. Medical terms are used clearly and supported by a glossary. The aim is to tell it as it is, clearly, uncomplicatedly, positively, and this is helped by straightforward colour photographs which provide much supporting information. Women and their partners appear 'just like you' going through the stages of this human experience, feeling a bit of fear but confidently following the correct advice. A book for thoughtful reading, both in school investigation and on that more hidden level of personal discovery.

SH

Age range: 14–17

GAMLIN, Linda

THE HUMAN BODY

Franklin Watts, 1988, Hdbk, 0–86313–753–9

Series: Today's World
Contents list, glossary, index, colour line
drawings and photographs

Fascinating for nine-year-olds onwards, this book explores the inner workings of the body. A few photographs of people doing things are interspersed with cut-away colour diagrams of how their bones, blood vessels, muscles and inner organs are operating. The book is well planned and incorporates not only the effect of pollution on breathing and health, but aspects of health and disease including infections, immunization and dentistry and surgery; a very modern, current and interesting book.

JF

Age range: 9–14

PARKER, Steve

THE BRAIN AND NERVOUS SYSTEM

Franklin Watts, 1989, Hdbk, 0–86313–865–9
Contents list, glossary, index, black and white
and colour photographs

This is a highly professional production covering important areas of the syllabus. The book is full of excellent colour photographs including gorgeous electron microscope photographs and very clear diagrams. There are some images published here for the first time, but what are so useful are the explicit diagrams showing, for instance, neural transmission, reflexes and cortex functions. The book has been really well thought out and will be avidly used by older primary children and at secondary level where it will be invaluable.

JF

Age range: 10–14

PARKER, Steve

THE EYE AND SEEING

Franklin Watts, 1989, Hdbk, 0–86313–739–3
Series: The Human Body

Contents list, glossary, index, colour line
drawings and photographs

This revised and redesigned edition of *The Eye and Seeing* explains the complete story of the eye, from its intricate structure of nerves, cells and delicate tissues, to its relationship with the brain and, finally, to its interpretation of what we see – or think we see! Several chapters are dedicated to eye problems and eye care – very essential considering the vital part our eyes play in our everyday lives. Each two-page chapter has large, simple, clearly labelled and captioned diagrams, and some are supported by colour photographs. The information is kept as simple as the subject allows, and any technical terms are written in bold type and explained immediately in the text and clarified later in the glossary. Some pages have a 'blue box' containing further, more specific, details about a topic under discussion. An extremely valuable addition to a top junior or secondary school library.

RG

Age range: 10–adult

PARKER, Steve

FOOD AND DIGESTION

Franklin Watts, 1989, Hdbk, 0–86313–864–0
Series: The Human Body
Contents list, glossary, index, colour line
drawings and black and white and colour
photographs

This is an excellent book that can be recommended for its clear, informative text and its superb illustrations. The detailed anatomical artwork is well labelled and attractively coloured and the significance of each of the well chosen colour photographs is concisely explained by a paragraph, below or beside it.

The author, who has written other books in this series, has set out the text as double-page spreads, each under its own heading. Certain technical terms are in bold type and explained in the glossary.

The human digestive system is described and certain related topics considered. The emphasis is on health education and the importance of diet in looking after our bodies. ('We are what we eat!')

WFW

Age range: 9–15

PARKER, Steve

TOUCH, TASTE AND SMELL

Franklin Watts, 1989, Hdbk, 0–86313–740–7
Series: The Human Body
Contents list, glossary, index, colour line
drawings and photographs

Our senses provide us with important information about the world outside our bodies. Touch can detect heat, cold, pressure and pain, as well as tactile stimuli. Taste and smell are perhaps not quite so important as touch, though they help us to appreciate and enjoy food, and give us warning if it has deteriorated (e.g. by the onset of decay). All these points, and many more, are clearly explained in a well written text, in which the technical terms are in bold type and are explained in the glossary. The colour photographs and detailed anatomical artwork have excellent titles and labelling: they contribute greatly to the clarity of the text.

An interesting book which (like that on hearing in the same series) gives some sound biological explanation.

WFW

Age range: 10–14

PLUCKROSE, Henry

TOUCHING

Franklin Watts, 1985, Hdbk, 0–86313–276–6
Series: Think About
Colour photographs

Human awareness, from a very early age,

depends to a large extent on the sense of touch. This book is a collection of brightly coloured photographs of various surfaces with which young children would be familiar. By talking about them, children will not only develop use of language and expression but also focus their attention on their sense of touch.

The few words of text that come with each picture should promote curiosity and enquiry, and a parent could share this book even with the pre-school child.

JW

Age range: 3–6

PLUCKROSE, Henry and FAIRCLOUGH, Chris

HEARING

Franklin Watts, 1985, Hdbk, 0–86313–280–4
Series: Think About
Colour photographs

Listen and you will hear – what? Pluckrose brings his usual flair and insight to bear on this everyday but mysterious process, much helped by Fairclough's imaginative colour photos. Their aim is to get children listening and making sounds, but, conceptually deeper still, to consider what sounds are like, why some are pleasant and some frighten, what some symbolize and predicate. Loud and soft, gentle (the purr of a cat), alarming like a fire engine, the sounds of talk and machines and animals, noise and music: these are the experiences of sound which children and their parents or teachers will explore with and through this book. Embedded in the simple text and photos are further questions, like why protect ears against noise, why do people travel about in noisy machines, and, most elusive of all, what is silence. So listen and learn, and be made a little more self-aware.

SH

Age range: 4–6

PLUCKROSE, Henry and GALLETLY, Mike

LOOK AT FEET

Franklin Watts, 1987, Hdbk, 0–86313–553–6
Series: Look at . . .
Index, colour line drawings and photographs

Looking at feet could be so obvious as to be dull. But the clever design of this book makes this impossible. There is no superfluous information, no hint of a misplaced register in accent or tone. Bright photographs work in perfect unity with text to give the subject real impact. Feet can do many things, walk and run, pump up tyres, tap dance. We see feet doing them. Colour contrasts between shoes and socks are witty and unexpected. There are all kinds of things for the young reader to do on top of simply reading and looking: questions based on pictures, things to try out (like identify different textures with feet), even measure feet. Is it true that right feet tend to be bigger than left feet? What about words with 'foot' in them? An active activity and awareness book, worth putting into every primary collection and giving as a present.

SH

Age range: 5–7

SOLOMON, Joan

EVERYBODY'S HAIR

Black, 1988, Hdbk, 0–7136–2985–1
Series: Friends
Colour photographs

Everybody has hair, but doesn't think about it all the time. Some theme books for lower primary get a bit earnest about that. But this book assumes that, although hair is interesting, children get on with other things too. The colour photographs are full of narrative interest, and speak volumes about why people (children and parents) wear hair as they do. Rasta, Sikh, and Afro styles are shown, and they can

all be made beautiful. The storyline is unselfconscious, because infant school children are getting on making models for a Rapunzel fairy story. Sophie is not worried that her hair is short: 'I would escape from the tower by myself', she says. It is all very unforced and credible: young readers will get really involved in this book, and be encouraged to notice differences without prejudice or pride getting in the way.

SH

Age range: 5–7

STONES, Rosemary and SHARRATT, Nick

WHERE BABIES COME FROM

Dinosaur, 1989, Pbk, 0–85122–766–7
Colour line drawings

Sex education at worst can be coy, earnest, and patronizing. Stones, whose involvement with The Other Award reveals her pedigree against bias and prejudice in children's reading, has in this book produced an honest, happy, and relaxed account of where babies come from. Text and pictures structure the subject simply and naturally. Side issues are left in smaller type for parents and teachers to develop. It's not just information, of course: it's attitudes too. Sex feels 'exciting and loving and good'. It's being practical, because other children are affected. Dads take part like mums in bringing up baby. Things are called by particular names, and why not be straightforward about it? This small book succeeds because of how it says it, and what it leaves out. Ideal for children to read, and great help for adults trying to put it all into words.

SH

Age range: 5–8

THOMSON, Ruth

TEETH AND TUSKS

Franklin Watts, 1989, Hdbk, 0–86313–830–6
Series: Look at . . .
Colour line drawings and photographs

Five-year-olds can manage this book. It has a straightforward approach based on simple statements interspersed with plain questions which go with the large photographs on each page. The photographs move from children looking at their teeth in mirrors to gnawing and tearing teeth, to tusks, while at the same time explaining the difference between herbivorous and carnivorous teeth. Gaping jaws of lions, hippos and horses almost stand out from the pages. The killer whale and sharks get their places of course. Other topics such as birds' beaks and reptiles' horny mouths are also shown. At the end of the book there is a diagram of man's dental arrangement and a 'things to do section'.

JF

Age range: 5–8

WARD, Brian R.

THE LUNGS AND BREATHING

Franklin Watts, 1988, Hdbk, 0–86313–706–7
Series: The Human Body
Contents list, glossary, index, colour line drawings and photographs

This is an excellent book, with a clear, highly informative text and superbly illustrated by detailed anatomical artwork and colour photographs. The significance of each of the latter is explained by a paragraph below, beside or opposite each photograph, while the biological diagrams are clearly labelled and attractively coloured. The book is well designed and set out in double-page spreads, each with its own heading. The text is concisely written by an experienced writer, who trained as a biologist. The emphasis is on health education and the importance of looking after our bodies. As would be expected, the dangers of smoking and of aerial pollution are stressed.

WFW

Age range: 10–15

WARD, Brian R.

THE SKELETON AND MOVEMENT

Franklin Watts, 1988, Hdbk, 0–86313–707–5
Contents list, glossary, index, black and white and colour photographs

Fascinating detail enough to grip the attention of upper primary and secondary children is expounded here. It reads like an encyclopedia of bone and muscle facts and figures – impressive indeed – all overseen by a medical doctor. The quality of all the images is superb and the use of colour throughout brings the latest in fascinating skeletal and locomotory theory to the tables of all children who can make easy interpretations. An excellent book for the school library.

JF

Age range: 10–14

GENERAL HEALTH

BALDWIN, Dorothy and LISTER, Claire

FIRST AID IN AN EMERGENCY

Wayland, 1986, Hdbk, 0–85078–996–6
Series: First Aid
Bibliography, contents list, glossary, index, useful
addresses, colour line drawings and photographs

When children are involved in accidents, it is often their friends who are first on the scene. They may also have to cope with accidents involving their parents or families. This book is part of a series designed for children. It deals with the first aid treatment that will ease pain, prevent any further injury and even save life. It sets out step-by-step explanation of the immediate first aid necessary after a serious accident. This includes instructions for mouth-to-mouth ventilation and external chest compression, as well as how to deal with shock, bleeding, fractures, burns and choking. The text is clear and well illustrated by photographs.

JW

Age range: 9–15

COLEMAN, Jill and GREENHILL, Richard

SIMON GOES TO THE OPTICIAN

Black, 1984, Hdbk, 0–7136–2338–1
Bibliography, colour line drawings and
photographs

Simon is nine and striker in the school football team. The last thing he wants is to wear glasses. But the letters on the board look fuzzy. So he goes to the optician. Books dealing with things like this succeed when they do three things well: first, tell it like it is; second, recognize how you may feel about it; and third, show you what it's like. This book does all three. Material is well structured for a young reader who knows nothing about it (and possibly their parents), and goes from simple to difficult and back easily (looking at the letters, having your inner eye inspected, putting the glasses on for the first time). Simon is worried and gets bored during the test, just like anyone his age. Despite better vision, he is still worried what his friends will say at school. Good colour photographs show it clearly, even the feelings. Books like this are useful for general knowledge and for people who suddenly feel life is making victims of them.

SH

Age range: 6–8

MACFARLANE, Aidan and McPHERSON, Ann

THE DIARY OF A TEENAGE HEALTH FREAK

OUP, 1987, Pbk, 0–19–286083–6
Contents list, index, black and white line
drawings

Two Oxfordshire doctors hit on the idea that an 'Adrian Mole' style diary would be a good way to talk about health and sex for teenage readers. Twelve printings in two years proves their point. Peter Payne is 14 and thinks that everything is wrong with him – acne, too small a penis, odd personal smells, not enough sexual experience (although he's afraid of it). The colloquial and satirical 'Mole' voice is used within the diary format to enable him to talk to the reader confidentially and irreverently about these preoccupations. There are times when he reads his sister's diary (and so learns about periods and tampons), gets a leaflet from school (on sex abuse), and reads magazine letters about teenagers and weight. The authors come in from time to time and give authoritative (but good-humoured) information (about depression, asthma, hayfever). It's a witty way of swallowing a pill for a readership group jaded with the earnest approach.

SH

Age range: 11–15

McPHERSON, Ann and MACFARLANE, Aidan

I'M A HEALTH FREAK TOO!

OUP, 1989, Pbk, 0–19–282232–2
Contents list, index, black and white line drawings

This is the sequel to *The Diary of a Teenage Health Freak* published in 1987 (reviewed above). The same two authors, two doctors, use an Adrian Mole diary format to tackle preoccupations about life, and particularly hidden parts of it, which research (from sources like English schools and responses to surveys by *Just Seventeen*) has shown matter to teenagers today. The witty self-deprecating style, with clippings from newspapers, announcements from booklets, quips about her dreadful family (and her allegedly famous brother Peter, the author of the original), and coyly secretive comments which she believes only she will read in her diary, are imaginatively used as a way of looking quite seriously at issues like anorexia and AIDS, divorce and glandular fever, animal rights and examination stress. The language is medical, vernacular, direct, humorous, human, and the device is light-hearted enough not to make reading the book awkward or rigged. A good book to promote among people of any age over ten in a school or family.

SH

Age range: 11–15

PARKER, Steve

SKELETON

Dorling Kindersley, 1988, Hdbk, 0–86318–272–0
Series: Eyewitness Guides
Contents list, index, black and white line drawings and colour photographs

The wonderful books in this series are to browse in, and to me are like a visit to a good museum. Lots and lots of photographs with informative captions. The pictures are all of very high quality and show a wide variety within the subjects.

In *Skeleton* I like the way the human skeleton is stretched over three double-page spreads, so as to show it on a reasonably huge scale, the captions expressing many aspects of the word skeleton. There are sections devoted to the skeletons of different groups of animals (mammals, birds, fish, external skeletons); then sections comparing bone groups (legs, shoulders, arms, hips, ribs, backbones, skulls and teeth) in humans to animals in general, explaining the general purposes of the groupings and marking differentiation where it occurs. Then a section on the structure and repair of bones and finally a name chart detailing all 206 bones in the human body.

SS

Age range: 5–adult

RICHARDSON, Joy

CLEAN AND DIRTY

Hodder & Stoughton, 1989, Hdbk, 0–340–42678–0
Series: Giraffe
Colour line drawings

This book is one of a series that claims to encourage very young readers to look more closely at their surroundings, and to help them understand what they see.

Certainly it has a story text (about a little girl who gets dirty and how she gets clean) that is colourfully illustrated, but I see its use as much as an early reader as a book for introducing scientific ideas. The pictures on the last two pages are like flash-cards for words.

JW

Age range: 5–7

ROWAN, Peter

ASK DOCTOR PETE

Cape, 1986, Hdbk, 0–224–02869–3
Contents list, black and white line drawings

Being ill is one thing, but thinking something is wrong is quite another. For young people (and adults!), there are all kinds of questions we should like to ask but dare not because we think they're stupid. Like eating fish making you brainy, getting piles from sitting on radiators, and damaging your eyes watching TV. Dr Peter Rowan has appeared on TV am's *Wide Awake Club* and on BBC Radio's *Outlook* answering questions like this. The privacy of a book helps when young readers are shy of asking questions directly, particularly when Quentin Blake's quirky line drawings make it all sound so normal. Rowan can be very serious and authoritative, on eating uncooked bacon and smoking; witty, when telling us that a sneeze has the force of a hurricane, and that baked beans really do make you fart; and surprising in confirming that carrots really do make you see better. Very much a book to leave lying around to be discovered: it informs and debunks, and will make even know-it-alls smile to themselves wryly.

SH

Age range: 10–14

ROWAN, Peter

NEVER SHAVE A CAMEL

Cape, 1988, Hdbk, 0–224–02607–0
Contents list, glossary, black and white line drawings

The best teachers can never resist a good ramble on, their captive audience sitting with their eyes out on stalks; this book is just like that. It is actually about first aid, but so presented, through hilarious, often irreverent anecdotes, that I found out things without realizing, as I rolled off my chair with laughter. A paradigm of the way to share one's knowledge, understanding and experience with children.

SS

Age range: 9–15

SANDERS, Pete

ON THE ROAD

Franklin Watts, 1989, Hdbk, 0–86313–788–1
Series: Be Safe
Contents list, index, colour line drawings and photographs

This book aims to increase children's awareness of the need for safety precautions when they are on or near roads. Realistic photographs of children are used to point out the potential dangers involved in crossing a busy road, skateboarding or playing in the street, and cycling two abreast, etc. Children are reminded of the value of using safety equipment which already exists on roads, such as pelican crossings and traffic islands. Likewise, road safety rules which have to be learned and practised, such as the Green Cross Code, are also highlighted. As well as drawing attention to road hazards and how to improve their own safety, ideas about what children can do to help make road environments safer for other people are also given. To help youngsters undertake active thought about road safety, there is a quiz and suggestions for several simple projects throughout the book. A useful topic book.

RG

Age range: 7–11

WARD, Brian R.

THE ENVIRONMENT AND HEALTH

Franklin Watts, 1989, Hdbk, 0–86313–731–8
Series: Life Guides
Contents list, glossary, index, useful addresses,
colour line drawings and photographs

Personal reading and the curriculum can equally well draw on books like this. Their coverage of issues is broad, kept focused by a common approach, layout per page, and tone. At the heart lie the well-being of the environment and our health (this series extends the *Human Body* series, also from Franklin Watts). Air and smoke and lead in petrol are all connected and affect our lives, while individual action (e.g. smoking) as well as industrial pollution (e.g. toxic waste, nuclear leukaemia) may serve to end them. Each topic is presented in a lively, summarizing way, stimulating further research. Getting personal, there are additives to diet, noise, stress and exposure to sunlight, ordinary enough but increasingly recognized as potentially dangerous if taken to excess. These things do not exist in isolation: they are everyone's business, and we must not ignore that. Photos and well designed diagrams help an unpatronizing but concise text to get the facts – and the message – across.

SH

Age range: 10–14

ADDICTIONS

BEVAN, Nicholas

AIDS AND DRUGS

Franklin Watts, 1988, Hdbk, 0–86313–779–2
Series: Understanding Social Issues
Contents list, glossary, index, sources of help,
colour line drawings and photographs

There are two kinds of drugs associated with AIDS. One kind is drug abuse, involves sharing needles, and helps to spread AIDS. The other kind is medical drugs, like AZT, which are allegedly helping to control AIDS. Bevan's leisurely conversational tone and expansive manner should not disguise the urgency of his information, that AIDS is here, now, and you can be next. 'With AIDS, once is enough', once with the wrong needle or unprotected sex. Many people simply don't seem to care; others have erroneous ideas about it (like doing it with friends). With dramatic real-life photographs, and clear scientific diagrams of the effect the HIV virus has on the body, he emphasizes that it is a one-way ticket. All sorts of activity – tattooing, sharing toothbrushes, oral sex – could be risky, while fear of AIDS can lead partners to give sex up, even if it destroys a friendship. Direct advice with sources of help at the end. No case studies in this one, as usual in the series, but many issues for discussion, research, and personal moral choice.

SH

Age range: 13–16

BROWNE, David

CRACK AND COCAINE

Franklin Watts, 1987, Hdbk, 0–86313–544–7
Series: Issues
Contents list, index, useful addresses, colour line
drawings and black and white and colour
photographs

The speed with which crack developed from cocaine is frightening. Browne tells young adults that 5000 people a day take cocaine for the first time. He hopes it won't be you. But this book does not preach: in fast-moving and compassionate prose, helped by vivid photographs and telling graphics, it describes the crack explosion, the drug barons of South America, the easy way it can be bought and become addictive. Browne is pessimistic about it being a losing battle for the seizure and treatment experts, but optimistic about education and individual choice ultimately being able to win out. Most of the material in the book concentrates on the United States, but no one can fail to see what a universal (social and personal) set of choices it implies. The pictures tell stories of their own, and can be used as discussion points as well as models for readers' own collection and evaluation of evidence.

SH

Age range: 10–15

CONDON, Judith

SMOKING

Franklin Watts, 1989, Hdbk, 0–86313–944–2
Series: Issues
Contents list, index, black and white and colour
line drawings and photographs

There is no doubting what Judith Condon thinks about smoking: 'the largest single preventable cause of death', a 'lethal cocktail' damaging personal health. Simple persuasive evidence on the subject and the choice. In a series of forceful double-page openings, modern, far from boring, and varied, she develops a subtler, broader argument: that of big business and economic imperialism, sponsorship and tax incentives for the production of cigarettes, the size of marketing budgets and the insidious power of the grown-up image. All these demand further examination and research, making this book a good departure point for it. There are problems for your own health, for babies yet unborn, for lobbies keen to create a smoke-free society. Pictures are well chosen and suggest how easy it is to accept and succumb. Main text and captions, in two type sizes, suggest a range of uses with readers of different abilities, for projects and leisure information.

SH

Age range: 10–14

HAWKES, Nigel

THE HEROIN TRAIL

Franklin Watts, 1986, Hdbk, 0–86313–483–1
Series: Issues
Contents list, index, chronology, black and white and colour line drawings and photographs

Issues is a series which assumes that no one is protected from reality and that living means making difficult choices. Here the issue is heroin, a drug bringing little pleasure and a lot of pain, bringing pushers profit at the expense of people's lives. Hawkes is a journalist on *The Observer* and uses a hard-hitting reporting style to get facts and opinions across in a way which gives a model of how readers should approach the matter themselves. The 'trail' from poppy field to street addict is, conceptually, an easy structure to work with. Within that, questions confront the reader, about the mixed success of suppression, and above all about the consequences of saying 'yes' to heroin. It does not sermonize, but lets the facts speak for themselves, and provides a way of getting into that broader literature which serious students will wish to explore for themselves, for formal or informal study.

SH

Age range: 12–15

HAWKSLEY, Jane

PREGNANCY, DRUGS AND SMOKING

Franklin Watts, 1989, Hdbk, 0–7496–0041–1
Series: Teen Guides
Contents list, glossary, index, colour line drawings and photographs

This book deals with the effects of drugs and smoking on babies before they are born. It works on the assumption that young adults, particularly those serious about an active approach to pregnancy, will already be asking questions and wanting advice. The practical information here should, as it says, not be seen as a substitute for proper medical advice. Hawksley is systematic and unsensational about what can go wrong. She is anxious to dispel the myth that damage can only be serious if AIDS, cocaine, uppers or downers are involved: it can be serious, too, if the pregnant mother consumes alcohol, smokes, or overdoses on caffeine or aspirin. The physical consequences on the foetus are plainly described. Throughout, there is a frank, down-to-earth, and scientifically authoritative approach taken, alert to feelings and attitudes, and never moralizing. Others in the series (on childbirth, birth control, safe sex, and single parenting) are worth acquiring for school/library and less formal uses.

SH

Age range: 15+

LEIGH, Vanora

LET'S DISCUSS SMOKING

Wayland, 1986, Hdbk, 0–85078–914–1
Series: Let's Discuss
Black and white line drawings and photographs

Frankly anti-smoking from the outset, the book tries to be fair to why people smoke, and outlines all the issues involved, including that of the civil liberty of those who smoke. This is what prevents a straightforwardly propagandist book from becoming tiring or off-putting.

Specially attractive are the eight real-life case studies, which should provide plenty of discussion material for readers and others. The history of tobacco, the purported link between smoking and cancer, smoking and general health, child smokers, the tobacco industry, the campaign against smoking, and the difficulty of stopping the habit are all discussed.

PMR

Age range: 12–16

POWNALL, Mark

INHALANTS

Franklin Watts, 1987, Hdbk, 0–86313–622–2
Series: Understanding Drugs
Contents list, glossary, index, sources of help, black and white and colour line drawings and photographs

Drugs are easy to get, particularly if they are everyday household substances like glues and aerosols. Any of these can be made 'sniffable', and Pownall's simple message is that doing it adds problems to your life. He asks why young people do it (boredom, fads, rebellion, copycat behaviour, getting a buzz) and wonders if headlines really tell the truth about sniffing sessions in derelict buildings when substances are everywhere. He is plain-speaking about the effects, from loss of balance and sniffer's rash to choking on your own vomit or suffocation. Throughout, comments from young people forcefully highlight what the author is saying, giving it credibility, avoiding any patronizing. Information is provided on the biochemical effects of benzene, toluene, and the rest, and on organizations which can help. The implied effect, too, is what society at large is doing about it, and what choices rest with the readers themselves. Well mediated material with an overall tone of honesty and a reluctance to over-simplify.

SH

Age range: 12–16

SANDERS, Pete

WHY DO PEOPLE SMOKE?

Franklin Watts, 1989, Hdbk, 0–86313–940–X
Series: Let's Talk About
Index, colour line drawings and photographs

Smoking is an issue for people at any age, and North London teacher Pete Sanders targets his book at upper primary. The facts are one thing, the tone or style another: he gets them both right. Many people smoke, he says, and you have to make up your own mind. It's not easy, but most adults now do not smoke, if you want encouragement. Then there are the facts: the infections to blood and liver and lungs, the addiction to nicotine and kicking the habit, the mixed-up way in which people use it to cope with stress. There are the dilemmas, about advertising images, sponsorship, government taxation and the law about buying cigarettes in shops. Using bold displays, realistic contemporary photos, full-page openings for easy understanding and analysis, and a sympathetic and authoritative tone, this is a book which gets across a topic probably over-bandwagonned by publishers but at a level and in such a way as to give it a distinctive place in its field.

SH

Age range: 7–10

STEPNEY, Rob

TOBACCO

Franklin Watts, 1987, Hdbk, 0–86313–621–4
Series: Understanding Drugs
Contents list, glossary, index, sources of help, colour line drawings and black and white and colour photographs

This book is dead against smoking, and recommends the reader to trash the ash. The best thing about smoking is never to start: it makes death closer, and takes away your freedom of choice. It looks big, you feel 'in', but really it's a big con. People make excuses about not being able to give it up, denying self-evident proof about lung and mouth cancers, and harm to unborn babies. The physical effects and psychological self-deceptions are sad and powerful. This book is intended to stimulate debate and influence personal and social decisions. It is appreciative of how hard it is to give up, to legislate smoking away, to change people through education. It places these issues firmly in the reader's lap, and recent figures about young people smoking suggest that it is not preaching to the converted. At times a little shrill (smokers think less and act more than non-smokers), this book informs, warns, stimulates, just at a time when young adults confront choices like these.

SH

Age range: 12–16

WARD, Brian R.

SMOKING AND HEALTH

Franklin Watts, 1986, Hdbk, 0–86313–401–7
Series: Life Guides
Contents list, glossary, index, black and white and colour line drawings and colour photographs

Life can be better when you look after yourself and know what you're doing.

This is the message of this series, the general editor of which is Chief Medical Officer for the Health Education Council. Ward's hard-hitting and persuasive analysis of smoking uses familiar arguments, but expresses and illustrates them with exemplary clarity and relevance for young readers. Understand the risks, he says, see what effects smoking can have upon your body. If you're a woman, there is evidence to show it affects both you and your baby: consider that. The risks in society at large, to countries producing tobacco, to people suffering other people's bad habits, are plainly there. There is hope: although 250 out of 1000 die of smoking before 65, there are also 10 million ex-smokers in Britain. You too can give it up (cartoons here to help), but it's not easy. Uncomplicated sentence structure, objective tone, and a well planned match between text and picture make this book a first-class addition to a school or personal collection.

SH

Age range: 10–12

SEXUALLY RELATED MATTERS

CHARLISH, Anne

ABORTION

Wayland, 1989, Hdbk, 1–85210–646–8
Series: Let's Discuss
Bibliography, contents list, glossary, index,
helpful organizations, black and white line
drawings and photographs

Having views on an important social issue
is no guarantee that you know enough
about it to argue well or decide properly.
This responsible and provocative
discussion will help young adults sort
both out. In objective terms it opens up
the medical, emotional, and legal
dimensions of abortion. Its own position,
for greater freedom of choice for women,
is clear but not strident or distorting.
Medical reasons exist for recommending
abortion, and these are outlined, holding
nothing back, plainly stating the case.
Facts and figures about unwanted
pregnancies to women under 20 speak
for themselves, and part of the book's
agenda is to encourage young adults to
get contraceptive advice: there is a final
section on 'avoiding unwanted
pregnancy' with a list of helpful
organizations. Case studies
(photocopiable for class use) and
excellent discussion points make this a
valuable resource.

SH

Age range: 12–16

HAWKES, Nigel

AIDS

Franklin Watts, 1987, Hdbk, 0–86313–628–1
Series: Issues
Contents list, index, colour line drawings and
black and white and colour photographs

A difficult subject, handled objectively
and fairly. Starting with the horrifying
facts about the numbers who have died

and those at risk from the disease,
Hawkes looks at its origins (that is, those
belonging to medical history, not those
belonging to the wilder imaginations of
people who would like to attribute the
disease to Africa, though the African
incidence of the disease is also
examined). He looks at how the virus
spreads, how it behaves, the symptoms of
infection, how it is spotted through tests,
how it can be caught – and therefore how
it can be avoided. The question of
treatment, and the more difficult question
of living with AIDS are also covered.

PSG

Age range: 13–16

SANDERS, Pete and FARQUHAR, Clare

AIDS

Franklin Watts, 1989, Hdbk, 0–86313–939–6
Series: Let's Talk About . . .
Glossary, index, colour photographs

This is a series which addresses itself to
subjects children ask questions about, like
smoking and drugs. 'You have probably
heard people talking about AIDS'. This
book presents the very questions children
would ask, and then, calmly, sets out to
answer them. Its assumption is, the more
we know, the less we fear. Toilet seats,
swimming pools, and saliva: don't worry!
So, how does it pass from one person to
another? No judgement, just plain facts in
the answer: dirty needles, unprotected
sex, being born with the HIV virus. These
other issues may need to be discussed
with children in their turn. Each page has
a question, and issues are discussed
alongside a straightforward photograph:
both are needed to get the facts across.
The tone is optimistic without being
facile: most of what we do together is
safe. We can talk to each other and to

adults about AIDS. Children, teachers and parents will all find this book very topical and a great help.

SH

Age range: 6–10

SAUNDERS, Deborah

SEX

Wayland, 1987, Hdbk, 0–85078–916–8
Series: Let's Discuss
Bibliography, contents list, glossary, index, black and white line drawings and photographs

From issues of morality and personal responsibility to sex education in schools and gay partnerships, the author, a marriage counsellor, covers a wide brief in a challenging way. Any one of the major aspects of her theme, like pregnancy or infertility or prostitution, can be taken further in class or in the library. There are questions for discussion and analysis on highly relevant topics like what to teach children in sex education and the extent to which parents should know if their daughter is on the pill. Case studies about a pregnant teenager, arguments at home, and making a young marriage work (these can be reproduced for classroom use) bring home the complexity of the dilemmas, which are not just sexual but interpersonal and social too. The material is structured clearly and interspersed with apt photos all of which extend the text validly. Unsermonizing is Saunders's message that freedom goes with responsibility, and this is a series which formally and informally extends valuable opportunities young people have to consider it.

SH

Age range: 12–16

STONES, Rosemary

LOVING ENCOUNTERS: A YOUNG PERSON'S GUIDE TO SEX

Collins, 1989, Pbk, 0–00–673247–X
Series: Lions 'Choices'
Contents list, index, 'Where to get help and advice', black and white line drawings.

Many encounters are not loving and damage self-esteem. Rosemary Stones emphasizes the loving and sharing aspects of sexual relationships in this classic paperback worth having available in any library and bookshop. She is confidential without being coy, practical without reducing sex to mechanics, and intuitively aware of the fearful questions boys and girls ask themselves on the theme: am I grotesquely different from other people? She puts sex into the setting of growing up and growing together (and apart), physically and emotionally. The book is comprehensive (saying 'yes' to sex, contraception, oral sex, orgasms, the law, body changes, being gay) and allows itself no sexist stereotypes. What it says about AIDS needs updating since it's a fast-moving area of science and behaviour. A book to hand confidently to other people, who will know you care if you say – and show – you believe what it says.

SH

Age range: 12–17

STONES, Rosemary

TOO CLOSE ENCOUNTERS AND WHAT TO DO ABOUT THEM

Magnet, 1987, Pbk, 0–416–03162–5
Bibliography, contents list, index, illustrations

It would be surprising if readers agreed with everything in this book (e.g. 'You are your body . . . '). Sex is a notoriously difficult area about which to write in a way that does not offend or irritate someone or other. But Rosemary Stones writes straightforwardly and unpatronizingly, offering advice on an enormous variety of topics about which it is difficult to find anything at all. These topics include: group pressure, self-preservation, keeping fit, self-defence and defensive weapons, safety in all sorts of situations including when you babysit, the messages given by what you wear, privacy and nudity, sexual fantasies, pornography, running away from home. Most tellingly, she explores why sexual harassment and assault happen in the first place, and what can and might be done about: reporting sexual harassment, obscene phone calls, flashing, touching and rubbing, peeping Toms, whistling, leering, commenting, sexual harassment and assault at school, by strangers, acquaintances, incest and abuse of care, and so on. Some of what she offers is common sense; some of it is the result of advice from experience and considerable thought. So, even if you don't agree with her suggestions or conclusions, this book will at least get you started on thinking through issues to which very few books and people address themselves.

PSG

Age range: 13+

WILKINSON, Graham

AIDS

Wayland, 1987, Hdbk, 1–85210–295–0
Series: Let's Discuss
Bibliography, contents list, glossary, index, black and white line drawings and photographs

Graham Wilkinson works as a counsellor for the Sussex AIDS Advice Centre, and speaks with authority and knowledge about AIDS and HIV problems. He objectively disabuses readers of myths – it's not just gays, the pill won't stop it, take care with everybody. His approach is caring, not punitive, but he places the issues firmly in society's lap: how do and should we deal with it, personally, socially? His advice is directly to young adults: his is a safer sex message where men and women are both responsible, a 'don't share needles' message if you're into drugs. Frank speaking and case studies (copiable for class use) give the book impact without sensationalism. Most poignant of all is the AIDS patient, how they feel and how others see them. A fast-moving subject like this will impel teachers to update the book, already a little out of date.

SH

Age range: 12–16

DISEASES

ALTHEA

I HAVE CANCER

Dinosaur, 1989, Pbk, 0–851–22770–8
Series: Talk it over
Colour line drawings

This is the story of Ben, who has had leukaemia, and tells how he has had to combat the disease. He explains simply and clearly the treatment he has had and how this helped him to get well again. The text is very straightforward and easy to understand and it is colourfully illustrated.

It is an *excellent* book to have in school, particularly when a pupil is undergoing this treatment. (Cancer chemotherapy usually results in the complete, but temporary, loss of hair.)

Althea Braithwaite has donated her royalties from this book to the Malcolm Sargent Cancer Fund for Children.

WFW/JW
Age range: 5–11

BREARLEY, Sue

TALK TO ME

Black, 1989, Hdbk, 0–7136–3192–9
Useful addresses, colour line drawings and photographs

This book focuses attention on speech. It is illustrated by colour photographs, taken at Charlton Park School by Jenny Matthews, of disadvantaged children with speech problems, deafness and other disabilities.

Most children take speech for granted but, in many classes there is the child, lacking friends, and in danger of isolation because of some speech impairment or disability, or some difficulty in verbalization or emotional expression. Even where this is not severe enough to warrant speech therapy, elocution lessons or other professional help, it may tax the patience of other members of class.

Children aged 7–9 may, at times, seem impatient, impulsive, selfish and more willing to talk than to listen, but they are capable of being thoughtful, considerate and caring. This excellent book should be in their class library.

Its title says it all: 'Talk to me . . . '

JW
Age range: 7–9

PARKER, Steve

BLINDNESS

Franklin Watts, 1989, Hdbk, 0–7496–0043–8
Series: Living with . . .
Contents list, glossary, index, people to contact, colour line drawings and black and white and colour photographs

We can see blindness in others easily enough, but it is a complex subject. Steve Parker, with RNIB help, uses cut-away diagrams and photographs to explain what seeing is and how things go wrong. Openings and paragraphs are clearly signposted, and colour is used imaginatively to reveal the optical and surgical aspects of visual disability and cure. Text and picture have to be used side by side, and at times both demand concentration, particularly from younger readers who will need help. Problems (like cataract and squint) can be cured in many cases (laser surgery, corneal transplant). This emphasis might encourage purchase for a collection where the 'living day-to-day' aspects of blindness are already well covered. Practical tests and advice are a good feature, like taking care with computers, sunlight and hygiene.

SH
Age range: 7–12

PETTENUZZO, Brenda

I HAVE ASTHMA

Franklin Watts, 1988, Hdbk, 0–86313–745–8
Series: One World
Contents list, glossary, index, the address for
publications of the Asthma Society, facts about
asthma, colour photographs

This book is part of a series which looks at the everyday life of young people with disabilities.

Here, we meet Alex Wood, a nine-year-old asthmatic who tells his story in his own words, and through specially taken colour photographs. With the help of Great Ormond Street Hospital for Sick Children and the Asthma Society, the author explains the treatment he is given and the effects of his illness on himself and his family. Alex is a plucky lad who enjoys a full and active life in spite of his recurrent illness.

This book will help children, both with and without asthma, to appreciate the problems and difficulties of those who have this condition.

It has the approval of the National Library for the Handicapped Child and bears the 'Handi-read' logo.

JW

Age range: 7–13

PETTENUZZO, Brenda

I HAVE CYSTIC FIBROSIS

Franklin Watts, 1988, Hdbk, 0–86313–746–6
Series: One World
Contents list, glossary, index, colour photographs

As this book is written positively and interestingly, the reaction of child readers on finishing it is likely to be 'Thank God I don't have that'. However, if they come across someone who suffers from it, they are likely to respond with understanding of the condition, the different exercises and diet which help, and of the constraints imposed by it. A useful book for sufferers to hand to friends and relatives, making it possible to avoid having to explain all the gory details oneself.

PMR

Age range: 8–13

PETTENUZZO, Brenda

I HAVE DIABETES

Franklin Watts, 1987, Hdbk, 0–86313–561–7
Series: One World
Contents list, glossary, index, colour photographs

Disability can be worrying and embarrassing. Books like this can help people understand disability better and increase acceptance in society. It deals directly with a boy of ten who lives with diabetes. Unemotional and unmoralizing commentary works, with a series of un-selfconscious and revealing photographs, to tell Marcus's story almost as if in his own words. Positive images of his family, direct photographs of him using the syringe and the blood test machine, explanations of what happens when you get diabetes, all these are set in a real-life world of a boy that age, keen on sport and able, with treatment, to live normally. He has control over his own life: that is an important message (not that the book preaches). Information on the disease and on the British Diabetic Association is provided for young readers and their parents/teachers.

SH

Age range: 8–10

TAYLOR, Barbara

LIVING WITH DEAFNESS

Franklin Watts, 1989, Hdbk, 0–7496–0042–X
Series: Living with . . .
Contents list, glossary, index, health care, first
aid, people to contact (useful addresses), black
and white and colour line drawings and
photographs

At least one in a thousand children is born profoundly deaf, but many more have

by clear colour photographs of helicopters involved in oil rig supply, hunting submarines and air–sea rescue work. As always, in this series, the information is reliable and the text is simple but thorough. There is a glossary for the several technical words used in the book. This is a useful title in a series which has benefited from not being padded out and stretched to a larger format.

RG

Age range: 7–12

KERROD, Robin

MOTORCYCLES

Franklin Watts, 1989, Hdbk, 0–86313–935–3
Series: How It Works
Contents list, glossary, index, colour line drawings and black and white and colour photographs

Some of the explanation is over-technical for the age range, and somewhat dry. However, it does cover every area of how motorcycles work, from the fuel system and the engine to the gears and transmission, the lubrication brakes, suspension, and gripping the road. There are brief explanations of some special bikes and a double-page spread of interesting facts relating to motorbikes.

PMR

Age range: 11–13

LITTLE, Kate

THINGS THAT FLY

Usborne, 1987, Pbk, 0–7460–0105–3
Series: Usborne Explainers
Contents list, index, colour line drawings

In typical Usborne style, this 24-page booklet is packed with brightly coloured pictures and diagrams. Nowhere is there a chapter introduction or an explanatory paragraph longer than seven short sentences. In fact, most of the illustration captions are either single or double

sentences. Essentially, *Things That Fly* is a basic introduction to air transport. There is no mention of bird or insect flight. Over half the book describes aircraft: how they fly, what powers them, their internal structure and what happens to them at an airport. The diagrams explaining the principles of flight, aeronautics and the workings of jet engines etc. are clear and very simple. The text does not go into great scientific detail. Lighter-than-air craft, i.e. hot air balloons and dirigibles, are covered briefly as well as gliders and parachuting. Round-up chapters describe pioneer plane flights, rocketry and facts about the biggest and fastest aircraft.

RG

Age range: 7–11

NORMAN, C. J.

THE PICTURE WORLD OF MOTORCYCLES

Franklin Watts, 1989, Hdbk, 0–86313–851–9
Series: Picture World
Contents list, glossary, index, colour photographs

A wonderful introduction to the world of motorcycles. Every conceivable aspect of that world is presented here: road bikes, race rider, grand prix racing, off-road sport, track racing, other motorcycle sports, custom bikes, stunt riding etc. There is a two-page spread of intriguing facts about motorcycles. And suitably anti-sexist too.

PMR

Age range: 8–10

NORMAN, C. J.

THE PICTURE WORLD OF RACING CARS

Franklin Watts, 1989, Hdbk, 0–86313–850–0
Series: Picture World
Contents list, glossary, index, colour photographs

Although there is a chapter on other

motor sports, such as karting, banger and drag racing in this attractive, large format book, most of the space is concerned with Formula One racing. The spectacle, prestige and glamour of a Grand Prix race is captured well by the excellent colour photographs of cars competing recently at Monaco and Budapest. Basic facts, neither in great depth nor technical detail, are given about the cars, their drivers and the supporting teams of mechanics which travel the international circuits. The content of the written information is shared fairly evenly between the main text, which is in a bold typeface, and the expanded captions, which make what is happening in each photograph very clear. There is a double spread of miscellaneous racing facts in ordinary text and a simple glossary at the back of the book. Recommended for young and partially sighted motor racing enthusiasts.

RG

Age range: 7–12

STEPHEN, R. J.

THE PICTURE WORLD OF AIRLINERS

Franklin Watts, 1989, Hdbk, 0–86313–848–9
Series: Picture World
Contents list, glossary, index, colour photographs

As the series title and cover picture suggest, all the visual information in this large, attractive book is conveyed through superb colour photographs. There is no artwork. More and more children fly each year and this title shows them what to expect: how passengers are cared for, the role of air traffic controllers and the flight crew, etc. There is also a

small gallery with information about several well known short-, medium- and long-haul airliners. The main text in each chapter, in bold sans serif type, uses simple language and carries relatively few concepts per page. The ideas in the text are linked extremely well to the photographs and are extended by excellent captions. Accessibility and ease of reading has been the conscious design effort here. The whole book has an uncluttered, spacious look to it and should appeal to a wide audience, including children with special reading needs.

RG

Age range: 7–12

STEPHEN, R. J.

THE PICTURE WORLD OF BMX

Franklin Watts, 1989, Hdbk, 0–86313–853–5
Series: Picture World
Contents list, glossary, index, colour photographs

It must be my age, but I didn't know exactly what distinguishes a BMX from an ordinary bike on one hand and a mountain bike on the other. Or what distinguishes a 'whoop' from a 'berm' or a 'moto'. The bikes, the riders, the racing, freestyle (which is what most of us associate with BMX), and mountain bikes are all discussed here, along with the history of the bike from its start to the formation of the world body for BMX in 1981 and the first world championship in 1982.

PMR

Age range: 6–8

SPACE

ATKINSON, Stuart

JOURNEY INTO SPACE

Viking Kestrel, 1988, Hdbk, 0–670–82014–8
Contents list, index, black and white and colour
line drawings and colour photographs

This is a highly readable account of the sort of Grand Tour of the Solar System and beyond that may indeed take place in the twenty-first century. Based on current research and plausible predictions about the future of space exploration and space colonization, the author weaves a credible narrative around the astronautical milestones of our past and makes educated guesses about those to come. Our imaginary tour includes a moon visit, a close encounter with the sun and, passing planets all the way, we venture to a space colony on a planet orbiting Proxima Centauri – the nearest star to our sun. The commentary is full of facts and figures and the beautiful photographs, from recent space sorties, make the whole journey throughly believable. The book will best suit those who are already space aficionados but the engaging style and enthusiasm should fire most able readers who have a scientific bent. Recommended.

RG

Age range: 11+

FURNISS, Tim

THE EXPLOITATION OF SPACE

Wayland, 1989, Hdbk, 1–85210–608–5
Series: World Issues
Bibliography, contents list, glossary, index,
colour line drawings and black and white and
colour photographs

This book manages, very successfully, to examine the past, present and future issues of humankind's great technological adventure in space. The great benefits from past space programmes and current satellite technology are outlined, namely the revolution in communications, vastly increased knowledge of the universe and, perhaps most important, a greater understanding of the need to protect and conserve our fragile planet. Future benefits from space are described, such as the manufacture of new drugs and materials on board satellites. The author then presents the counterbalance to this optimistic picture by describing the many problems, challenges and dilemmas that face scientists and governments when considering the future of space exploitation. These are the increased militarization of space, the staggering costs and the criticism that this incurs and, perhaps the most difficult of all, the huge build-up of space debris, which, if not rectified, threatens the very possibility of future space launches.

RG

Age range: 11–14

FURNISS, Tim

SPACE ROCKET

Franklin Watts, 1988, Hdbk, 0–86313–776–8
Series: Engineers at Work
Contents list, glossary, index, chronology of
rocket development, colour line drawings and
photographs

This attractively illustrated book outlines the history of space rocketry. It emphasizes that during the R & D stages, rapid problem solving was made possible only by team-work that involved not just engineers but many others, experienced in all sorts of disciplines, such as design, technologies, maths and sciences (e.g. of fuels, structural materials, aeronautics and astronautics, physics, telecommunications, health and safety).

Many different aspects of rocketry are

considered and some of the problems mentioned.

Finally, there are a few very simple experiments and fun activities for the young reader.

WFW

Age range: 9–14

GRAHAM, Ian

SPACE SHUTTLES

Franklin Watts, 1989, Hdbk, 0–86313–937–X
Series: How It Works
Contents list, glossary, index, colour line
drawings and photographs

This title in the *How It Works* series sets out to explain, to a middle school audience, what the world's first re-usable space craft look like, their history, how they work and how they are currently being deployed in space. The book does this job very well. Its particular strengths are the many colour photographs and large, often cut-away, simple diagrams. The text, in two columns, is clear and concise. The many inevitable technical terms and abbreviations are explained immediately after they are introduced, even though there is a glossary for further clarification. To give the young readers a broader perspective of advancing space technology the American shuttle is contrasted with other international designs, particularly the Soviet version, which has also flown. However, the chapters on the shuttle's robotic arm and the backpacks astronauts use for space walking are likely to be the most appealing. Recommended.

RG

Age range: 7–13

HAWKES, Nigel

SPACE SHUTTLES – A NEW ERA?

Franklin Watts, 1989, Hdbk, 0–86313–811–X
Series: Issues

Contents list, index, colour line drawings and
black and white and colour photographs

By using a less formal journalistic style, plus a commercial-looking combination of text and illustration, this title takes a refreshing look at the development and current use of re-usable space vehicles. There are also commentaries on the past performances of these space work-horses, as well as chapters which describe the very ambitious plans for their involvement in future space-age ventures. These programmes include a role for shuttles in the building of space stations for zero-gravity manufacturing, grand-scale space exploration and, ultimately, as launch-pads for human migration and space colonization. The book compares the various existing and proposed international designs for shuttles, including the futuristic British HOTOL idea. The text, in single columns with largish print, is interspersed with many easy-to-interpret diagrams and fact boxes. This makes all the information very accessible. There are plenty of prompts and questions, designed to initiate discussion. Recommended.

RG

Age range: 9–14

SANDAK, Cass R.

THE WORLD OF SPACE

Franklin Watts, 1990, Hdbk, 0–86313–529–3
Series: New Frontiers – Exploration in the 20th
Century
Contents list, glossary, index, colour line
drawings and photographs

Through a chronological approach and in a workmanlike way, this book charts the development of space exploration from Sputnik One to the current space shuttle programme. It stops just short of the Hubble Telescope launch. The milestones of the space race, on both the Russian and United States side, are recorded and contrasted in some detail. There is a profusion of famous names, events and dates, such as Laika, Gagarin, the Apollo–Soyuz link-up and, of course, Armstong and Aldrin on 21 July 1969. This is all valuable stuff for space fans and projects on the history of space exploration but, as a leisure read, it is occasionally heavy going. The accompanying, often spectacular, colour photographs along with a dateline at the back of the book do, however, help pin down some of these events and remind us just how far space technology has come in a little over 30 years.

RG

Age range: 11–14

COMPUTERS

FIDDY, Pamela and FOX-DAVIES, Dick

SUPERMARKET COMPUTER

Black, 1985, Hdbk, 0–7136–2652–6
Series: Computers in Action
Index, colour line drawings and photographs

This title leads the reader cleverly and thoroughly through the reasons why supermarkets can operate more efficiently and effectively with the help of computers. By asking questions, the text convinces us that computers cut out human error, speed up check-outs and make the life of the store manager very much easier when stocktaking and price changing, etc. Some supermarkets have computers in the form of electronic cash registers, but these rely on an operator typing in the price of each article at his/her own speed, whereas supermarkets which have a scanner attached allow the computer to 'look' at the articles and put in the correct prices automatically. This highly efficient method uses barcodes – and the pages dealing with the 'what', 'how' and 'why' of barcode labels are particularly good. All these fairly complex concepts are made interesting and very accessible by combining clear colour photographs with lively, eye-catching and well captioned diagrams.

RG

Age range: 9–14

GODMAN, Arthur and TREGEAR, Tim

ACORN CAMBRIDGE ILLUSTRATED DICTIONARY FOR YOUNG COMPUTER USERS

CUP, 1986, Pbk, 0–521–27419–2
Contents list, glossary, 'Timeline', colour line drawings and photographs

An introduction to computers and a history of computers complement this full and rich dictionary, which seems to have everything which a child may be interested in looking up. Five years have passed since the Dictionary was first published and so there are things which would be worth including in any future edition (AT and XT, for example). But all the information here has been put in the simplest and briefest possible manner. There are lots of colour illustrations, and an excellent page explaining how this book is best consulted.

PSG

Age range: 10–14

AGRICULTURE

BOLWELL, Laurie and LINES, Clifford

FARMING THE LAND

Wayland, 1987, Hdbk, 0–85078–934–6
Series: The Countryside
Bibliography, contents list, glossary, index,
colour line drawings and photographs

This title takes a clear and objective look at all the varieties of current British farming practices – from crofting to horticulture, from mixed to fish farms. The authors stress that, in order to be efficient, our farmers have to make the right decisions, both in the light of the land they have and the prevailing market forces that the EEC imposes on them. The book describes how, because of the need for profits, farms have had to become more specialized and highly mechanized. Furthermore, where pigs and poultry are concerned, new factory farming methods have become the norm. The authors also point out that many people consider these new farming methods have actually been detrimental because of alterations to our landscape and over-production of commodities, as well as being cruel to animals. On the other hand, they point out that farmers are becoming more sensitive to green issues and the public's demands for more healthy eating.

RG

Age range: 11–14

FITZGERALD, Janet

SPRING ON THE FARM

Hamish Hamilton, 1989, Hdbk, 0–241–12580–4
Series: Science Through the Seasons
Contents list, index, extension activities, colour
photographs

Children naturally explore and books like this help stimulate and focus their investigation. One of four about farms (on each season), the book uses large, very accurately printed colour photographs to give exact pictures of creatures and their lives. Eleven short topics are presented, all leading to observation, measurement, sorting, and other activities. Many questions are simple – which bird do you see most often? – while others involve more demanding concepts, like why birds' beaks are the shape they are, or more dedication, like how plants grow or what baby chicks like to eat. All can be carried out in a well organized school, many at home, and collaboration with teachers and parents is assumed (and guidance for adults provided). This, and another series on woods, can be added to the other imaginative books of this type for junior age children and adults who live alongside them.

SH

Age range: 5–7

MILLER, Jane

FARM MACHINERY

Dent, 1987, Hdbk, 0–460–06255–7
Colour photographs

There are many books on farms, but this attractive book will find its place for its useful colour photographs of farm machinery. An economic script-like text acts as a pointer to the pictures and helps young readers look carefully and hard. The machines are all at work, ploughing or crop spraying, transporting pigs or sorting potatoes, themes which serve as organizing principles for the layout. Technical words are not avoided: many can be 'found' by looking in the pictures; others may need further explanation and research. But it can be assumed that many readers will have other books to hand, or even models which help them

understand how they work. Well
designed pages give impact and clarity to
the learning and looking, and will make
a trip into the countryside, or simply an
imaginative one in the classroom, a more
interesting and informed experience.

SH

Age range: 6–8

MILLER, Jane

SEASONS ON THE FARM

Dent, 1986, Hdbk, 0–460–6234–4
Colour photographs

By outstanding full colour photographs,
showing a variety of farm animals and
farm machinery, and a few well chosen
words to encourage and practise reading,
Jane Miller introduces the very young to
farm activities during the four seasons.

This attractive book will prove as
popular as her earlier books, *Farm
Alphabet* and *Farm Counting*, and delight
children, whether at school in town or
country.

JW

Age range: 5–8

CROPS

BJÖRK, Christina

LINNEA'S ALMANAC

R & S, 1989, Hdbk, 91–29–59176–7
Index, colour line drawings and black and white and colour photographs

A great deal of attention has gone into the production of this book – which cannot be said for all natural history books! It is the story of one little girl's calendar of events, of what she does in her garden, in the house and how she is attuned to nature. It shows a deep sensitivity to the environment. The book is arranged on a month-by-month basis with all the things she gets up to – from flying kites, to pressing flowers, to collecting leaves, to looking at the stars. It's like a holistic earth book with fascinating things for older children who like to read and discover – with a great Linnaeus connection.

JF

Age range: 7–12

COLDREY, Jennifer and BERNARD, George

STRAWBERRY

Black, 1988, Hdbk, 0–7136–3052–3
Series: Stopwatch
Index, black and white line drawings and colour photographs

The life cycle of the strawberry fruit is described in intimate detail in this book. Closer than life inspection of the bisected flower and fruit reveal the development of the flower, pollination and fruit set and changes in maturation of the fruit. The colour pictures are supported by line drawings. The position of the seeds on the fleshy fruit are well shown on several occasions, and the book further describes effects of rotting, and of fruit loss by a woodmouse.

JF

Age range: 6–10

DAVIES, Kay and OLDFIELD, Wendy

MY APPLE

Black, 1990, Hdbk, 0–7136–3200–3
Series: Simple Science (Through Play)
Colour line drawings and photographs

This is one of a series of simple science books for very young children, showing how to make observations from familiar objects. Its format, with large colour photographs and a few simple sentences, makes it attractive to children. They are invited not only to look at apple blossom and mature apples, but to examine them carefully – their stalks, their waterproof and brightly coloured skin; the way they float; to cut them open and count the seeds; to grow the seeds; to taste the fruit and to cook it; to make prints with blocks of apple.

There are notes at the back for adults on the scientific concepts behind the activities.

JW

Age range: 4–7

GODDARD, Susan

SOYA

Wayland, 1986, Hdbk, 0–85078–791–2
Series: Focus on Resources
Bibliography, contents list, glossary, index, sources of further information, colour line drawings and photographs

Focus on Resources is a series of topical surveys of key natural resources. *Soya* uses a concise authoritative commentary to outline the versatile range of uses this product has. Information is logically structured, from the plant and its harvesting and processing to the variety of foodstuffs available for animals and human beings. Double-page openings break up the material into manageable chunks, each one decorated with colour photographs or diagrams which complement the discussion and identify products which readers will recognize from shopping expeditions. The author is a representative of the American Soybean Association, and so claims like soya being the most efficient and least costly source of protein in the world, and an obvious choice for vegetarians and slimmers, should be seen for what they are. Yet this dimension makes the book good for comparative discussion about foodstuffs and environment, as well as for the soya product itself.

SH

Age range: 10–14

WATTS, Barrie

DANDELION

Black, 1987, Hdbk, 0–7136–2855–3
Series: Stopwatch
Index, black and white line drawings and colour
photographs

With the use of stunning close-up photographs of dandelions, a story is told of the development of seeds from the flower. The text is simple and straightforward with no scientific jargon; one feels that the text is sometimes too simple in this series of good photo-guides, and that opportunities have been missed. Youngsters will enjoy this volume since it has interesting pictures of

dandelion 'clocks' and seeds wafting away.

JF

Age range: 6–10

WATTS, Barrie

POTATO

Black, 1987, Hdbk, 0–7136–2929–0
Series: Stopwatch
Index, black and white line drawings and colour
photographs

We get chips from potatoes. But other things happen too, like new potatoes. Using full-page illustrations, in which subjects are strikingly lit against a black ground for definition and impact, Watts takes young readers through the process of growth and decay. Shoots grow in the surface of the potato, so close that it looks like the moon. The potato dies as shoots grow to the surface of the soil, and roots spread out to support tubers which become new potatoes. Each opening has text in two sizes (for beginners and those further on), and a diagram–photograph combination for analysis and comparison. Young readers will need help at the flowers and fruit stage. Tips on the dangerous green bits are sound. At the end, readers can go through it all again on their own, helped by six key pictures showing the main stages of the book.

SH

Age range: 4–7

DAIRY PRODUCTS

DIXON, Annabelle

MILK

Black, 1987, Hdbk, 0–7136–2933–9
Series: Threads
Contents list, index, more things to do, colour line drawings and photographs

Most of us see and drink milk every day. *Threads* is a series which looks at products like this, asks how they are made, and how to find out more. Colour photographs show cows and milking and bottles and milkmen, organized on the 'how it gets to us' principle. Products sold in shops are shown to identify them in children's minds, make them better shoppers and researchers (because looking at products is a good way to find out more). Emphasis is placed on how clean milk is, even in the milking shed. It can go off, and cheese is a way of stopping it doing this too quickly. Primary girls and boys are shown making cheese, butter and yoghurt, with simple layouts showing how the recipes are carried out. Steps are clearly numbered, and materials are close at hand. It really is quite versatile stuff.

SH

Age range: 6–10

129

INSECT CULTURE

ROWLAND-ENTWISTLE, Theodore

FOCUS ON SILK

Wayland, 1988, Hdbk, 1–85210–072–9
Series: Focus on Resources
Bibliography, contents list, glossary, index,
sources of further information, black and white
and colour line drawings and photographs

The author sets himself the daunting task of writing a clear, concise history of the discovery of silk in China; this is followed by a description of silk production in the mulberry silkworm; finally, the process of silk manufacture and the many uses of silk are discussed. The morality of killing the chrysalis by baking or steaming isn't raised, but might well be by child readers. Adults need to be prepared.

All this assumes an enormous concentration and a determination of understanding on the part of the reader and help will surely be needed to interpret. As with all books that discuss textiles, this one needs embedding in a wider learning context. Children need to know silk for themselves – the touch, the smell, the feel. If they come to this book with prior knowledge they will read it more responsively and will be more likely to make use of the valuable list of contacts provided.

HM

Age range: 9–11

FOOD AND DRINK

BASKERVILLE, Judith

BREAD

Black, 1987, Hdbk, 0–7136–2930–4
Series: Threads
Contents list, index, colour photographs

A book in the *Threads* series covering everyday products and their manufacture and usage. An attractive cover – a girl eating a brown bread sandwich surrounded by a border of brown bread – invites the reader inside. The whole process of bread making is covered, from the raw materials to finished product. The bit about tasting water, flour and salt on their own and then thinking about mixing them together to improve the taste is particularly effective. There's a quick, easy recipe for bread rolls and the multi-cultural aspect of 'bread around the world' is good too.

The origin of sandwiches is mentioned; the Earl of Sandwich wouldn't stop playing cards for long enough to eat, so he asked for a piece of meat between two slices of bread – so the 'sandwich' was born!

The page of 'things to do' at the back of the book will extend the topic still further with more recipes and experiments, all involving bread.

SD

Age range: 4–7

DESHPANDE, Chris and DAS, Prodeepta

FINGER FOODS

Black, 1988, Hdbk, 0–7136–2986–X
Series: Friends
Things to do, colour photographs

Finger foods are the kind you can eat with your fingers. Primary school children are the stars in this televisual book built around realistic colour photographs of them preparing for a picnic. Text and pictures show foods of many kinds – dumplings, bhaji, chapatis, pitta bread – making sure the text is not daunting on its own. Even so, it will need practical as well as vocabulary help from adults to carry the tasks through completely. The structure is cognitively and visually subtle, from showing what the children want, getting ideas from shops and restaurants, and then making the picnic itself. Tasks like making spring rolls and hummus are tricky, and the 'things to do' section (for the teacher) is just a clue to how much preparation is required. This is why the book succeeds: it's not just a 'look and go away' kind of experience.

SH

Age range: 5–7

DOWNER, Lesley

JAPANESE FOOD AND DRINK

Wayland, 1987, Hdbk, 0–85078–943–5
Series: Food and Drink
Bibliography, contents list, glossary, index, some useful addresses, colour line drawings and photographs

This series aims to show a country's food and drink, and to give younger readers an idea of why it is so. Lesley Downer brings her experience of Japan and Japanese cookery to this readable book. Geography and social customs have influenced what people grow – rice, mushrooms, tea – and use for food – particularly fish and seaweed. Meal-times through an ordinary day show what the table looks like, in a family home or in a sushi bar. Photographs show the people, settings, markets, clothes, all giving vivid information in a structured and well signposted way to younger readers. Half-a-dozen recipes can be tried out, most with adult help, and suppliers in the UK and elsewhere are given at the back. A useful and attractive book worth introducing to readers who like knowing more about the way other people live.

SH

Age range: 8–13

LAFARGUE, Françoise

FRENCH FOOD AND DRINK

Wayland, 1987, Hdbk, 0–85078–895–1
Series: Food and Drink
Bibliography, contents list, glossary, index, maps, French words and phrases, colour line drawings and photographs

Nowadays, many children go to France on holiday: this would be a good book to dip into beforehand and then take with them. It explains the meaning of many of the words they would encounter in shops and restaurants and helps them to enjoy the great French tradition of good food and drink.

It starts with a good clear map of the country and a brief account of its geography, which is varied in view of its large size. Some chapters on the production and selling of food and wine are followed by more detailed sections on specialities. The typical daily meals are named and described, as well as more festive celebrations. Certain regions of France are dealt with separately, each marked clearly on an outline map and then its food and wine described. There are nine simple recipes for children to try, to create a taste of France for themselves.

A few French words and phrases about food and a booklist for further reading completes this excellent survey of French food.

JW

Age range: 9–13

OSBORNE, Christine

MIDDLE EASTERN FOOD AND DRINK

Wayland, 1988, Hdbk, 1–85210–313–2
Series: Food and Drink
Bibliography, contents list, glossary, index, colour line drawings and photographs

Christine Osborne has written other books on life and cooking in the Middle East and, with sure-footed insight into what young readers want and understand, presents an exciting account for this series. The principle is to set food and drink in the setting of country and culture. Information is structured clearly and logically: the region and its variety, food from figs to lamb, the selling of it (in suqs or markets, where men do the shopping) to the preparation of meals. A feeling for middle eastern meals comes across through informative colour photographs, with rituals like eating by hand and coffee drinking. Emphasis is placed on food you can make, and seven recipes with easy-to-follow diagrams are included (hummus, kebabs, Persian chicken), all well within the capacity of the young reader. Festival meals give Osborne a chance to give us more about local customs. A readable, practical book which knows how to keep things to an attractive minimum.

SH

Age range: 10–14

PARAÏSO, Aviva

JEWISH FOOD AND DRINK

Wayland, 1988, Hdbk, 1–85210–030–3
Series: Food and Drink
Bibliography, contents list, glossary, index, appendix on the three languages associated with Judaism, colour line drawings and photographs

This attractive, well written book first outlines the history and geography of Israel and the food laws stated in the books of Deuteronomy and Leviticus. It look at Jewish eating habits and the dietary specialities in Israel and throughout the Diaspora, and describes certain Jewish festive foods.

The colour photographs are fascinating and illustrate well different aspects of Jewish life and culture.

Simple recipes are included so that the young readers can experience Jewish cooking for themselves.

The author, an experienced teacher, has travelled widely and written several educational books on food and cooking.

WFW

Age range: 11–16

SHUI, Amy and THOMPSON, Stuart

CHINESE FOOD AND DRINK

Wayland, 1987, Hdbk, 0–85078–896–X
Series: Food and Drink
Bibliography, contents list, glossary, index, colour line drawings and photographs

This book gives an accurate and fascinating picture of the very important and all-pervasive relationship the Chinese have with their food. For instance, did you know that people in China usually greet each other with, 'Have you eaten?' instead of 'Hello'?. The conventional reply is, 'Just now!' (whether true or not) and this implies everything is fine. Comprehensive information about the history and geography of the country is brought together with chapters on how the food is grown, processed and preserved. Likewise, Chinese culture, manners and traditions are discussed alongside how food is cooked, served and eaten. Simple, step-by-step recipes of dishes from the four regional cuisines of China are included throughout the book and these enable the reader to get an actual 'taste of China'! The well captioned colour photographs give excellent support to the clear and easy-to-read text. This title would provide valuable

background reading for G.C.S.E. Home Economics coursework. Recommended.

RG

Age range: 10+

SPROULE, Anna

BRITISH FOOD AND DRINK

Wayland, 1988, Hdbk, 1–85210–312–4
Series: Food and Drink
Bibliography, contents list, glossary, index, safety hints, colour line drawings and photographs

A country's food and drink come into being for good reason, and a concise introduction attempts to map out the diversity of race (English, Welsh, Scottish), geography and social custom behind what the British eat and drink. Ethnic minority tastes are not included. One claim of the series is that of dispelling myths about national habits. This book gets rid of the traditional fry-up for breakfast, but portrays British life as a succession of meat meals, TV dinners, and baked beans at school. Half-a-dozen recipes, otherwise well displayed in instructions and diagrams, reinforce the meat-based character of British eating (hotpot, Sunday lunch, steak and kidney pie), and no mention of trends towards vegetarianism appears. It is not always easy to follow: 'processing' ties itself up in knots, while some syntax and vocabulary (including search-terms in the index) is unhelpful. In pragmatic terms, a book with some use, but in need of others to set it in balance.

SH

Age range: 10–14

TAVLARIOS, Irene

GREEK FOOD AND DRINK

Wayland, 1987, Hdbk, 0–85078–941–9
Series: Food and Drink
Bibliography, glossary, index, Greek words and phrases, colour line drawings and photographs

Food and drink are set within geography and culture as Tavlarios trots through the various parts of Greece (history, too), saying what grows where. Once on shopping and the food itself, things get more practical. She wants to tell us not just what is eaten, but where and why, and a feel for authentic Greek life comes across. Eight easy-to-follow recipes, with safety tips and ingredients you can buy outside Greece, are an attractive feature. Cooking and eating fish or meat, however, is not all there is: we are told when they are eaten, how ancient some of the recipes are, and what to expect if you go to a Greek restaurant or home. Photographs are not just cookbook in style, because Greek life, shops, people, ceremonies are shown too. A nice way to blow clichés away and get young readers thinking seriously about why people (not just tourists) eat what they do.

SH

Age range: 10–14

THOMSON, Ruth and DAS, Prodeepta

RICE

Black, 1989, Hdbk, 0–7136–3105–8
Series: Threads
Contents list, index, colour line drawings and photographs

Rice comes in bowls and packets, mostly cooked, on the table at home. Only then does it grow in fields and get harvested and milled. This order of presentation is wholly logical: start with what young children know, and go on to things they don't. Thomson's introduction to this

familiar product, assisted by aptly positioned colour photographs and diagrams, is firmly set in the young child's world. It is full of things to think about and do, like cook rice, grow rice in a pot, and try out a rice and carrot cake. Simple practical guidance for the recipes is given in attractive layouts which children can read and follow, as they choose. These things can be done at home or in school. Ideas are given for further research.

SH

Age range: 7–10

WILKES, Angela

MY FIRST COOK BOOK

Dorling Kindersley, 1989, Hdbk, 0–86318–356–5
Contents list, colour photographs

The appealing part of this book is its size – it's enormous! and all the photos of food are life size to make for easy identification. The text is kept to a minimum, but the important points are all included, especially a list of rules for the kitchen, e.g. be very careful with sharp knives, turn saucepan handles inwards.

The book takes a young cook through the whole process – from a list of cook's tools to a detailed description of the finishing touches. Many basic recipes are included – easy bread, short pastry, sponges – right through to more fun goodies like ice cream sundaes and chocolate truffles.

A really excellent first cook book for a young child, one that could lead to a lifetime's interest in cooking and food.

SD

Age range: 4–7

SHOPPING

LINES, Cliff

EXPLORING SHOPPING

Wayland, 1988, Hdbk, 1–85210–349–3
Series: Exploring the Past
Bibliography, contents list, glossary, index, places to visit, black and white and colour line drawings and photographs

Bringing the past to life and closer to the reader is no small challenge. This series combines an investigative approach to local history with practical tasks which young readers can carry out for themselves. Shopping through the ages is described in text and pictures, providing background and concepts (e.g. the chain store, barter). Around that there is a raft of activities which children can do in their neighbourhood: look for old shops, old adverts, go to a local market, ask old people what it used to be like, look through old newspapers, compare then and now, consider what shopping will be like in the future. This makes the book highly useful for personal discovery reading and organized work in school and library. Topics are displayed so that the immediate past comes first and the remote past last. Logical, useful, well mediated information, with the fun of doing thrown in.

SH

Age range: 9–14

CHEMICAL TECHNOLOGIES

CACKETT, Susan

GLASS

Franklin Watts, 1988, Hdbk, 0–86313–768–7
Series: Resources Today
Contents list, glossary, index, colour line
drawings and black and white and colour
photographs

Though this book is written very much
from an adult's point of view, and written
down to children, glass is such an
interesting material and so common a
part of our lives that children are likely to
get drawn into the book.

The cartoon-style 'story of a drinks
bottle' is especially appealing, and there
are 'Fact Files' on handmade glass,
decorating glass and stained glass, and on
fibre optics, mirrors, glass ceramics and
soluble glass.

PMR

Age range: 9–11

CASH, Terry

PLASTICS

Black, 1989, Hdbk, 0–7136–3104–X
Series: Threads
Contents list, index, colour photographs

A book not immediately of interest to me,
turned out to contain some interesting
facts. In fact the whole subject was
opened up for me on reading this book.
Did you know for instance that the bits on
the bottom of plastic buckets are called
sprues? They are cut off when the bucket
is made. The cover of the book is
illustrated with a border of 'sprues' – they
look a bit like mini-candles!

This is one of the *Threads* series, all
covering aspects of everyday products.
Many items made of plastic are covered
in this book, explaining the process
involved in their manufacture, e.g. egg
boxes, buckets, bottles, tubes.

On many of the pages are questions or
suggestions for further explorations; the
ideas for making a mould are especially
good. The back page has more questions
and experiments to try to encourage
further study. A good index and contents
page complete a fascinating book.

SD

Age range: 4–7

CHANDLER, Jane and BARBER, Ed

GLASS

Black, 1987, Hdbk, 0–7136–2931–2
Series: Threads
Contents list, index, more things to do, colour line
drawings and photographs

Many everyday products deserve a
proper look, and glass is one of them.
After all, we find it in mirrors, magnifying
glasses, shop windows and milk bottles.
The *Threads* series encourages this
approach, and uses its topics to stimulate
activities and discovery learning.
Processes for making round and flat glass
are difficult to understand, but Chandler,
using simple text with diagrams and storytelling colour photographs, gets the main
principles across. Further research and
back-up materials (e.g. on lenses and
toughened glass) would be essential for a
systematic class exercise/project.
Illustrations here are revealing, realistic,
functional, suggesting what to examine
and how, and doing it together can be the
best way. Follow-up suggestions (e.g.
optical fibres, artefacts from the past)
need the infrastructure and advice a
teacher or librarian can provide.

SH

Age range: 7–10

MERCER, Ian

OILS

Franklin Watts, 1988, Hdbk, 0–86313–770–9
Series: Resources Today
Contents list, glossary, index, two fact files,
colour line drawings and photographs

This book, attractively presented by the design and production team of Aladdin books, to appeal to the junior school child, is by Ian Mercer, an educator at the Geological Museum, London, but, as the colour photograph of sunflowers on the cover makes clear immediately, it deals not just with mineral oil, but also with vegetable oils: indeed, the book starts off by classifying oils as animal, vegetable and mineral – as in the game 'Twenty Questions'!

It is set out as a series of double-page spreads, each well illustrated by colour photographs or coloured diagrams: only the first photograph in the book is problematic (it is not labelled).

There are two fact files, a glossary of eight terms, and a short index (20 entries).

The text is straightforward and informative, and I found only half-a-dozen or so misleading things in the book to which, as a science teacher, I took exception.

WFW

Age range: 7–11

NEWSON, Lesley

DEALING WITH DIRT

Black, 1988, Hdbk, 0–7136–3046–9
Contents list, index, black and white line
drawings

As a former school librarian, I view with enthusiasm this attractive little book, as a superb introduction to the Science of Cleaning. I feel certain that children will find it interesting, informative, easy to understand and quite thought-provoking. They will enjoy the illustrations, which show a good sense of humour. (The characters could easily have been labelled with names like Dan Druff, Fred Bear, Cur Rosentein, Poor Lou-Ted, Washingtum, Also-ran Sid, Hugh Wotapong etc.)

But, as a science teacher, who has always insisted on concise English, accuracy, thoroughness, and the correct use of scientific terms, I find it difficult to allow the author of a science book the same degree of artistic licence as I am prepared to grant an illustrator. I soon found myself analysing the shortcomings of the text, the glaring omissions, the misuse of scientific terms and the misconceptions they could engender.

My review grew in length, rapidly, till I realized it was too long, and would have to be cut. I then stopped nit-picking and decided to be charitable!

WFW

Age range: 7–11

METALLURGY

LAMBERT, Mark

IRON AND STEEL

Wayland, 1987, Hdbk, 0–85078–970–2
Series: Focus on Resources
Bibliography, contents list, glossary, index,
colour line drawings and photographs

For several years the *Focus on Resources* series has provided reliable information on world commodities but the series design is beginning to show its age now. When this title tries to describe the large-scale and complicated chemical processes involved in modern iron and steel production, there is a serious problem of lack of space. There are insufficient small diagrams to help make clear many of the chemical and technical points in the text. Those diagrams that are included, although perfectly good, are isolated to a single page or double-page spread, away from the text they are trying to support. The many photographs, often spectacular, are mostly too small to show clearly the big plant involved. Similarly, because each chapter is always confined to two pages, many technical terms are insufficiently explained in the text, even though some are picked up later in the glossary.

RG

Age range: 11–14

MANUFACTURES

BROOKS, Felicity

HOW THINGS ARE MADE

Usborne, 1989, Pbk, 0–7460–0277–7
Series: Usborne Explainers
Contents list, index, colour line drawings

This short paperback in the *Explainers* series is subtitled 'Finding Out About' and Usborne have, in their usual colourful style, made industrial technology fun and quite easy to understand. The double-page spreads are full of information about the manufacture of everyday items which are interesting and relevant to children, e.g. drink cans, shoes, pencils and even Lego bricks. The cut-away diagrams which outline manufacturing stages for each of these products, although small, are bright and clear enough for infants to follow. The captions cannot avoid being technical occasionally and, because of the small format of the books, tend to crowd the pictures in some places. Nevertheless, this is a book most children will want to look at and use to get information for special topics. Having dipped in, better readers may well be inspired to read it from cover to cover.

RG

Age range: 6–11

DIXON, Annabelle

WOOL

Black, 1988, Hdbk, 0–7136–3049–3
Series: Threads
Contents list, index, colour line drawings and photographs

An extremely practical book that helps children to take on learning for themselves. A book to use, to do things with; children will recognize and respond to the presenter's tone in the text – a clear, humorous and direct message, inviting participation to smell, feel and experiment in order to discover the special properties of wool. Each experiment carries a careful explanation, well supported by photographs and illustrations. Children are shown how to card, spin, dye and weave wool, in ways which are all possible and with materials that are readily available at home or in a busy classroom. Children should come away from this book feeling that wool is something really rather special. Top marks too for attention to equal opportunities: boys and girls in photos represent different ethnic groups and are shown taking part equally in each experiment and activity.

HM

Age range: 7–11

JENNINGS, Terry

WOOD

Black, 1989, Hdbk, 0–7136–3103–1
Series: Threads
Contents list, index, colour line drawings and photographs

The thread in this title is the sequence of events, from seed to sawmill, occurring in forestry and in the manufacture of wood products, such as veneers and plywood. Interspersed with these chapters, children are shown doing various activities and investigations to do with wood. These comprise the usual planting of seeds and taking wood rubbings etc., but also include making your own chipboard and a fair test for the strength of wooden dowling. The language is never technical and the photographs clarify the industrial processes and show how the experiments are done. There is a valuable 'green' chapter on the need for tree conservation and paper recycling, which explains that 17 trees can be saved for every tonne of waste paper collected. This is another useful title in the series with good ideas for teacher which are, just as importantly, accessible to children as well.

RG

Age range: 7–11

PATTERSON, Geoffrey

THE STORY OF WOOL

André Deutsch, 1987, Hdbk, 0–233–97923–9
Index, colour line drawings

This book outlines the history of wool production and its use from the Stone Age through to the present. It is necessarily brief, resulting in a dense text supported by illustration, and with interesting insights into the nature of sheep breeding, and spinning and weaving techniques across cultures and millennia.

Understanding the process of wool production – carding, spinning, weaving, knitting, fulling, cropping and so on – requires a grasp of specialist language; the author offers careful explanations of each process, but in the end I wonder if a child can imagine the movement of person and loom. I missed a moving image and wonder how books like this will compete with explanations on TV.

Children will understand better what wool production is about when they are given practical experience of what is involved. This book, then, needs to be used as part of a wider classroom project.

HM

Age range: 9–11

RICKARD, Graham

DIAMONDS

Wayland, 1987, Hdbk, 1–85210–070–2
Series: Focus on Resources
Bibliography, contents list, glossary, index,
colour line drawings and black and white and
colour photographs

Diamonds, the 'king of gems', are the hardest, most brilliant and beautiful of jewels. This book, from Wayland's *Focus on Resources* series, takes a thorough look at the history, mining and processing of diamonds. Early mining methods, including those in eighteenth-century Brazil, where black slaves were lucky to be fed in return for their labour, are described. Modern mining techniques used in South Africa and Namibia, where the workforce is still black, are also outlined. Fascinating background information is given on the unique physical properties of diamonds, which make them indispensible in today's high-tech industries, as well as information on the traditional skills involved in gemstone cutting and diamond valuation. The history of famous and infamous stones, such as the Cullinan, is provided. Superb colour photographs are used throughout. One afterthought: perhaps this book would benefit from an updated series cover design and conversion to a larger format.

RG

Age range: 11–14

WOOD, Tim

PAPER

Franklin Watts, 1987, Hdbk, 1–86313–570–6
Series: Making
Contents list, index, colour line drawings and
photographs

This book details very methodically with each stage in the international production of a particular type of high-quality writing paper. From the opening chapter, where all the raw materials for making this product are shown, the clear text is supported by excellent, specially commissioned, colour photographs. As well as helping to clarify the procedures at the tree plantation, pulp mill and paper mill, these photographs give a true feeling of the grand scale of the operations and the huge plant required. It is a pity, however, that apart from a useful forest-to-finished-product flowchart at the back of the book, there are no other child-friendly diagrams to illustrate the internal goings on at both mills. It is also surprising, perhaps, that there is only one small paragraph which mentions paper recycling and no mention at all of the need for tree conservation.

RG

Age range: 8+

BUILDING

CASH, Terry

BRICKS

Black, 1988, Hdbk, 0–7136–3048–5
Series: Threads
Contents list, index, colour line drawings and
photographs

Tapping a child's curiosity about where
bricks come from and how they are
made, this book interests them in brick
patterns, in experimentation with the
strength of various kinds of bricking, in
collecting different types of brick, in their
colours and texture and shapes.
Excellent.

PMR

Age range: 6–8

EDOM, Helen

HOW THINGS ARE BUILT

Usborne, 1989, Pbk, 0–7460–0279–3
Series: Usborne Explainers
Contents list, index, colour line drawings

In 24 busily illustrated pages,
explanations are given of the building of
houses, roads, bridges, dams, tunnels and
oil rigs. Each opening is full of brightly
coloured line drawings, and many objects
shown are labelled and arrowed for
information. Insets, blow-outs, and other
graphic devices are used to zoom in on
specific activities like welding or blasting.
This is also a way of structuring
information, the detail within the general
design of the open page. It can be used
on several levels, easy to difficult, and in
informal and formal reading situations
(from fun book in the car to research tool
in the library). Its very succinctness means
that some teachers will want it used in
context with other resources, while its
paperback format may make it more of a
personal gift than a school book.

SH

Age range: 7–10

THE ARTS

◆

Possibly the most difficult subject area to convey adequately to young people, for after all, why should they be reading about this when they could be out there doing it? Books, however, can serve as both a vicarious indulgence and as an enticing introduction.

GRIFFITHS, Vivien

MY CLASS VISITS A MUSEUM

Franklin Watts, 1987, Hdbk, 0–86313–550–1
Series: My Class
Colour photographs

A class of young children are trying to imagine what it was like to live a hundred years ago, so they go on a visit to the City of Birmingham Museum. The story is told through photographs and in the words of Lorraine Copes, one of the class. They enjoy being dressed in Victorian costume and handling some now obsolete household utensils. Then they write up their visit back at school. Perhaps this book will suggest practical activities like this, that brings the past to life and makes history really enjoyable.

JW

Age range: 5–9

LEE, Vicky and FAIRCLOUGH, Chris

MY CLASS VISITS A PARK

Franklin Watts, 1985, Hdbk, 0–86313–324–X
Series: My Class
Colour line drawings and photographs

This series shows primary children outside the classroom, at the library or swimming bath, and here in a London park with their teacher. Chris Fairclough's near full-page photos show in detail who they are and what they do, from getting ready to going on the bus, to having lunch in the open air and coming home on the underground. For young readers these will be familiar or exciting experiences, with memories and hopes of their own. There is an activities emphasis, as they draw the birds they see, look at flowers and talk to a gardener, play tag and have fun. Conversational caption-like language is intended to be the words of Kirsty, a girl in the class, a credible device most of the time (except when the ducks are said to have their own noisy language), but the main interest is looking and learning. Lee works as an educationist with the London Borough of Ealing.

SH

Age range: 6–8

ARCHITECTURE

CLEMENTS, Gillian

THE TRUTH ABOUT CASTLES

Macmillan Children's Books, 1988, Hdbk, 0–333–47067–2
Contents list, colour line drawings

A marvel of colour and design, this book will draw in even the most disinterested reader. Clements has an excellent sense of humour which shows itself in both text and illustration, and is able to include an enormous variety of information because she takes seriously not only the actual fabric of castles, but also the life which went on inside them: there are double-page spreads on people in the castle, on preparing a feast, on why castles declined, and so on.

PMR

Age range: 8–12

GOODALL, John S.

THE STORY OF A CASTLE

André Deutsch, 1986, Hdbk, 0–233–97879–8
Colour line drawings

Much happened to this Norman castle between the twelfth century and today when people pay to go round it. Goodall takes us through the centuries in pictures, letting scenes from different times speak out to us of how the castle was used by rich and poor, friend and foe. There is no text, apart from one page of notes at the start. Each opening has an interleaved half-page, covering up and revealing new scenes like *trompe l'oeil*. In this way outer scenes give way suddenly to inner, kitchen to banquet, family croquet to a wedding reception on the lawn. During the Civil War, the family wait in terror on the battlements, and then, at a turn, fight the Roundheads to the death in the hallway. Edwardian balls turn to hospitals for war-wounded soldiers. It is a place now empty, now full, always full of atmosphere evoked by his subtle colours and accurate historical research. An ideal way to give younger readers a sense of place and history.

SH

Age range: 6–8

MACAULAY, David

CASTLE

Collins, Pbk, 0–00–192158–4
Glossary, black and white line drawings

David Macaulay's architectural picture books – on cathedrals, pyramids, cities, and now castles – have attracted much deserved critical acclaim. This time his tale is of a castle and surrounding town built between 1283 and 1288 when King Edward was trying to subdue the Welsh. The story is simple enough: land is chosen, the buildings built, people live there. The astonishing originality lies in how it is done: bit by bit the castle is built, and with line drawings of elevations and plans, sections and aerial views, with people and without, Macaulay plants the reader firmly on the site. Young readers can see how and why walls and moats and drawbridges were built that way, and what it was like when enemies tried to break in. The castle is a place designed by men to be lived in, and, final irony, with the passage of centuries, the town overwhelms and forgets the castle. This mix of history and design, story and information is irresistible as a classroom/ library resource and for personal ownership.

SH

Age range: 8–12

MACAULAY, David

CATHEDRAL

Collins, 1973, Pbk, 0–00–191260–6
Glossary, black and white line drawings

David Macaulay is widely recognized for his architectural picture books and this one is about a fictional cathedral built in France between the twelfth and fourteenth centuries. Macaulay's books have been called the most outstanding picture books of recent years, and the carefulness of his research, the beautiful accuracy of his drawing, the blend of history and architecture, and the clarity of his text have all been praised unstintingly. I find the entire black and white line drawings a bit severe after all the colour by which one gets spoilt in modern books, but Macaulay has a genuine gift for getting readers interested in the text because of his eye for fascinating details.

PSG

Age range: 11+

MACAULAY, DAVID

UNDERGROUND

Collins, 1978, Hdbk, 0–00–195850–X
Glossary, black and white line drawings

David Macaulay's books about buildings (castle, cathedral, pyramid, mill) make readers of any age look at them in a wholly different way. He goes underground in this one, looking at the 'massive root system' of part of a cityscape, out of sight and so out of mind: until this book. Using architectural drawings and plans, cut-aways and breathtakingly futuristic angles on what is usually hidden away in the ground, he shows us foundations to buildings, water and gas pipes snaking their way under the streets, how tunnels are built and how they avoid all the rest. The line drawings are full of detail and compel looking and looking by the reader. Most impact will probably come from streets stripped of their surface layers, a mass of pipes and vaults and chambers, making our normal street sights wafer-thin. A crystal-clear, properly technical text makes no concessions and has no real upper age limit.

SH

Age range: 9–12

ARMOUR

BYAM, Michel

ARMS AND ARMOUR

Dorling Kindersley, 1988, Hdbk, 0–86318–271–2
Series: Eyewitness Guides
Contents list, index, black and white and colour
line drawings and photographs

Comprehensiveness is of course impossible for a book of this size on such a subject, but Byam has provided an excellent range of arms and armour, from all corners of the globe. Japanese, Indian and African weapons and armour are found side by side with European ones. The photographs are generous, lavish and detailed, and the most attractive feature of the book is its psychological insight into the mind of the potential reader of the book: there are sections on the weapons and armour of the North American Indians, the guns that won the West, duelling swords and pistols, and so on. In other words, the book is organized in a way that will appeal. Here is a tribute to all the instruments of death that the evil imagination of man has been able to dream up, and even beautify, from prehistory to the present.

PMR

Age range: 8–12

CRAFTS

COLEMAN, Anne

FABRICS AND YARNS

Wayland, 1989, Hdbk, 1–85210–674–3
Series: Craft Projects
Contents list, glossary, index, notes for parents
and teachers, black and white and colour line
drawings and colour photographs.

This book is full of ideas for creative fun
with all kinds of fabric and yarns. It has
clear, easy instructions and step-by-step
drawings to take the reader through each
project. Some of the projects require the
use of a sewing machine, but all are
straightforward. As well as providing
ideas for school use, the simple text and
clear layout make the book suitable for
children to use on their own, at home.

It provides an excellent introduction to
the use of an exciting, colourful and
versatile medium and such creative
activity can develop in many directions
and last a lifetime.

JW

Age range: 7–11

EVERETT, Felicity

FASHION DESIGN

Usborne, 1987, Pbk, 0–7460–0188–6
Series: Usborne Guides
Bibliography, contents list, glossary, index, career
advice, black and white and colour line drawings

Careful attention to layout and text
enables the reader to visit the big names,
to glimpse the fashion shows of the world
and to spend time inside a fashion studio
to see how garments are designed, made
and sold. It's good to see an equal
emphasis on male and female fashion
design too. A clear message: the fashion
industry is a highly organized, exciting
and pressured operation, full of creative
potential. There *are* ways of entering this
world – and this book tells you how. It

concentrates particularly on ways of
getting started as a fashion illustrator, with
plenty of advice on how to draw.

The book is written with the young
student in mind, but will hold appeal for a
younger readership too. Ten-year-olds I
know who enjoy designing and making
their own clothes and putting on school
fashion shows will delight in what this
book has to offer.

HM

Age range: 9–18

EVERETT, Felicity and GARBERA, Carol

MAKE YOUR OWN JEWELLERY

Usborne, 1987, Pbk, 0–7460–0077–4
Series: Usborne Guides
Contents list, index, useful addresses, colour line
drawings and photographs

A well organized set of simple ideas for
making your own jewellery, using various
inexpensive materials. Different
techniques are shown, each with clear,
precise instructions which leave nothing
to chance and are carefully illustrated to
show what to do at each stage. The text
really does encourage the reader to have
a go at making the different kinds of
jewellery shown, and to be innovative
with ideas too. Jewellery making looks
enormous fun done this way, and it could
be made at home or in the classroom.

The decision to show the finished
jewellery modelled exclusively by one
young white woman is sad, and serves to
exclude. I would certainly put this book in
the way of older primary children and
encourage both boys and girls to be
creative with the ideas presented here.

HM

Age range: 9–16

HULL, Jeannie

CLAY

Franklin Watts, 1989, Hdbk, 0–86313–898–5
Series: Fresh Start
Contents list, index, colour photographs

A very practical book with the early basics of clay work being very well detailed. The description of thumb pots left me longing to 'have a go', since it's some time since I had 'hands-on' experience.

The photos are clear, showing in fine detail the tools required and the materials. The supporting text is very simple but at the same time contains enough detail to make things work and avoid frustration setting in.

The book not only covers the practicalities of working with clay but gives a brief history of pottery, addresses for materials and a page of further ideas for pots.

SD

Age range: 7–11

McDERMOTT, Catherine

DESIGN

Wayland, 1989, Hdbk, 1–85210–454–6
Series: The Arts
Bibliography, contents list, glossary, index, careers in design, black and white and colour line drawings and photographs

We live in a society that relies heavily on the skills of the designer. This book discusses the work of some of the main schools of design that have emerged since the Industrial Revolution. It contains examples of design in many different media and from many different countries. The appearance and form of an object can often be used to identify the country and era of its origin.

The book is most interesting and is generously illustrated to provide a survey of the world of design and should encourage readers to find out more for themselves. There are suggestions for further reading and for careers in design.

JW

Age range: 11–16

POTTER, Tony

LETTERING AND TYPOGRAPHY

Usborne, 1987, Pbk, 0–7460–0093–6
Series: Usborne Guides
Bibliography, contents list, glossary, index, black and white and colour line drawings and photographs

Being able to write is not the same as being able to use lettering effectively. This practical guide explains the basic techniques about calligraphy and typography. It is the kind of book to have beside you when trying out new layouts on the page, designing a poster or school newsletter, or experimenting with special effects like shadow letters. There are exercises to copy, original alphabets to use, and advice on how to do stencils and rubbings. Grids, nibs, ems, paste-ups, serifs: not mystique but plain getting down to it. Everywhere you look on the busy page there are ideas and things to do, at novice and expert levels. Where text gets hard, pictures make the methods clear. This is a working manual for readers of all ages, for young people keen to experiment, and adults, in school or at home, to get ideas from. There is another in the series, on technical drawing, likely to be of interest. I hope for advanced users there will soon be one on desktop publishing.

SH

Age range: 11–16

ROUSSEL, Mike

CLAY

Wayland, 1989, Hdbk, 1–85210–533–X
Series: Craft Projects
Contents list, glossary, index, notes for parents and teachers, colour line drawings

Mike Roussel's experience as a primary teacher and contributor to *Art & Craft* show through in this attractive and practical guide to making things out of clay. He anticipates all kinds of questions and difficulties – what kind of clay to use, what tools, what to make, and how to do it. Stage-by-stage diagrams, with clearly numbered instructions in simple, unambiguous text, will give children confidence that they can make clay birds and pots, piggy banks and badges, and that they will look right at the end of their efforts. Basic techniques are described and demonstrated. More ideas and safety tips are provided in windows on many of the pages. As things get more demanding (particularly using a kiln), sensible advice about working with adults is provided. Notes for teachers and parents stress that such creative fun is not just making things, but developing imaginative and collaborative skills.

SH

Age range: 7–11

ROWE, Christine

THE CHILDREN'S BOOK OF POTTERY

Batsford, 1989, Hdbk, 0–7134–5995–6
Bibliography, contents list, glossary, index,
potter's quiz, potter's materials (where to buy
them), black and white line drawings and black
and white and colour photographs

A book of clear practical information for the child (or the teacher!) who wants to do some pottery. It starts with a list of equipment, and some sensible health and safety rules. Then there are instructions for hand building pots (from thumb pots to more elaborate coiled and slab work). Throwing and turning pots on a wheel and glazing and firing in a kiln are described in detail, without dwelling on difficulties and possible pitfalls. The two-colour step-by-step diagrams are very clear, and there are plenty of photographs of children's work, to show what can be done. It is a book of lively

ideas, which should encourage anyone to get some clay and 'have a go'. For those whose interest has been really fired, there are some useful addresses at the back.

JW

Age range: 9–13

WRIGHT, Lyndie

PUPPETS

Franklin Watts, 1988, Hdbk, 0–86313–743–1
Series: Fresh Start
Contents list, index, museum collections and
puppet theatres, black and white line drawings
and colour photographs

Using crayons and lettering, paints and printing is great fun but you need good ideas and plenty of practical advice. Lyndie Wright provides just that. In a friendly conversational tone, she takes the reader through puppet making step by step. Colour photos, text and captions work well together to display the various techniques needed for making string and rod, glove and shadow puppets easily. The pictures show while the text explains, and all the time you can check to see what to do and what things should look like. Good advice is there in plenty on being careful with materials, washing, using non-toxic pens, not using Bostik with polystyrene, keeping cellophane away from hot lights. The artistic side is not swamped by technicalities, because colours and expressions on faces and using puppets in puppet theatres are enthusiastically described. Equipment and places to visit (mostly in the south of England) add to the information provided by the delightful book.

SH

Age range: 8–15

WRIGHT, Lyndie and FAIRCLOUGH, Chris

MASKS

Franklin Watts, 1989, Hdbk, 0–86313–899–3

Series: Fresh Start
Contents list, index, further information, black
and white and colour line drawings and colour
photographs

Making masks seems easy enough when
you have an experienced guide. In this
step-by-step series of practical guides,
clear instructions are coupled with bright
easy-to-copy photographs. The effect is
to convince even unartistic kids and
embarrassed adults to get making. From
simple (paper plate masks) to complex
(masks with moving parts, full body
masks and shadow masks), the book
covers many types, made from many
materials, most easy to get. Using
balloons you can make paper masks, and
add toilet roll eyes, give it fringes of curly
wild hair. Face and monster size, some
with raffia beards and string hair, masks
appear on logically designed openings
for easy reading and practical work.
Advice on taking care, finding things,
getting ideas is down to earth. This is an
ideas book for primary teachers and
parents, but one also for children keen to
do something practical and not wait too
long to have fun with what they've made.

SH

Age range: 6–10

PAINTING

CUMMING, Robert

JUST LOOK . . . A BOOK ABOUT PAINTINGS

Viking Kestrel, 1979, Hdbk, 0–670–81288–9
Index, black and white and colour photographs

This is an attractive book about pictures and paintings, and their appreciation. It contains illustrations, mostly in full colour, of a wide selection of the masterpieces (fourteenth to twentieth century) most often seen in reproductions.

The young reader is invited to look at them, to read the brief comments on them and to answer questions about them. The answers, in most cases, are to be found in the pictures, though some answers are given on p.59. (In a library copy of the book, this page is likely to become well worn with use!)

As the author says, once you start to look at paintings, and to think and imagine, there is no reason ever to stop. To visit the many galleries to study the originals, so beautifully illustrated in this book, would certainly take a lifetime.

WFW

Age range: 11–16

NEWLANDS, Anne

MEET EDGAR DEGAS

CUP, 1988, Hdbk, 0–521–37192–9
Colour photographs

In *Meet Edgar Degas*, the artist speaks directly to children, taking them on a visual tour through his art and his Paris in the mid-1800s. Sixteen of his works of art are reproduced in full colour and, opposite each colour plate, there is a short account written as if Degas were giving his own documentary, and guiding us backstage at the ballet, where young

dancers fidget; to the races where horses tense before the start; to the outdoor café, where a singer entertains the customers. We look with him at his self-portrait and at pictures of his friends and relatives. A most enjoyable introduction to Degas from an educator at the National Gallery of Canada, where works of Degas (from other galleries) were exhibited in 1988.

WFW

Age range: 9–16

POWELL, Jillian

PAINTING AND SCULPTURE

Wayland, 1989, Hdbk, 1–85210–345–0
Series: The Arts
Contents list, glossary, index, career information, black and white and colour line drawings and photographs

A brief look at the history of painting and sculpture throughout the world, from Stone Age cave paintings to the art styles of modern times. There are short sections on Islamic and Oriental art, as well as art in tribal cultures, and on the different influences on the development of art in Europe. There is also a short section on techniques and materials.

The illustrations are well chosen and there is a short list of major art galleries to visit, where you can see these masterpieces for yourself.

JW

Age range: 11–16

RICE, Melanie and Chris

I LIKE PAINTING

Kingfisher, 1989, Hdbk, 0–86272–447–3
Series: I Like
Contents list, index, black and white and colour line drawings and colour photographs

This colourful and interesting introduction to the world of art is sure to spark an interest in painting and paintings in any child. The book is well designed as a series of double-page spreads, each under some short heading (such as 'Style', 'Line', 'Pattern') with the emphasis on looking and doing rather than reading: the text is short but well illustrated. For instance, the importance of shape and shadow is dealt with under the heading 'Silhouettes', and activities are suggested. Indeed, the emphasis is on 'look and see', 'think and do', and 'question and answer', throughout. The authors – Melanie is a teacher and Chris a freelance writer – have children of their own and have a clear vision of what is required in information books for children – be they from urban East London or rural Dorset. They end their introduction to this book with the words 'Have fun!' It will provide hours of amusement and fun for children, as well as bring more than 40 famous paintings of widely different genres to their attention.

WFW

Age range: 9–13

MUSIC

ARDLEY, Neil

MUSIC

Dorling Kindersley, 1989, Hdbk, 0–86318–339–5
Series: Eyewitness Guides
Contents list, index, black and white line
drawings and colour photographs

Music is similar to other books in this
series: first a section attempting to explain
how sound works, which I find very hard
to understand, but this is a good try; then
sections on blown instruments (including
organs), instruments with strings
(including keyboards), percussion and
electronic music (including electric
guitars). A wide variety of instruments is
shown so that the instruments of the
orchestra can be identified, but many
unfamiliar, rare and unusual ones are also
illustrated. There are stripped down
instruments showing how the parts fit
together and the functions they fulfil and
sections showing the making of various
instruments, which explains why they are
so expensive. A glorious book to
treasure.

SS

Age range: 5–adult

BLACKWOOD, Alan

MUSIC

Wayland, 1988, Hdbk, 1–85210–343–4
Series: The Arts
Bibliography, contents list, glossary, index, black
and white and colour line drawings and
photographs

Music is presented as the most popular
and widely practised of all the arts. The
book starts by describing briefly the
elements of musical sound and some of
the various types of instruments around
the world and how they work. There are
short sections on the music of different
cultures, popular music, as well as a brief
account of Western 'classical' music and
opera. The book is simply written and in
general terms: though so attractively
presented, it would have little appeal as a
background reader to the serious young
musician, while some young people may
be disappointed to find so little mention
of the popular 'groups' of today. On p.45
the headings ('Where to hear and see
"live" music' and 'Getting involved in
Music') have been interchanged.

JW

Age range: 11–16

DESHPANDE, Chris

SCRAPE, RATTLE AND BLOW

Black, 1988, Hdbk, 0–7136–2988–6
Series: Friends
Colour photographs

As the title suggests, this is a book about
making sounds. Renuku recounts how
her class made, from a pile of 'rubbish' on
their classroom floor, a variety of 'musical
instruments'. They were first shown a
collection of authentic instruments from
all over the world. A photograph of these
(and a key to their names) is shown in the
book, together with photographs
showing them at work on their project,
and playing the 'musical instruments' that
they had made.

At the end of the book is a page of
useful 'things to do' in relation to such a
project.

JW

Age range: 7–11

HAWTHORN, Philip

THE USBORNE FIRST BOOK OF THE
RECORDER

Usborne, 1986, Pbk, 0–7460–0069–3

Series: First music
Contents list, glossary, index, colour line
drawings

The recorder is one of the few musical
instruments which can be learnt from a
book. This colourful and informative
book explains how to play the different
notes and provides plenty of tunes for the
beginner to practise. The presentation is
clear and witty. There are cartoon
characters to help, and games and
puzzles for extra fun.

At the end of the book there is a
buyer's guide with details of the more
available makes of descant recorder. A
useful book!

JW

Age range: 7–14

MILES, John C.

THE USBORNE FIRST BOOK OF THE PIANO

Usborne, 1988, Pbk, 0–7460–0197–5
Series: First Music
Contents list, glossary, index, colour line
drawings

Just the book to give children who are
beginning to learn to play the piano! It is
not a piano-tutor but would be an
excellent supplement to their first lessons.
The colourful fact-filled pages would help
them to learn to read music and to
understand music theory. The amusing
cartoon characters guide them from first
notes to simple tunes, though those
printed on blue paper are more difficult
to read. In addition to interesting facts
about the piano, there are little puzzles to
solve.

JW

Age range: 7–11

PETTIGREW, Mark

MUSIC AND SOUND

Franklin Watts, 1986, Hdbk, 0–86313–392–4,

Pbk, 0–7496–0383–6
Series: Simply Science
Contents list, glossary, index, colour line
drawings and photographs

A pneumatic drill hardly gives the 'sound
of music', yet, in a sense, the cover
illustration of this book creates an image
that sets the scene as much as the
'splendid, wonderfully pneumatic girl' in
Aldous Huxley's Brave New World. For
the picture is not taken from a doubly (or
trebly) exposed film but is a clever trick
photograph made from a collage of
superimposed offset images to suggest
vibrant energy.

Indeed, the book contains a number of
superb photographs and some vivid
drawings which, together with clear text,
briefly explore a wide range of topics, as
an introduction to the first principles of
the science of sound.

However, the scientific content of the
32 pages seemed so little, that the last
line of Blake's poem To the Muses is
brought to mind: 'The sound is forc'd, the
notes are few!' Nevertheless (to quote
from the same verse), the book will be
'enjoy'd [by] the languid [kids] that do
scarcely move [and whose] notes are
few!'

WFW

Age range: 7–10

TURNER, Barry Carson

I LIKE MUSIC

Kingfisher, 1989, Hdbk, 0–86272–448–1
Series: I Like
Contents list, index, black and white and colour
line drawings and colour photographs

Music is such a wide subject that it must
have been difficult to decide what to
include in a short book designed to
encourage children to make and play
their own instruments. This attractive,
colourful book clearly shows the diversity
of music. There are very brief sections on
the playing of the piano, recorder and
guitar; a section on the standard

instruments of the orchestra; a description of instruments commonly used in pop music and of less familiar instruments from around the world.

Of more practical use are the sections on making your own instruments and creating your own music, in which are presented activities which any reader should enjoy.

JW

Age range: 7–11

CINEMA

MANN, Brenda

CINEMA

Wayland, 1989, Hdbk, 1–85210–399–X
Series: 20th Century
Bibliography, contents list, glossary, index,
further information, black and white and colour
line drawings and photographs

Cinema has had a brief but vigorous history. Through TV and video, it has become a dominant form of communication and image making for young people. It is therefore all the more important to understand its role in our lives. Mann uses an opening-by-opening presentation of text and picture to achieve this. The structure is historical, from the early days of D. W. Griffith through the Hollywood star system to recent films like *Crocodile Dundee*. Within that, important themes emerge, like animated film, documentaries, and propaganda. There is, too, the film-going public and its social habits. Even when it seems just a catalogue of names, we know that they are surely chosen. Stills and posters complement the text well, and give visual substance to films which readers may not have seen but will now want to. This useful attractive sourcebook is ideal for projects, but, for class and library use, needs planned reading and viewing to back it up.

SH

Age range: 10–14

THEATRE

RICE, Melanie and Chris

I LIKE THEATRE

Kingfisher, 1990, Hdbk, 0–86272–516–X
Series: I Like . . .
Contents list, index, black and white and colour
line drawings and photographs

This attractive well illustrated book is an introduction to all types of theatre from the world over, and aims to stimulate interest by suggesting activities such as making a toy theatre, constructing puppets and masks, giving a shadow play, playing miming games and staging a play. It deals with different aspects of the theatre, e.g. actors and acting, stage sets and machinery, stage lighting, costumes and make-up, props and sound effects. The emphasis throughout is on amusement and having fun trying out things.

WFW

Age range: 9–13

DANCE

DODD, Craig

THE PUFFIN BOOK OF DANCE

Puffin, 1989, Pbk, 0–14–03–2530–1
Contents list, glossary, Who's who in dance,
Dances in time, Time chants of dance, black and
white line drawings

This little information-packed book for young dance fans, may well prove as much a source of inspiration as a fine ballet performance, or the musical *A Chorus Line*, with its song 'I can do that . . .' (sung by a boy who goes along to a dance class with his sister) or the TV series *Fame* (that portrayed the dedication and upward mobility of pupils of the New York High School for the Performing Arts).

The book deals not only with the evolution and recent history of dance, the life of professional dancers and describes, with diagrams, certain dance steps, but it tells how dances are made and looks at the toil and talent behind the glamour and excitement of this spectacular art form.

JW

Age range: 11–16

MITCHELL, Pratima

DANCE OF SHIVA

Hamish Hamilton, 1989, Hdbk, 0–241–12550–2
Series: The Way We Live
Colour photographs

The selection of beautiful photographs here make the colour and attractiveness of the oldest of Indian classical dances come alive. Two girls, one Indian and one Western, are learning Bharata Natyam from an Indian lady teacher in a London home accoutred in an opulent Indian manner. Mita's younger sister tags along for the lesson and finds some of the

dance easy to do. There are close-ups of half a dozen of the hand poses. Mita and Magdalene are invited to perform a dance for the local Hindu Club.

PMR

Age range: 5–8

THOMAS, Annabel

BALLET

Usborne, 1986, Pbk, 0–7460–0085–5
Series: Usborne Guides
Contents list, glossary, index, colour line
drawings

This colourful book explores various aspects of ballet – from doing it yourself to the enjoyment of watching it at the theatre. The fully illustrated text gives help with technique, with simple steps and exercises to try – all explained with step-by-step pictures. It discusses ballet as a career, and describes the colourful world of the dancer. It ends with some brief synopses of famous ballets and notes on famous dancers and choreographers. A useful book, full of information for the young dancer.

JW

Age range: 9–16

THOMSON, Ruth

MY CLASS LIKES DANCING

Franklin Watts, 1987, Hdbk, 0–86313–559–5
Series: My Class
Colour photographs

A class of young children in Nottingham have been photographed as they enjoy a variety of dance-based activities.

The writer, Ruth Thomson, meets a boy in the group, Paul Gadsby, who tells us in his own words what is happening in the pictures.

The children learn dances from the Caribbean, China, India and Britain, and we see them planning and making their costumes as well as enjoying the final presentation.

Children will enjoy this colourful book, and they and their teachers may be inspired to do a little dancing in their own class.

JW

Age range: 5–7

VAN ZANDT, Eleanor

DANCE

Wayland, 1988, Hdbk, 1–85210–342–6
Series: The Arts

Bibliography, contents list, glossary, index, Where to see and learn dance, colour line drawings and black and white and colour photographs

The author discusses the origins of dance, believed to be the earliest of all arts, and examines the dance traditions of many different countries and cultures. There are sections on social dance – from medieval courts to modern discos; folk dance to classical ballet; modern dance and show business.

The aim is to encourage readers to take part in and enjoy dancing, and there is a useful page of suggestions on where to see and learn dance.

JW

Age range: 11–16

SPORT

BARRETT, Norman

GYMNASTICS

Franklin Watts, 1988, Hdbk, 0–86313–680–X
Series: Picture Library
Contents list, glossary, index, colour photographs

Given that modern gymnastics are acrobatic skills there will not be a majority of youngsters in any one institution taking up the high level required at an open gymnastic meeting. For those with the aptitude and body build and who are already performers, as well as for those who wish to increase their knowledge, then here is a simple, well illustrated introductory guide book to artistic gymnastics, sports acrobatics and work on and with apparatus.

JH

Age range: 9+

BARTLETT, E. G.

JUDO

Wayland, 1988, Hdbk, 1–85210–150–4
Series: World of Sport
Contents list, glossary,, index, colour line drawings and photographs

Judo is descended from the ancient martial art of ju-jitsu. It is a sport full of legend and the word means 'the gentle way'. The performers and keepers of the sport's traditions like to think of the sport as emphasizing self-defence and mental discipline.

Having looked at the history and the development in the outside world of what was once taught in secret, the important basic ideas like balance, efficiency and the need to help each other in the learning process are dealt with first.

Other matters like breakfalls, clothing, training and throws follow while skills and tactics in competitions are not forgotten. All are well illustrated and photographs of boys and men, women and girls, feature and make for a lively production. A knowledge of the glossary of mainly Japanese words would help with one's identification with the sport.

JH

Age range: 10+

BETTERIDGE, John

SPORT FOR DIABETICS

Black, 1988, Pbk, 0–7136–2473–6
Bibliography, contents list, index, black and white line drawings and photographs

This claims to be a self-help book. It will certainly help many of the significant number of diabetic sports people participating today and who in time past would have been ruled out. It will also help parents of diabetic children. The modern treatment which controls blood glucose is explained and the author quite rightly draws attention to those physical activities where hypoglycaemia could cause problems for others as well as the patient. Examples are cited. John Betteridge is a lecturer in Medicine at University College London and here makes an excellent contribution to sports medicine.

JH

Age range: 15+

BLUE, Adrianne

FIELD ATHLETICS

Wayland, 1988, Hdbk, 1–85210–316–7
Series: World of Sport
Bibliography, contents list, glossary, index, colour line drawings and photographs

In America track and field athletics take place mainly in the schools, colleges and universities with the result that standards are high and the scientific approach to coaching and training has been a feature for much longer than in this country. There was a time when American books were the only ones available on athletics. This book is by an American. With the increase in field athletics (though a majority of athletic club members are runners, not throwers and jumpers) to a more respectable level, there will be interest in this little book by many junior and secondary school students.

It covers the jumps and throws and is about training techniques and equipment. The American author is a sports correspondent and interested in the emergence of women in sport in general and athletics in particular.

Excellently illustrated with action photographs in colour, it has hints and tips for would-be performers.

JH

Age range: 10+

CLARIDGE, Marit

SKIING

Usborne, 1986, Pbk, 0–7460–0097–9
Contents list, glossary, index, colour line drawings

A book for beginners but also useful for more competent and advanced skiers. Lots of good material with few wasted words. Pithy, direct, colourful and very full of excellent advice help and direction. It is about Nordic and Alpine skiing, starting with the basics and going on to competition work. Very practical and good value for money.

JH

Age range: 8–adult

COOK, Janet and WAY, Penny

WINDSURFING

Usborne, 1988, Pbk, 0–7460–0196–7
Contents list, glossary, index, colour line drawings and photographs

A guide to a fast-growing activity. Once the basic techniques have been mastered, it is only a matter of weeks before one can enter competitions and perhaps in months rather than years compete nationally. This is what the reader is encouraged to think. The coloured pictures and diagrams are excellent. The theory and thinking behind techniques are a great help and contribute enormously to a first-class book for all windsurfers.

JH

Age range: 10–adult

DEAN, Nick

TRACK ATHLETICS

Wayland, 1988, Hdbk, 1–85210–317–5
Series: World of Sport
Bibliography, contents list, glossary, index, colour line drawings and black and white and colour photographs

For those who run, aspire to run better or who wish to know about track athletics, this guide deals with those aspects of athletics.

It is specific about some of the techniques involved and generalized on others. Photographs of athletes in action are used to illustrate the text which covers clothing, equipment, venues and championships as well as having information on the professional side of an amateur sport, if that is not a contradiction in terms. The compilation is by a photo-journalist who is a keen athlete and is a useful general introduction to track athletics for the young person.

JH

Age range: 10–18

GRIFFITHS, Vivien

MY CLASS GOES SWIMMING

Franklin Watts, 1986, Hdbk, 0–86313–322–3

162

Series: My Class
Colour photographs

Swimming has lovely full-page coloured photographs which form the bulk of this book. Simple sentences about what 'we' do on the day 'our' class goes swimming take up only a small amount of page space.

I am not sure about the book's purpose. It is certainly not about swimming techniques. It might encourage reluctant youngsters to overcome possible cultural objections and participate more readily in a happy activity at primary school level.

JH

Age range: 5–11

IRELAND, Donald

RUGBY

Wayland, 1988, Hdbk, 1–85210–159–8
Series: World of Sport
Contents list, glossary, index, colour photographs

Donald Ireland, who has compiled the material for this book, is a man of experience in teaching and coaching Rugby Football. It is good to see that Rugby League, American Football, Gaelic Football and other versions of football get more than a mention.

In the main, however, the book is for those who play to the Union rules with the techniques and tactics which are used in that game being clearly explained and useful practices outlined and illustrated.

The section on fitness and individual skills is applicable to almost all players in all these basically similar games where catching, passing, running, tackling and kicking are common elements.

Well illustrated with lots of useful additional material to help create and maintain the ethos and spirit of the rugby world.

JH

Age range: 9–adult

MOHUN, Janet

DRUGS, STEROIDS AND SPORTS

Franklin Watts, 1988, Hdbk, 0–86313–780–6
Series: Understanding Social Issues
Bibliography, contents list, glossary, index,
colour photographs

A thoroughly researched information book with plenty of well presented good material under suitable headings with interesting quotes as in 'The Trade in Sports Drugs': 'I hear that weight lifters have trouble carrying their suitcases, they are so full of drugs.'

Aspects covered include the effects and use of drugs, the harm and trade in them together with sections on drug profiles and sources of help. The publication aims to help young adults and may do just that.

JH

Age range: 12+

PEACH, Susan

IMPROVE YOUR RUNNING SKILLS

Usborne, 1988, Pbk, 0–7460–0166–5
Series: Super Skills
Contents list, index, colour line drawings and
photographs

Very little about running at all speeds from a jog to a sprint is left unmentioned in this excellent handy publication. Kit, fitness, competition, race tactics and even injuries are included as are many other aspects. There is hardly a wasted word and all the essentials are put simply so that one has a compendium of running information succinctly put and well illustrated. David Moorcroft makes his contribution together with other consultants, e.g. Norman Brook, a national coach, and Charlie Spedding, a London Marathon winner.

JH

Age range: 9–adult

PERCHARD, Peter

CRICKET

Wayland, 1988, Hdbk, 1–85210–156–3
Series: World of Sport
Bibliography, contents list, glossary, index,
colour line drawings and photographs

Ian Botham is on the front cover and many contemporary international players demonstrating attacking and defensive batting are to be seen inside. Bowlers and fielders showing their art and craft are fewer in number in this colourful and attractive book of hints and comments on cricket. There is enough for the young enthusiast to grasp in the way of skills and attitudes and the advice is sound and quite detailed.

A book to consult in order to make practice purposeful and profitable while also encouraging a wider view of the game as part of history and culture. Peter Perchard is highly qualified to write on cricket, being executive editor of *The Cricketer* magazine and a well known writer on the subject.

JH

Age range: 9–18

PINDER, Steve and STEEN, Rob

SPORTS WATCHING

Puffin, 1988, Pbk, 0–14–032617–0
Bibliography, contents list, index, black and white
line drawings

A reference book with some answers for all those who ask questions about games and sports and what goes on between players themselves, and between players and those controlling them. Aimed at the TV watcher, it could prove to be a useful book and will help to provide insight into the activities and language of sports people and those who commentate. It professes to be an armchair guide.

JH

Age range: 8–16

SHAPIRO, Harry

FACTS ON DRUGS AND SPORT

Franklin Watts, 1989, Hdbk, 0–7496–0047–0
Contents list, glossary, index, colour photographs

The topic is explained first. Next the drugs used and what they can do, the dangers and what is being done and could be done to combat the problem are presented in a straightforward manner with coloured illustrations helping immensely.

The book does what its title says. It presents in a readable succinct way the social and medical facts. Good for secondary school students.

JH

Age range: 13+

TATLOW, Peter

GYMNASTICS

Wayland, 1987, Hdbk, 0–85078–992–3
Series: World of Sport
Contents list, glossary, index, colour line
drawings and photographs

It is mainly girls and young women who feature in the photographs chosen to illustrate activities in this book, but then they do tend to be more supple or more lithe than their male counterparts and somehow have the aesthetic advantage generally speaking, though the strength of the men has its points. Gymnastics requires strength and also those qualities of body awareness, good timing, courage and suppleness, which do not come to the majority of us in full measure.

It is an individual sport with a number of aspects or forms related to particular pieces of apparatus and most are well covered. Sports acrobatics performed to music is a more recent addition to the Olympics programme and is briefly touched on since it is really allied to circus work though it is a branch of gymnastics.

The author, a freelance sports writer, explains the techniques and skills which judges look for in competition performances. A useful contribution to writings on gymnastics.

JH

Age range: 8+

TRUMAN, Christine

TENNIS

Wayland, 1987, Hdbk, 1–85210–155–5
Series: World of Sport
Contents list, glossary, index, colour line
drawings and photographs

Lawn Tennis, though quite an old game, has not until recent times been a majority sport and, being a non-contact sport, has been seen mainly for women though today it is the hard-hitting top men who attract attention. Christine Truman draws on her experience (she was in the finals at Wimbledon at sixteen) to produce a useful book of suggestions and helpful tips for improved performance. With diagrams and colour photographs to help she covers various aspects of the game, its history and variety, its venues and personalities. Diagrams are used where necessary to illustrate technique.
Clothing and equipment are discussed, as is the need for fitness and a knowledge of tactics.

A useful contribution in the *World of Sport* series.

JH

Age range: 10+

WILSON, Charlie

SWIMMING AND DIVING

Wayland, 1988, Hdbk, 1–85210–149–0
Series: World of Sport
Bibliography, contents list, glossary, index,
colour line drawings and photographs

Much has been written in books, magazines and newspapers and on TV and radio a great deal has been seen and said about swimming and diving. One is tempted to ask if there is anything new to say. There is little new here except, of course, the pictures, the arrangement of the material and the selection of it. Most people learn to swim so that they can feel safe in the water and after that they love splashing about in the medium and that is what most of us seem to do. This book is for the keen swimmer who may have aspirations to do it competitively, though there is much general information which might please the TV watcher of swimming competitions and diving contests.

There is simple analysis of techniques for the learner in particular while the coach will find a few useful ideas he or she might apply.

As with all the books in this series it is well and colourfully illustrated. It is written by a Great Britain and Olympic coach.

JH

Age range: 9+

WOODS, Paula

IMPROVE YOUR SOCCER SKILLS

Usborne, 1987, Pbk, 0–7460–0168–1
Series: Super Skills
Contents list, glossary, index, colour line
drawings and black and white and colour
photographs

A handy information-packed book in a good series. Brief explanations, apt diagrams and generally easy-to-follow explanations, instructions and illustrations make this a very good self-help reference book. As well as the basic techniques with the ball, there are sections on set plays and team work, how to become a professional, the rules of the game and a quiz or two to round off a well packaged collection. There is professional advice from Ian St John.

JH

Age range: 8–adult

GEOGRAPHY

◆

An area which has been traditionally the backbone of information books on publishers lists from the dawn of publishing. The selector has to find how to establish a way between the exotic 'Let's go' approach and a book which conveys the real flavour of a country.

CHAMPION, Neil

COUNTRIES OF THE WORLD

Usborne, 1986, Pbk, 0–86020–978–4
Series: Facts and Lists
Contents list, index, colour line drawings

Although this small book is packed with information, and uses three columns of smallish print, most juniors will find some absorbing stuff in it and will not be intimidated at all. The *'Facts and Lists'* series has had the usual Usborne high-quality commercial design job done on it. Each double-spread chapter in this title has incidental facts and amusing trivia packaged inside boxes with neat little 'Did you know?' and 'Amazing but true' headings. Harder information is conveyed using straightforward text, lists, tables and a colourful map of the world. The small, easy-to-read pictograms are printed on blocks of pastel colour. The whole book is liberally sprinkled with cartoons to break up the text and make it easy to read. Subjects covered include: population, languages, and rich and poor countries. This is far from a serious reference book; it is meant to be fun and it does contain useful information.

RG

Age range: 7–11

ATLASES

COOPER, Michael

CHILDREN'S ATLAS

Collins, 1989, Hdbk, 0–00–190071–4,
Pbk, 0–00–190072–2
Indexes, maps, flags, colour line drawings

Although primarily a book of maps, this atlas starts with a brief introduction to our planet, its formation and its structure. The maps that follow, of all the countries of the world, are very clearly printed, uncluttered, and show the main cities and towns, as well as the physical features. Then come brightly coloured illustrations of the flags of the countries, with useful descriptions of their origins and symbolism. The tables of population and country size are undated, so may, even now, be of only comparative interest.

A very good atlas for juniors.

JW

Age range: 7–13

WIEGAND, Patrick

OXFORD RAINBOW ATLAS

OUP, 1987, Hdbk, 0–19–831662–3
Contents list, index, keys, colour line drawings
and photographs

This colourful atlas is specifically designed for the age range and the clear (uncluttered) maps are surrounded by coloured drawings to give a visual picture of the countries.

The inset of the British Isles gives a good idea of size to the maps of other countries, while on the sectional maps of the UK, the similar inset map of the whole UK, with the relevant map section highlighted, is helpful.

The keys to symbols are also clearly shown and explained. The frames round some of the maps are too narrow near the central crease, so that the close juxtaposition of facing maps can give the impression of a double-page spread: this may confuse a child into thinking the two adjoining maps are continuous.

JW

Age range: 6–9

EUROPE

BUTTERFIELD, Moira

THE USBORNE BOOK OF LONDON

Usborne, 1987, Pbk, 0–7460–0051–0
Contents list, index, colour line drawings

Though it claims only to give a flavour of London's past, everything is here which you might possibly want to know, if you were a child. There are pages devoted to London's beginnings, to Anglo-Saxon London, to medieval London, Tudor and Elizabethan London, and to each century from the seventeenth to the twentieth. There are double-page spreads on each of the sights which a child might see: Westminster Abbey, the Houses of Parliament, the City, the Tower of London, St Paul's Cathedral, and so on. There are double pages on parks and museums and on some of the attractions in outer London. There is information on some of the better known shops and on London shopping in general, on transport, people and places, on arts and theatres, and on London traditions and festivals. To cap it all, there is a sightseeing map of central London and a visitor's guide. My only criticism is of the colours used in printing the book, which seem a bit strong to me.

PMR

Age range: 10–14

DICKS, Brian

GREECE

Hamish Hamilton, 1988, Hdbk, 0–241–12453–0
Series: Focus on . . .
Contents list, index, colour line drawings and photographs

Greece is many things: a Mediterranean country, a tourist trap, a place of classical culture and archaeology, an EEC member, a Greek Orthodox society, and home to football teams like Panathenaikos. All these factors present writers like Dicks with the challenge of balance and inclusion. Key topics such as Athens and Crete, farming and tourism get told in all these ways, showing how Greeks live now, what change is doing to their country, and what goes on behind the scenes (industry, family meals, religion). Text is layered so that, alongside the main narrative, there are panels of detailed text on focal topics like Knossos or Athos. Photographs are functional, though some are tourist brochure by reason of the popularity of their subjects. Dicks knows Greece well, but so distilled is the topic here that almost certainly young readers will have to use this book with others.

SH

Age range: 8–12

HUBLEY, Penny and John

ITALIAN FAMILY

Black, 1986, Hdbk, 0–7136–2731–X
Series: Beans
Map, colour photographs

Francesca Rossi is 8 years old and she lives with her family in Grassina, a small town near Florence. An account of her daily life is given in this book, using colour photos, closely allied to a brief text. We go with her to school, and see the classroom and school dinners. We see her father and mother, both at home and at work. We visit her grandparents' farm and learn a little of country life. In short, we see a happy family, living their ordinary lives, in another country. As we move nearer to 1992 and to closer integration in Europe, it is, perhaps, a good idea to stress how similar our European neighbours are to ourselves, rather than the differences. Some differences will be noticed in the photographs by observant children, but very few would notice three mistakes in the text: two typographical spelling mistakes in the Italian (Elementare, p.6; Popolo, p.9), and the fact that 'Feragosto', p.11, refers specifically to 15 August, rather than to a factory holiday fortnight in August, or to an Autumn Fair (a fair is 'fiera').

JW

Age range: 7–11

NORBROOK, Dominique

FRANCE

Franklin Watts, 1985, Hdbk, 0–86313–287–1
Series: Passport to . . .
Contents list, index, fact files, colour line drawings and black and white and colour photographs

With books like this, 'what' and 'how' are the challenges. 'What' is content, and this book scores high, with an astonishing coverage of aspects of modern France from Paris to farming, perfumes to transport. For practical research in upper primary and lower secondary, this is a valuable resource book. One opening distills the essence of topics like news and broadcasting, education, or the arts, but, since it is concise, such material will form the starting point for more extensive and systematic research, say for a project. The 'how' is presentation, concise but clear, documentary and at a level of news broadcasts on TV, and likely to present slow readers with problems of interpretation. An excellent feature is the good-humoured self-critical tone of the text (e.g. on farming policy and holiday traffic jams), encouraging readers to be the same, and debunking the travel guide euphoria which sometimes creeps into children's books like this. Four fact files, with striking graphics, will give information and example to young readers.

SH

Age range: 9–12

WHINES, Nicholas

A CHILD'S HISTORY OF LONDON

BBC, 1984, Pbk, 0–563–21358–2
Contents list, index, black and white and colour line drawings and photographs

A chatty conversational style invites children to look at paintings, photos, and other illustrations in order to discover the enormously varied history of this great metropolis. Tower Hill, Roman and medieval London, Moorfields, the Coronation of Edward VI, London Bridge, a frost on the Thames, a wedding feast at Bermondsey, the Plague, the Great Fire, the gradual expansion of the city through the eighteenth and nineteenth centuries, the age of the car, the War – all these are explored with a view to what might most catch a child's eye or fancy. In a couple of pages, London since the War can only be touched on.

There are many ways to interest a child in history, and this is one of the best.

PSG

Age range: 7–12

SCANDINAVIA

JAMES, Alan

LAPPS – REINDEER HERDERS OF LAPLAND

Wayland, 1986, Hdbk, 0–85078–739–4
Series: Original Peoples
Bibliography, contents list, glossary, index, black and white line drawings and black and white and colour photographs

The Lapps are one of the oldest and most interesting of the European peoples. They are known to have wandered Northern Scandinavia for over ten thousand years, during most of which time their nomadic way of life remained much the same. In the seventeenth century, the arrival of missionaries began to introduce outside influences. Since that time, many traders and settlers have come to their lands and, in recent years, even tourists. Modern life-styles have now caught up with most Lapps. There are now new methods of reindeer herding. Modern technology and some measure of prosperity have changed their traditional pattern of life.

This book, with its attractive colour photographs, shows both their traditional and modern way of life and how the Lapps are adapting to the pressures of European culture.

JW

Age range: 7–11

ASIA

ASHBY, Gwynneth

KOREAN VILLAGE

Black, 1986, Hdbk, 0–7136–2812–X
Series: Beans
Map, colour photographs

The story of Ochun, a village between the cities of Seoul and Pusan, is centred on the Chun family: eleven-year-old Chun Yung Mee tells us about her family and their life in their village, which shows a mixture of old and new features. They still have to fetch water, but they have a freezer, a TV, and a video recorder. They grow rice and vegetables for themselves, and sell their apples. Yung Mee goes on a class visit to the ancient town of Kyongju: there is an authentic ring to this – from the getting up much too early, wanting to look at the many shops rather than the antiquities, to the falling asleep on the bus on the way home. She also visits, with a friend, the city of Taegu and goes to see her friend's sister weaving silk in a factory in Seoul. The references to the Seoul Olympics date the book. We see the family's Buddhist altar and learn that they also follow the teachings of Confucius. The pictures show both the traditional way of life in the countryside, and the recent incursion of Western ways that have greatly influenced life in the cities.

JW

Age range: 7–11

HUSAIN, Shahrukh A.

INDIA

Hamish Hamilton, 1986, Hdbk, 0–241–11823–9
Series: Focus on . . .
Contents list, index, colour line drawings and photographs

Though the section on Religion has some

inaccuracies and some bias, and science and technology are underplayed, the rest of the book forms, for this age group, one of the most balanced and comprehensive introductions to India of which I know. There is information on the cities, on the villages, on farming, on power and industry, on sports and entertainment, on food, on the Ganges, on the mountains, on trains, on wildlife, and so on. With one or two exceptions, the photographs are excellent.

PMR

Age range: 8–12

MORRIS, Rick

FROM DAWN TO DUSK IN CHINA

Collins, 1989, Pbk, 0–00–191189–9
Contents list, colour line drawings and photographs

This is a no-gimmicks account of a day in the life of Wang Ying Yan, who is 10 and lives with her doctor parents in an apartment in Nanchang in southern China. Her coach journey to school passes through urban landscape in mid-March. Morris takes us through her day using a mass of small colour photographs, and narratives through captions and main text running in parallel. The tone is realistic, unselfconscious and non-judgemental. At school, she reads stories, does maths, works on a computer, learns Chinese, meets friends, makes things from paper for a project. Surrounding the photographs are drawings of everyday objects like comic books, paints, and toothpaste, which are part of her life. The reader is drawn in (she doesn't force herself upon you), and can recognize differences (exercises to music, few cars on the streets) as well as feel a lot of things in common. A project can highlight these and develop them imaginatively.

SH

Age range: 8–10

TAYLOR, Allegra

TAL NIV'S KIBBUTZ

Black, 1987, Hdbk, 0–7136–2851–0
Series: Beans
Maps, colour photographs

This attractively presented book is illustrated with colour photographs, integrated with the text. This tells the story of the Kibbutzim, through the eyes of a 10-year-old boy, and gives an informative account of the customs and social life of Israel.

The book is designed to have a wide appeal (not just for Jewish children); it should prove particularly popular with those interested in the human geography of Israel, besides those seeking information upon the Spring festival of Shavuot.

WFW

Age range: 7–11

WATERLOW, Julia

CHINA

Wayland, 1989, Hdbk, 1–85210–043–5
Series: Countries of the World
Bibliography, contents list, glossary, index, maps, colour line drawings and photographs

It is always a problem to keep Geography books up to date in our fast-changing world. This book on China not only relates how the Communists took over from the ancient emperors but even mentions the student riots of 1989.

The book is about China and its people, and how they live and use their land. Although it is the third largest country in the world, its one thousand millon people live crowded lives as two-thirds of the land is unsuitable for farming

and settlement. This is not the only problem. There is a great need for modernization of industry and agriculture if the standard of living is to be improved. This well illustrated book shows clearly the China of today and points the way for the future.

The author speaks and writes Chinese and has travelled extensively throughout China. I feel sure that her transliteration of Chinese names is correct even when they differ from those used by the Press, but to render Mao Tse-Tung as Mao Zedong and the Yangtze as Chang Jiang is rather confusing. Perhaps we should be thankful that the book is entitled simply *China* and not Zhonghua Renmin Gongheguo or some other transliteration!

WFM/JW

Age range: 7–11

WHITAKER, Janet

VISITING JUNJUN AND MEIMEI IN CHINA

CUP, 1988, Pbk, 0–521–35933–3
Index, colour line drawings and photographs

Junjun is a boy of 10, Meimei a girl of 8, and they live in a village called Hua Shan in China. You get there by flying first to Shanghai. Whitaker did this in 1986 to make radio programes for BBC Education. Differences and similarities will strike young readers and form part of the learning and enjoyment with a book like this. Structured clearly around topics like home, school, work and shopping, the discussion is objective, interesting, never coy, nicely pitched in language difficulty and tone for the reader. Complicated ideas like the morality lessons in school are described intelligently, and new things (an abacus for calculating in the shop, changes from communes to personal incentives for the children's parents) and familiar ones made different (no frozen food in the shops, kite festivals) are all made accessible and readable. Colour photographs give authenticity to the children's lives. You feel you've gone there, and Whitaker is a thoughtful guide.

SH

Age range: 7–10

WOOD, Frances

CHINA

Batsford, 1987, Hdbk, 0–7134–5266–8
Series: People at Work
Bibliography, contents list, glossary, index, black and white line drawings and photographs

The aim of this series is to provide young adults with an understanding of a country and culture through direct exposition and through the lives of typical people there. Wood displays China, past and present, in a cool, analytical way, explaining why things are as they are, in industry, agriculture, and society generally. Through lives of real people, like farmers and factory workers, she is able to give at first hand not just how they live and feel about it, but also the broader context of their lives. For doctors, it may not be relative wealth, it may involve traditional medicine, and in the past it meant persecution. Personal values come through in what a teacher says about schools, what a guide says about the extravagance of tourists, what an art student says about the independence of young women, all issues worth developing for curricular and leisure discussion purposes. Unpretentious but authentic photographs give a feel for the hardship and dedication of many of the characters. Wood lets their lives speak to us, and lets us notice and consider the differences.

SH

Age range: 12–16

AFRICA

GRIFFIN, Michael

SALAAMA IN KENYA

Black, 1987, Hdbk, 0–7136–2852–9
Series: Beans
Map, colour photographs

Salaama is a 10-year-old girl who lives
near Mombasa in Kenya. Her father
works in that city, and in term time, she
and her brother live with him there, so
that they can go to a school and get a
good education. Their mother looks after
the younger children on the family farm
about ten miles away. The whole family
works very hard and there are few
modern aids to make life on the farm
easier, but the pictures show a happy and
quite prosperous family. (Their part of
Kenya is not affected by drought or
famine.)

Clear simple text is matched to good
colour photographs: together, they give a
vivid picture of life in Kenya.

JW

Age range: 7–9

STEWART, Judy and MATTHEWS, Jenny

FAMILY IN SUDAN

Black, 1987, Hdbk, 0–7136–2921–5
Series: Beans
Colour line drawings and photographs

Many different countries are explored by
this series, often using a device of having
a young story-teller. Dawalbeit lives in
west Sudan in Africa in an extended
family which owns a shop, land and
animals like cows and camels. Colour
photos, intended to rival TV coverage,
provide much local atmosphere and
detailed pictures of sieving millet, going
to school to learn the Koran, or travelling
to market by camel or truck. The climate
is harsh, with fierce dry winds and
drought. We read of a severe famine, and
rescue after much hardship, interestingly
personal because of the way of telling.
The boy is easy to understand – he likes
Bob Marley, plays football, likes peanut
butter – and the unforced likeability of
the character shows itself in the tone and
structure of the book, which is easy to
follow, allowing for stops for reflection
and investigation along the way. A useful
addition to other works on this general
topic.

SH

Age range: 7–9

AMERICA

CARY, Pam

THE USA

Wayland, 1988, Hdbk, 0–85078–851–X
Series: Countries of the World
Bibliography, contents list, glossary, index,
colour line drawings and photographs

Nobody could call this type of broad, first introduction to current life in the USA dull or dry. Over half the space, in this large-format book, is devoted to good quality colour photographs which show the differing peoples of America, a few of their industries, festivals, customs and transport systems, as well as some of the wildlife and landscapes in this huge and beautiful country. Most of the chapters are confined to double-page spreads which means there is no in-depth information on topics such as education, religions and government, but the coverage is meant to be general and not heavy going. There is more detail in the longer chapters on history, the American people and cities – where New York, Chicago and New Orleans are featured. The text is clear, in two columns, and there is a glossary and an extensive further reading list.

RG

Age range: 9–13

KENDALL, Sarita

AMAZON FAMILY

Black, 1987, Hdbk, 0–7136–2853–7
Series: Beans
Colour line drawings and photographs

People live all over the world, and this series aims to show how they do it. Silvia is 11 and her family live in a village in Peru on the Amazon side of the Andes, where her father works at a sawmill. High-definition colour photographs tell a vivid atmospheric story: the small hut full of a happy busy family, her life at school, her visits to the high Andes to visit relatives, a trip across the lake to the market in town. Efforts are made to make the first-person narrative credible, but it's difficult to make her seem less than a know-all at times ('wood sent to Lima for the building trade'). A glossary (guava, manioc, toucan) may be needed. Her register is 'terribly English', with expressions like 'all in all', 'gets up my nose', and 'we had a great time'. This could have been a really lovely book.

SH

Age range: 7–10

AUSTRALIA

BROWNE, Rollo

AUSTRALIAN MINING FAMILY

Black, 1986, Hdbk, 0–7136–2701–8
Series: Beans
Colour line drawings and photographs

David lives in Nhulunbuy in the Northern Territory of Australia. His dad works at the mine and David goes to see the blasting: the explosion is always exciting to watch. David and his brothers spend a lot of time at the Surf Club where they are on the Junior Boat Crew. They go swimming too, but they have to watch out for the crocodiles.

Easy to read, with at least 50 per cent of the space given to colour pictures, a couple of inadequate quality.

PMR

Age range: 6–10

GRINDROD, Warrill and GARRETT, Dan

KID'S OZ: AN INTRODUCTION TO AUSTRALIA

BBC, 1987, Pbk, 0–563–21342–6
Contents list, glossary, map, black and white and colour line drawings and photographs

Australia is the only country in the world to have a whole continent to itself. In this book you are taken on an adventurous journey through the country, to learn both of its diverse geography and its interesting history. You meet plenty of real children on the way, e.g. some who live in Sydney, some on a sheep station, some aborigines. Even the children and people from the past really existed. The numerous pictures and short paragraphs of text present a wide range of information in a most attractive way. This book really brings the country to life and is sure to appeal to the young reader.

JW

Age range: 7–11

BIOGRAPHY

◆

This still remains a popular *genre* where young people can learn about the past in an accessible and personal way.

BENNETT, Olivia

ANNIE BESANT

Hamish Hamilton, 1988, Hdbk, 0–241–12224–4
Series: In Her Own Time
Bibliography, contents list, index, black and white
and colour line drawings

Bennett explains, defends and celebrates
the life of this Victorian reformer who
found herself reluctantly abandoning her
husband and her Christian beliefs, and
becoming a pamphleteer and journalist
for greater freedom and justice in
marriage, working conditions, the law,
science, motherhood, birth control,
poverty, education and politics. Later in
life, she became a Theosophist, which
many of her earlier friends and admirers
found difficult to accept.

PMR

Age range: 13–16

BIRCH, Beverley

MARIE CURIE

Exley, 1989, Hdbk, 1–85015–092–3
Series: People who have Helped the World
Bibliography, glossary, index, important dates,
map, black and white colour line drawings and
photographs

Marie Curie is the amazing life story of the
woman who discovered radium. Her
story makes fascinating reading and
leaves one feeling quite helpless. Her
total dedication and willpower are shown
throughout the book: from the mammoth
task of isolating radium – 'like looking for
a grain of sand in a mountain of grains';
to her lecture at the Sorbonne in 1906 –
the first time a woman had ever lectured
there – right through to her determination
to carry on her research after her
husband's death in spite of her own
illness, caused by the effects of radium on
her body.

The book is clearly and concisely
written with no hint of sentimentality, just

a lot of empathy and admiration. It makes
compelling reading.

SD

Age range: 11–14

BLACKWOOD, Alan

TWENTY TYRANTS

Wayland, 1989, Hdbk, 1–85210–140–7
Series: Twenty Names
Bibliography, contents list, glossary, index, black
and white and colour line drawings and black and
white photographs

How do you show someone who is really
bad, and not make it boring or
sensational? It is difficult, particularly if
you exhaust words like 'ruthless' and
'appalling', and if people are bad in
different ways. That said, young readers
are fascinated by cruelty and so a writer
has a head start. Blackwood's catalogue
of 20 tyrants from classical to recent
times, each one getting a double-page
opening, brief text, portrait and revealing
tableau, just comes off. At times, rhetoric
trips him up, but he does succeed in
building up a varied picture of tyranny.
Some were tyrants when they pushed
good too far; others plain evil, like Hitler
and Pappa Doc. Many got bad when they
got old. Blackwood leaves loose ends
which need further explanation, but that
does not disqualify it for a useful role in
a highly popular history project for young
readers.

SH

Age range: 9–12

BROWN, Pam

FLORENCE NIGHTINGALE

Exley, 1988, Hdbk, 1–85015–117–2
Series: People who have Helped the World
Bibliography, glossary, index, maps, a list of
important dates in her life, black and white and
colour line drawings and photographs

Florence Nightingale is depicted more as

the tough campaigner, who was the founder of modern nursing, than as the saintly 'Lady of the lamp'. Although a good account is given of her long and active life, the stress is not on her family background (she came from an upper middle-class British family) but on the appalling social conditions (of poverty, squalor due to the Industrial Revolution and the deprivation resulting from war, injuries and illness) made worse by the class system of her day, and the way she transformed hospital care and public attitudes towards the nursing profession.

Thus this biography will appeal to those with an interest in social history, particularly those who aspire to medical or nursing careers.

This informative well written book has a compact format, with short lines for easy reading, with wide outer margins that are used for smaller illustrations, quotations and other notes.

It is well illustrated, partly in full colour, with some fine art reproductions.

WFW

Age range: 9–16

BUCHAN, Elizabeth

BEATRIX POTTER

Hamish Hamilton, 1987, Hdbk, 0–241–12051–9
Series: Profiles
Contents list, list of Beatrix Potter's books, black and white line drawings and photographs

The tale of Beatrix Potter is full of surprises and children who met her books when small will want to know something about it. From the wealth of material, diaries and illustrations, and from biographies like Judy Taylor's (1986), Buchan selects what slightly older children will want to know, and can understand: Potter's lonely childhood, her love of animals, how Peter Rabbit started in a letter, her final years as a sheep farmer in the Lake District when she did not wish to talk about her books. Many of her animal characters existed in real

life, and she drew them lovingly and accurately. Pictures, cruder than the originals but enough to encourage the reader to go back to them, abound in this compact, careful little study of a children's author very much her own woman in her time.

SH

Age range: 8–11

BULL, Angela

ELIZABETH FRY

Hamish Hamilton, 1987, Hdbk, 0–241–12084–5
Series: Profiles
Contents list, black and white line drawings

Angela Bull has a journalist's instinct for her audience and a remarkable sympathy with a child's mind. Engaging the child reader from the very first line, she enlivens the story of Elizabeth Fry's childhood with such episodes as the time when the seven sisters, for fun, joined hands across the main road to stop the mail coach as it galloped towards Norwich. Always with an eye to the child's mind and heart, Bull tells the story of the prophecy which guided Elizabeth Fry through her misfit childhood in a relatively idle and pleasure-oriented home, through an initially disappointing marriage, through the economic ups and downs of nineteenth-century business family fortunes. There is no unnecessary heroine worship: the warts are all here, but Fry emerges as the remarkable and humane woman she was. Excellent.

PMR

Age range: 8–12

DOUBLEDAY, Veronica

WOMEN AND LITERATURE

Wayland, 1988, Hdbk, 1–85210–389–2
Series: Women in History
Bibliography, contents list, glossary, index, black and white line drawings and photographs

181

The changing role of the woman writer in Britain, from the seventeenth century up to the present day, is examined in this book. It takes a wide view of literature, looking at social commentaries, journalism, diaries, poetry and fiction. Besides discussing main themes, such as the significant contribution women have made to the development of the novel, it gives some case histories of famous (some less so!) writers, illustrated by documentary evidence, contemporary pictures and quotations: the short line length not only makes for easy reading but gives room for these as marginalia. Thus, though so brief, this book is well illustrated, highly informative and includes chronological details. Moreover, there is a good reading list and some project ideas to encourage deeper investigations.

JW

Age range: 11–16

FORREST, Wendy

ROSA LUXEMBURG

Hamish Hamilton, 1989, Hdbk, 0–241–12685–1
Series: In Her Own Time
Bibliography, contents list, index, 'time chart',
black and white line drawings and photographs

Rosa Luxemburg's role in the development of international socialism is very important, but political history can be dry, a mere tapestry of characters spouting polemic. This under-recognized figure (1870–1919) lived a heroic and exciting life, afire with socialist ideals which she believed would save the world from chaos and capitalism. She lives on the page: her own arresting words appear as marginal notes, striking illustrations show the tumultuous times she lived through. Succinct but never elliptical, Forrest's style is cool and clear, showing how Rosa opposed World War I and was murdered in the turmoil in the defeated Germany after it. This is a book about ideas and commitment, inspiring,

thought-provoking, demanding careful reading. It is also a historical comment on what was to become the new Europe, and the values and ideologies we live by, for good or bad.

SH

Age range: 12–14

GATTI, Anne

ISABELLA BIRD BISHOP

Hamish Hamilton, 1988, Hdbk, 0–241–12150–7
Series: In Her Own Time
Bibliography, contents list, index, black and white
and colour line drawings

Fascinating story of the inspiring woman traveller and travel writer, who remains little known, though several of her books are in print. She struggled against physical frailty and discovered her metier almost by accident at the age of 40. She was planning another visit to China when she died at the age of 72! Her travels took her also to parts of North Africa, the Middle East, Tibet, the Indian subcontinent, Japan, Korea, New Zealand and Canada. She struggled against Victorian attitudes to women, remained a devout Christian all her life, and was elected the first woman Fellow of the Royal Geographical Society.

PMR

Age range: 11–16

GRAY, Charlotte

MOTHER TERESA

Exley, 1988, Hdbk, 1–85015–093–1
Series: People who have Helped the World
Bibliography, glossary, index, map, important
dates in her life, black and white and colour
photographs

Mother Teresa is written in a concise fashion. It left me awestruck. Here is a woman totally dedicated to her cause and not afraid to try all possible avenues in her quest to help people less fortunate than herself. Some of today's generation may find her work and selflessness beyond their imagination! Not just a book for a school library but a good addition to anyone's personal collection.

SD

Age range: 11–14

MARTIN, Christopher

H. G. WELLS

Wayland, 1988, Hdbk, 1–85210–489–9
Series: Life and Works
Bibliography, contents list, glossary, index, list of dates, black and white line drawings and photographs

Most readers know H. G. Wells for his science fiction, and this is often studied in secondary school. This book shows how Wells's ideas about science and society were developed through a lifetime of visionary and partly autobiographical writing. He put his science fiction into familiar settings, which gives them their power. There were stories of little men like Mr Polly, attacks on greed and wealth, and works advocating a united world. In the end, war and inequality brought on a disillusioned death in 1946. We see Wells in his time, helped by period photographs and lively illustrations from magazines and films, and supported by well chosen background reading and extracts from his own books. Martin's style is straight, unpatronizing, authoritative and organized. A very helpful book for individual enjoyment and class and library use.

SH

Age range: 11–14

MARTIN, Christopher

SHAKESPEARE

Wayland, 1988, Hdbk, 1–85210–418–X
Series: Life and Works
Bibliography, contents list, glossary, index, list of dates, black and white line drawings and photographs

This compact little book is a most useful introduction to Shakespeare: it is informative, attractively set out and well illustrated in black and white, though the cover illustration, inspired by the famous Chandos portrait of Shakespeare, is in colour.

The carefully chosen quotations from his main works are brought to life by clear concise commentaries, which not only place them against the background of his life and times, but contrive to inspire enthusiasm for his plays and poems.

The book probes the mystery surrounding Shakespeare's life: the few facts we have to build up a picture of the Bard of Avon as a man are in stark contrast to the worldwide fame of his writings.

For school project work on 'Shakespeare the Man', this book would be most helpful.

WFW

Age range: 11–16

SANDERS, Catharine

ODETTE CHURCHILL

Hamish Hamilton, 1989, Hdbk, 0–241–12575–8
Series: In Her Own Time
Bibliography, contents list, index, time chart, black and white line drawings and photographs

Odette Churchill's exploits are the classic material of World War II drama. She was a British spy in France, courageous and resourceful. These qualities proved essential when she was betrayed. Imprisoned and savagely tortured, she escaped from Ravensbruck concentration camp by luck at the end of the war. These external events could be mere sensation, but at all times her down-to-earth realism shines through. She says that in prison 'the only way to escape is with your mind', and her mental battles as she coped with solitary confinement are as involving as the fears of Anne Frank. Sanders refuses to parade clichés about heroism: she wants to understand a woman who claimed she was only an ordinary person doing an ordinary job. Through Odette's thoughts, often revealed in her own words, and supported by well chosen photographs, she will involve young readers' sympathies completely. Useful background material on women in wartime, too.

SH

Age range: 12–14

SCHLOREDT, Valerie and BROWN, Pam

MARTIN LUTHER KING

Exley, 1988, Hdbk, 1–85015–086–9
Series: People who have Helped the World
Bibliography, glossary, index, important dates,
black and white and colour photographs

This series tells the stories of 'great humanitarians and peacemakers of our time'. This work's sub-title 'America's great non-violent leader, who was murdered in the struggle for black rights' gives the clue to its approach. Powerful and vivid, it uses a skilful journalistic mixture of commentary, quotation and picture to recreate King's path from preacher to leader of the civil rights movement, from 'I have a dream' in 1963 to his death from a sniper's bullet in 1968. It won the *Times Educational Supplement* Senior Information Award in 1988. Its content and style compels participation by the reader, and are ideal for encouraging responsible awareness of racism and prejudice which exist then as now. With excellent picture research, and further reading (for the teacher/librarian), this is a true journey through history and through the emotions. There is an abridged version for younger readers.

SH

Age range: 10–13

WARNOCK, Kitty

MARY WOLLSTONECRAFT

Hamish Hamilton, 1988, Hdbk, 0–241–12151–5
Series: In Her Own Time
Bibliography, contents list, index, time chart,
black and white line drawings and photographs

Mary Wollstonecraft (1759–97) was really a woman before her time. Her outspoken views on the equality of men and women were treated with hostility in her day. She reacted against the view that men born to rule and women to obey. The French Revolution led her to develop her ideas about political equality, between classes and the sexes. The lack of education held women down, making them either mistresses or mothers. Warnock introduces these complex ideas in clear, carefully structured prose. Concepts of equality and opportunity are defined and explored with young readers in mind. Simplification never becomes distortion. Mary's life was full of incident, and her books became bestsellers. They were rediscovered at the time of the suffragettes and have been popular ever since. Her ideas are highly relevant today, and confirm the view that feminism was not invented yesterday. This series is a useful classroom and library resource.

SH

Age range: 11–13

WINNER, David

DESMOND TUTU

Exley, 1989, Hdbk, 1–85015–087–7
Series: People who have Helped the World
Bibliography, glossary, index, 'Timeline', black
and white and colour line drawings and
photographs

Winner starts with the dramatic story of how Archbishop Tutu and all the other major church leaders protested against the banning of the last remnants of legal opposition to apartheid, and were arrested for their pains. Then he goes on to provide the historical background to apartheid in South Africa, before coming to Tutu's birth, upbringing, education and preparation for his life work. Tutu's gradual involvement in politics, his being thrust increasingly into the limelight, his contribution to fighting apartheid are all well told. Tutu emerges as the warm, friendly, humorous and lovable man that he is.

PSG

Age range: 11+

FLAGS

◆

CRAMPTON, William

FLAG

Dorling Kindersley, 1989, Hdbk, 0–86318–370–0
Series: Eyewitness Guides
Contents list, index, black and white and colour
line drawings and photographs

This popular topic is competitively covered by publishers. *Eyewitness Guides* aim to present photographs of objects as if they are really there, and the flags in this book are touchably real on the page. Competent introductions appear on the flag used in history, on battlefield and at sea, to send messages (semaphore, in sport) and represent symbolic and heraldic meanings. Concise text, captions and labels, and illustrations (of flags and where, when, and why they are used) fit together in attractive understandable layouts on each double-page opening. It is pleasantly free from flippant editorial touches. An excellent feature is a series of openings on major countries, their flags and how they developed, with historical scenes explaining how and why flags changed. A systematic display of flags of the world ends the work. A very useful sourcebook, usable by young readers throughout a wide age/interest range.

SH

Age range: 9–14

WOOD, Tim

FLAGS

Franklin Watts, 1989, Hdbk, 0–86313–801–2
Series: Spotlight
Contents list, glossary, index, colour line
drawings and black and white and colour
photographs

Total simplicity and direct artwork are the hallmarks of this book. They make it ideal for younger readers and those who find reading difficult. Bold sans serif typography make it like handwriting. A main feature is a ten-page sequence of flags of the world, all bright and clear, easy to copy and use as a basis for making a flag for a pageant or a game. Flags also have other uses, like on the race-track or at sea. The semaphore system is shown and would be fun for a group of children to learn. *Spotlights* are simplified versions of already published titles in the *First Look* series, with rewritten text but some illustrations reproduced. This book is a workmanlike presentation of a topic of continuing interest to younger readers, and can be used, in conjunction with others and news and illustrations from magazines and TV, to make a project on flags very interesting indeed.

SH

Age range: 5–8

HISTORY

◆

Although this subject constitutes a significant part of publishers' output, there are still some areas neglected while others have a large number of books devoted to them.

WORLD HISTORY

ADAMS, Simon and KRAMER, Ann

TRADE AND RELIGION: BARBARIAN INVASIONS, EMPIRES AROUND THE WORLD AND MEDIEVAL EUROPE

Kingfisher, 1990, Hdbk, 0–86272–424–4
Series: Historical Atlas
Contents list, glossary, index, black and white and colour line drawings and colour photographs

This work outlines major events between AD 456 (roughly the end of the Roman Empire) and 1450 (roughly the start of the Reformation). It equates trade with civilization, and that with empire and religion, both of which created recognizable conditions in which trade could occur. Empire itself is seen in various ways – Roman or Byzantine or Mayan or Viking – wealthy and ordered, or based on military strength. Religion could create wealth and trade, temples and scriptoria, trade routes and social systems. Conflict could arise between them, involving secular and religious power (like Crusades). Trade depended on and stimulated the development of technology. Around themes and propositions like this the work is constructed, using in the main a montage of illustrations (very useful for casual research), and a text which stresses breadth at the expense of depth. For a coherent view of history, even of one episode, other works and the guidance of teachers and librarians would be essential.

SH

Age range: 10–13

BRETT, Bernard

THE FIGHTING SHIP

OUP, 1985, Hdbk, 0–19–273155–6
Series: Rebuilding the Past

Contents list, index, colour line drawings and black and white and colour photographs

The Fighting Ship describes ten naval engagements ranging from the clash between Greek and Phoenician triremes at Salamis in 480 BC through to the high-tech jet and frigate conflict over San Carlos Water in the 1982 Falklands War. Old favourites such as Trafalgar and the Armada are also covered. Each event is accurately portrayed by a person who was there. Some of these personal accounts are better than others; frequently momentum is held up by too much factual detail. There are no sub-headings to highlight significant stages in the action and break up the dense text. Each chapter provides good historical background to either the sailor's, airman's or submariner's conditions, weapons and rations, etc. The illustrations are vivid; however, there is no consistent approach to the captioning and occasionally accompanying specifications to illustrations are given in different units. The loose overall production of the book is further exemplified by the omission of a much-needed glossary.

RG

Age range: 11–adult

BRIQUEBEC, John

THE ANCIENT WORLD: FROM THE EARLIEST CIVILIZATIONS TO THE ROMAN EMPIRE

Kingfisher, 1990, Hdbk, 0–86272–423–6
Series: Historical Atlas
Contents list, glossary, index, black and white and colour line drawings and colour photographs

The ancient world in this work extends from 30000 BC to AD 456, the earliest civilizations to the Roman Empire. Briquebec's approach is to present in text and pictures something of what is known about these early peoples, with maps, artefacts and seals, cave paintings and artists' reconstructions. It brings together peoples of many types (Egyptian, Persian, biblical, Greek, Roman) which are widely documented elsewhere, along with less obvious examples like early Chinese dynasties and North American and African aboriginal cultures. The emphasis on civilization is highlighted by key search terms (in bold in text, and in glossary and index) like kingdom and republic and democracy, as well as interpolated sections on writing and religion. The author is interested in the civilized-ness of these early peoples, and that is how the reader can compare them. The other use of this book is as a storehouse of ready illustrations of archaeological origin, copies of which can decorate a project.

SH

Age range: 10–13

CAMPLING, Elizabeth

THE 1970s

Batsford, 1989, Hdbk, 0–7134–5988–3
Series: Portrait of a Decade
Bibliography, contents list, index, key figures of
the decade, black and white photographs

Contemporary newspapers are a valuable source of information and opinion about a period of history. This series uses the format of newspaper pages, with columns and headings, along with topical black and white illustrations, to present and reveal the 1970s. Campling has contributed two others to this series (1900–1909 and the 1980s). It is a pre-selection without taking the personal discovery and initiative away from teenage readers, for scanning and investigative skills are certainly required with this book. Many key events are included (internment, SALT-1, Munich, Watergate, the Ayatollah), presented in the style of the period rather than with the wisdom of hindsight. Many issues have

not gone away and will form the start of many a productive discussion in class (drought in Africa, the EC, inflation, information technology), while others give the dated feel of the period with their own fascination. Quotations, reports from the Commons, lists of films and sportsmen of the year: an imaginative way to bring it to life now.

SH

Age range: 11–15

CORBISHLEY, Mike

THE MIDDLE AGES

Facts on File, 1990, Hdbk, 0–8160–1973–8
Series: Cultural Atlases for Young People
Bibliography, contents list, glossary, index, maps,
gazetteer, black and white and colour line
drawings and photographs

This well illustrated book is about the peoples of medieval Europe, beginning about AD 350 and ending in the fifteenth century. Because this was a time of power struggles, the land boundaries between countries frequently changed.

The first section looks at different cultures and traces the development of the more important empires of that period.

The second section examines, in greater detail, individual countries – some of which can still be recognized today.

By the excellent colour photographs of places, artefacts and documents, and detailed maps of Europe (both as it is now, and as it was then), a fascinating picture of Europe in the Middle Ages can be built up.

Though this is one of the series of *Cultural Atlases for Young People*, do not be misled by the word 'atlas': the maps it contains are excellent but it is far *more* than an atlas.

JW

Age range: 9–16

DUDMAN, John

THE SINKING OF THE TITANIC

Wayland, 1987, Hdbk, 1–85210–163–6
Series: Great Disasters
Contents list, glossary, index, black and white and colour line drawings and photographs

Most people are fascinated by disasters and the story of the sinking of the *Titanic* is one of the best known. Even so, this well written account manages to create quite an atmosphere of excitement as it tells the story.

She was the biggest liner ever built and details are given of her size and construction and pictures to show her luxury and opulence. She was thought to be unsinkable but this view changed within seconds of her collision with an iceberg. The full extent of the tragedy only emerged later at the subsequent inquiries. Only some of the questions were answered but now that the wreck has been discovered, perhaps more answers will be forthcoming.

JW

Age range: 7–11

GARRETT, Michael

THE SEVENTIES

Wayland, 1989, Hdbk, 1–85210–724–3
Series: Decades
Bibliography, contents list, glossary, index, black and white and colour photographs

Is a decade more than the sum of its parts? For Garrett the 1970s were a melting pot of old and new ideas, all rather mixed up, some sad, some happy. To make sense of the complexity, he looks at those changes which affected young people most, like fashion and music – hot pants, punk, reggae, David Bowie, The Who. Pictures work well to show how confident people were with these things: they are unashamed, creatures of their decade, but, just like now, trying to be themselves. Young readers can identify with that.

Similarities and differences abound, and suggest ideal topics for discussion in class and research in the library. Images of the 1970s include the Munich Olympics and Watergate, and are scattered at the reader like pieces of an old newspaper, in need of formal shaping by teacher or librarian. Despite bitty text and old-fashioned design, this book is certainly very useful.

SH

Age range: 10–13

GREY, Edward

THE EIGHTIES

Wayland, 1989, Hdbk, 1–85210–725–1
Series: Decades
Bibliography, contents list, glossary, index, black and white and colour photographs

Capturing a decade in terms of key images and events is not easy. Understanding them is harder still because the truth and context fade from memory quickly. This picture of the 1980s freeze-frames major news events like Chernobyl and changes in eastern Europe and famine in Africa, taking a *Newsround* approach to topics that will appeal to readers in the age range. Fashion and pop music, media and leisure get greatest attention, as Live Aid and rap, Boy George and TV soaps, keeping fit and video games rush past, concise, vivid, aptly cited, all stimulating further research. Pictures do a newsworthy job in giving literal shape to many of the images. Deeper questions lurk underneath, like why people lived like that, how ephemeral some fashions are, and how deadly serious issues like AIDS and famine are. A work-book to dip into, consult, use with others, and extend through personal and directed investigation.

SH

Age range: 12–15

HEALEY, Tim

THE 1970s

Franklin Watts, 1989, Hdbk, 0–86313–702–4
Series: Picture History of the 20th Century
Contents list, colour line drawings and black and
white and colour photographs

Healey knows his job: the 1970s was a decade long ago to most young readers, easy to caricature and misrepresent, to see things in terms of good and bad. His introduction suggests it was a thoughtful decade after the 1960s, showing caution (oil crisis and Watergate) and progress (detente, women's movement, natural foods). Each issue is given a double-page spread, with succinct commentary and a range of well displayed illustrations with captions. He simplifies without distortion, knowing that, for subjects like Vietnam and terrorism, SALT-1 and Three Mile Island, young readers can be encouraged to carry out individual and group research, probably in a G.C.S.E. curricular setting, with a range of support services from teachers and librarians. Sections on fashion, pop and film will be easy for such readers to extend, using video and own-culture materials. A year-by-year chronology of highlights is a helpful summary. A starting point for lower ages, a quick readable digest for older ages in the interest/reading range.

SH

Age range: 10–14

HEATER, Derek

THE COLD WAR

Wayland, 1989, Hdbk, 1–85210–656–5
Series: Witness history
Bibliography, contents list, glossary, index,
leading figures, black and white and colour line
drawings and photographs

The ideological differences between communism and capitalism kept power blocs, particularly the USA and the West set against USSR and China, in states of mutual and armed suspicion for decades.

Arrangements after World War II, the Iron Curtain and Berlin Wall, and the NATO–Warsaw Pact stand-off are early highlights. Heater argues that these forces triggered off flashpoints round the world for decades afterwards – in the Middle East and Korea and Vietnam. The effects of Soviet military control can be seen in Hungary in 1956, Prague in 1968, and modern Poland. There is a mix of narrative and analysis, using contemporary sources, like what Brezhnev said about Afghanistan or Gromyko about SALT-1. This allows young readers the chance to see how historical evidence can be used in understanding history. Rhetorical questions to the reader are intended to enhance this process, although they do sound teacherly. With recent developments in Eastern Europe, this book, stopping intellectually at 1986, seems a bit *passé* at the edges, but for the heyday of the Cold War it is sound research material.

SH

Age range: 12–14

KRAMER, Ann and ADAMS, Simon

REVOLUTION AND TECHNOLOGY: RAPID CHANGE AND THE GROWTH OF THE MODERN WORLD

Kingfisher, 1989, Hdbk, 0–86272–436–8
Series: Historical Atlas
Contents list, glossary, index, black and white
and colour line drawings and photographs

The term 'historical atlas' is a metaphor for what this book does: it maps out the main events between 1760 and the present day which can be said to represent change and growth. One strand is that of economic and social development by aggression, as the violent aspects of revolutionary change (like a world war, a cold war, an end to both) are sketched out, mostly through pictures and captions. A main text does its best to suggest cause and effect relationships. Revolutions (Industrial, American, French, Russian, technological) are similarly outlined, within a broad thrust of ongoing history. An assumption is that such change both led to, and relied on, technological advances, and all types of change led to the amalgam that represents modern times. This whistle-stop tour from the spinning jenny to satellite pop culture is stimulating but, even with chronologies and an index, needs much extra help for effective use. Very much a dip-into source book, for an overview and useful pictures.

SH

Age range: 10–14

LEYSER, Henrietta

MEDIEVAL WOMEN

OUP, 1988, Hdbk, 0–19–913347–6, Pbk, 0–19–913308–5
Series: Presenting the Past
Contents list, index, dates of sources, black and white and colour line drawings and photographs

If you believe that the information books in a school library should provide a resource to document the core curriculum, this book will disappoint you: it contains few relevant facts about medieval women (and even some of those named do not appear in the incomplete index). If you are an activist for women's rights, it may be a little more to your liking, but you may still be disappointed (as I was) by the superficial way this important topic has been treated in this book.

As a reviewer, I hesitate to write a negative review, but this 'fresh look at the hopes and achievements of women from all walks of life during the ninth to fifteenth centuries' (to quote from the publisher's blurb) is little more than a glance, taken through jaded eyes!

However, the questions set at the end of each section are sensible ones that

could be set for homework, if this book were used in school: perhaps the idea of the book is to stimulate creative writing from girls, using the colourful illustrations and provocative text? The book is interesting. As a class text it should stimulate discussion from the boys, anxious to expose what they may see as *mis*representing the past! As the book begins by treating so dismissively stories from Genesis and other books of the Bible, it will also exercise the skills of Jewish and Christian class teachers.

JW

Age range: 12–16

MESSENGER, Charles

THE SECOND WORLD WAR

Franklin Watts, 1986, Hdbk, 0–86313–389–4
Series: Conflict in the 20th Century
Bibliography, contents list, index, maps, black and white and colour line drawings and photographs

This well illustrated book is divided into four chapters: the European Conflict, 1939–1941; Global War, 1941–3; Victory Road 1944–5; and The Impact of War. It also has six appendices, including the useful chronology.

The author, who retired from the army to become a full-time military writer after 21 years' service in the Royal Tank Regiment has, with help from a distinguished editorial panel and production team, given a concise, but authoritative, historical account of World War II, all the havoc and horror and unprecedented scale of death and destruction it caused, and examined briefly some of the ways in which it has affected human society in the modern world.

WFW

Age range: 11–16

MIDDLETON, Haydn

THE AGE OF CHIVALRY

OUP, 1988, Hdbk, 0–19–913346–8
Series: Presenting the Past – Topics
Contents list, index, black and white and colour
line drawings and photographs

Chivalry is a difficult idea to get across: it's not only long ago, but it's also a set of values and attitudes. Medieval knights had to be kind as well as brave, like Chaucer's 'perfect gentle knight'. Their idealism and brutal energy came together in paradoxical activities like the 'just wars' of the Crusades. Out of their *recherché* courtly love arguably came greater appreciation for woman. This makes this book sound daunting, but in fact it's highly readable. Decorated with exciting illustrations, authentically modelled on or taken from manuscripts or tapestries, and told in witty down-to-earth expository prose, Middleton brings the period to life. He makes us believe that knights lived as well as believed tales of Arthur and Charlemagne, that rules of gentility enabled men to survive tournaments, and that, when chivalry died, it took some ideals with it. Inventive questions are posed G.C.S.E.-style so that students can imagine themselves into the age and its characters, easy to do with a book as evocative as this.

SH

Age range: 11–15

PARKINSON, Roger

ATTACK ON PEARL HARBOUR

Wayland, 1988, Hdbk, 1–85210–593–3
Series: Documentary History
Bibliography, contents list, glossary, index, black
and white line drawings and photographs

Eyewitness history often has the impact which cooler perspectives lack. Put it into context, and tell it well, and you have compulsive reading. This study of Pearl Harbour was first published in 1973, and this is its second impression. It is fascinating to watch the tragic momentum towards the destruction of the US Pacific Fleet in December 1941, and the dramatic irony of the diplomacy leading up to it. Parkinson uses contemporary documents (accounts of meetings, press releases, recorded interviews) to bring the issues and personalities alive. The impressions of the Japanese pilots themselves are reproduced, along with vivid tortured photographs of impregnable ships ablaze and sinking. Bluff, bravado, heroism, and pathos shine through the pages. Marginal headings highlight the thrust of the story, and generous references to further research (needing an update now) show how much more any reader needs to do to understand it fully at this distance.

SH

Age range: 12–16

PARKINSON, Roger

THE ORIGINS OF WORLD WAR I

Wayland, 1987, Hdbk, 1–85210–280–0
Series: Documentary History
Bibliography, contents list, glossary, index,
Timetable to War, Dramatis personae, black and
white line drawings and photographs

It is over 20 years ago that Roger Parkinson, an experienced teacher, made this careful and imaginative selection of material for pupils studying the origins of World War I. There will be those who express surprise that this book should have been reissued recently after it had been out of print for so many years: obviously it was to meet a need that the *Documentary History* series has been reissued. There are still many teachers who like to supply their students with contemporary accounts in order to introduce them to research from primary sources. Despite the alleged decline in reading standards and the apparent 'down-grading' of History's place in the Curriculum by the Education Reform Act, documentary history teaching continues apace – no doubt facilitated by the ease with which documents can now be photocopied. The more didactic teacher will, nevertheless, find this book of interest, and those who prefer a chronological approach will find Appendix 1 ('Timetable to War') useful.

WFW

Age range: 15–18

PARKINSON, Roger

THE ORIGINS OF WORLD WAR II

Wayland, 1990, Hdbk, 1–85210–279–9
Series: Documentary History
Bibliography, contents list, index, black and white photographs

Typically for the series, this book recreates the subject almost entirely through eyewitness accounts. The author's art, here, is more like an editor's: the challenge is to select material from a wide range of sources in order to portray history as it really happened, and it is a challenge to which the author rises honourably. Designed to introduce students to research from primary sources, the book has notes on sources, and provides a remarkably succinct and well rounded view of the worldwide events which led up to the War. The best kind of unbiased history, which will compel reflection in any mind, young or old.

PMR

Age range: 12–16

PIMLOTT, John and MATHER, Ian

THE COLD WAR

Franklin Watts, 1987, Hdbk, 0–86313–390–8
Series: Conflict in the 20th Century
Bibliography, contents list, glossary, index, maps, chronology, black and white and colour line drawings and photographs

The Cold War, that opposition between two superpower blocs born out of Yalta and World War II, stopped just short of fighting, but only just. Pimlott and Mather's analysis (up to 1986) is one of near conflict in a series of dangerous flashpoints. Their discussion of Cuba is superb. They document the SALT talks, take us through Reagan's rhetoric about 'the evil empire' and stop with the uneasy balance of power between NATO and the Warsaw Pact. Young readers know that this is more history than the authors intended, but the issues have not gone away. Both sides have strengths and weaknesses, militarily and intellectually, and it is for us to weigh them up as historians. If contemporary history is to be interpretative, books like this, in clear dispassionate prose, will help young people to understand what risks exist when power politics are mixed with nuclear arsenals. Maps, memorable photographs, and an excellent index will help readers with a demanding but rewarding discussion.

SH

Age range: 12–14

ROSS, Stewart (editor)

THE FIRST WORLD WAR

Wayland, 1989, Hdbk, 1–85210–796–0
Series: The World Wars
Contents list, glossary, index, places to visit (esp. war museums and war cemeteries), war on screen (suggested films), important dates, maps, black and white and colour line drawings and photographs

So much has been written about World War I that selection of books suitable for a school library is a problem. This book, though based on a French text contributed by several writers, can be recommended strongly: it has been translated ably by Paul Fowkes and then carefully re-edited for use in English schools by Stewart Ross, under whose name this English edition is published. The text is even-handed, but a slight

French bias of the superb illustrations (maps, photographs, paintings, drawings, original documents, news clippings and posters) serves to remind us that, though almost the whole world was drawn into the armed conflict, it was in France that most of the battles were fought, and in France that most of the millions who lost their lives were killed.

WFW

Age range: 11–16

WHITLOCK, Ralph

EXPLORING PEOPLE

Wayland, Hdbk, 1–85210–005–2
Series: Exploring the Past
Bibliography, contents list, glossary, index,
colour line drawings and black and white and
colour photographs

This title begins as an activity-based guide for juniors researching recent local history or family histories. There are sound ideas and techniques for interviewing aged relatives or neighbours. This is followed by ideas on how to put this remembered information into chronological order with other local and national events further back in time. Family tree research methods are explained, as well as advice on how to tackle parish and census records, when delving into nineteenth-century local history. After this, broader history topics such as surname derivations and events recorded in local folklore and traditions are dealt with. Later chapters are concerned with Middle Age sources, such as church brasses and entries recorded in the Domesday Book. Finally, the information archaeologists discover about our ancient ancestors is described. A useful introduction to primary research methods for school projects on local history.

RG

Age range: 10–13.

WILLIAMS, Patricia (editor)

CHILDREN AT WAR

BBC, 1989, Pbk, 0–563–34406–7
Contents list, chronology, black and white line
drawings and photographs

War involves armies and nations but is often most vivid when personal. This is even more so when the experiences happened when people were children, and they look back with fear and surprise at how they survived. Twelve writers from round the world tell their story about the effect of World War II on them. Each episode is short, powerful, evocative, ideal for showing young people today what it was like to be there. For one it was a lack of sweets, for another an uncle who did not come back, for a third watching the Jews being taken away, for a fourth surviving the holocaust of Hiroshima. Black and white photographs give a sometimes horrifyingly concrete realism to these memories, pictures repeated in the BBC TV companion series *Landmarks*. Writing like this comes alongside young people today, and the barriers of the years go down.

SH

Age range: 10–13

WINDROW, Martin and HOOK, Richard

THE HORSE SOLDIER

OUP, 1986, Hdbk, 0–19–273157–2
Series: Rebuilding the Past
Contents list, glossary, colour line drawings

With its companion volume on the foot soldier (OUP, 1983), this work is a unique and impressive introduction to wars and men who fought in them through the ages. In this work, the emphasis is on the cavalry man, fighting alone, like the adept Scythian warrior or the heavily armoured mediaeval knight, or in complex formations, like Napoleon's regiments of cuirassiers at battles like Jena and

Wagram. Crusaders and Wild West cavalry, Roundheads under Cromwell and the much-slaughtered horsemen of World War I, the pageant of carnage and glory is told. The authors use both fact and fiction, both based on accurate scholarship (worn lightly), both supported by detailed and atmospheric colour line drawings and informative captions. We often look up at horsemen, and see the terror they inspired. The compelling layout will help slower readers through the mature text, but all readers will come away infected for ever.

SH

Age range: 10–16

ANCIENT HISTORY

BURRELL, Roy

THE GREEKS

OUP, 1989, Pbk, 0–19–917101–7
Contents list, 'Timeline', colour line drawings

Written as a narrative, this really held my attention, presenting lots of readily digestible information. Much is in the form of dialogues with an imaginary historical person present at an event, putting forward their impressions and feelings. A wealth of pictorial evidence with clear helpful captions, coloured sketches of reconstructions of Greek life, closely following archaeological evidence. There are two short biographies of eminent archaeologists of Greece and the first section is a very effective comic strip of the Minotaur legend, something to grab a child's interest from the first.

However, some small criticisms. Not enough attention is given to women, children, slaves or plain old-fashioned work; there are too many generalizations of the 'everyone did . . .' style, which really means well-off men; in the sections about religion and the 'dark ages' many concepts difficult for children are not explored in sufficient depth.

SS

Age range: 8–12

CONNOLLY, Peter

TIBERIUS CLAUDIUS MAXIMUS:
THE CAVALRYMAN

OUP, 1988, Hdbk, 0–19–917106–8
Series: Rebuilding the Past
Contents list, index, colour line drawings and photographs

Author-illustrator Peter Connolly is widely known for numerous attractive and authoritative works for young people

on the military aspects of classical life. There are two books on Maximus of which this is the second. The man really existed, as tombstone and archaeological evidence shows, and Connolly reconstructs his life as a soldier in the Roman army under Trajan. Text and artwork design is carefully orchestrated for impact and accessibility for young readers. Around a spinal column of main commentary there are many notes and informative captions, encouraging the eye to roam about a highly organized page. Maps, diagrams showing armour and horse equipment, dramatic pictures of Maximus in action against the Dacians of the upper Danube, all contain a wealth of easily mediated information. For a study of the period, and for readers interested in soldiers, this book is irresistible.

SH

Age range: 9–13

CORBISHLEY, Mike

ANCIENT ROME

Facts on File, 1989, Hdbk, 0–8160–1970–3
Series: Cultural Atlases for Young People
Bibliography, contents list, glossary, index, maps, gazetteer, black and white and colour line drawings and photographs

This book is called an atlas, and that is partly what it is, for it is full of clearly drawn maps which help you to understand the story and to see where places are and where events took place. The first section – History of an Empire – tells how the Romans became important and the accompanying maps and charts assign a place and date to the principal events in Roman history. The second part – The Geography of an Empire – looks at the effect the Romans had on the lands they took over. Important towns and villages with their Latin and modern names can be located using the gazetteer and maps, and there is a useful glossary of Roman terms. The large colour photographs and drawings illustrate a concise text. This is an excellent addition to the wide range of books on this subject by an author whose other books will be known to most school librarians.

JW

Age range: 9–16

HARRIS, Geraldine

ANCIENT EGYPT

Facts on File, 1990, Hdbk, 0–8160–1971–1
Series: Cultural Atlases for Young People
Bibliography, contents list, glossary, index,
gazetteer, black and white and colour line
drawings and photographs

The pyramids and mummies of Ancient Egypt are *clichés* which any serious writer for young people has both to use and move beyond. Dr Harris, wearing scholarship lightly, presents her subject enthusiastically in this well designed and valuable information source book. We see Egypt as a place, with its dependence on the Nile, its Pharaoh god-kings, and complex social life. We see it chronologically, through the dynasties, with their feuds and misfortunes, to the time of Greece and Rome. We see it as a journey down the Nile, from Upper Egypt to the delta, ancient and modern, with sites like Abu Sinbel and the Valley of the Kings, accompanied by meticulous and well annotated maps. This arrangement makes it easy to know where we are, helped by a comprehensive index (to text and illustration) and gazetteer. It is an infectious way of coming to know. Reconstructions and vivid colour photographs, with informative captions, weave their way through the book.

SH

Age range: 9–15

MACAULAY, David

CITY

Collins, 1975, Pbk, 0–00–192157–6
Glossary, black and white line drawings

It has been said that David Macaulay's architectural picture books are among the most outstanding non-fiction books of recent years.

In this book, he shows the planning and construction of an imaginary Roman city. He demonstrates clearly his belief that 'the Romans knew that well-planned cities did more to maintain peace and security than twice the number of military camps.' This city is not just an architectural exercise; its design, based on careful research, was meant to meet the needs of those who built and inhabited it. Thus this book, with its clear text and accurate drawings, will interest students of history and classics – and even future city planners!

JW

Age range: 9–16

OLIPHANT, Margaret

THE EGYPTIAN WORLD

Kingfisher, 1989, Hdbk, 0–86272–411–2
Series: Kingfisher History Library
Bibliography, contents list, glossary, index,
'Timeline', colour line drawings, black and white
and colour photographs

Three thousand years of history are here retailed in 87 pages, the wordage reduced by a quarter because of the illustrations which make the book visually interesting. The book needs far more detailed maps if the curiosity of readers is to be served. For example, the 'Fortress of Buhen in Nubia' is illustrated on a page which happens to have a map as well; but there is no mention of Buhen or of Nubia on this map – or any other in the book.

This sort of fault lies not in Oliphant but in her editors. The author has an attractive approach to a long and complicated history: starting with what every schoolchild knows (mummies and pyramids), she discusses the world from which these originated before going back to the time before the Pharaohs. The bulk of attention is given to the life of the country (kingship, government, religion, armies, everyday life) though she returns to the Land of the Dead for the penultimate pages, and rounds off the book with a glance at Christian and Muslim Egypt which follow. There is a certain element of catalogue about the scores of kings whose achievements need to be mentioned, but Oliphant manages to counter some of the dullness by the various excitements of how that rich world has come to be rediscovered after an astonishingly long time and within a surprisingly short period.

PSG

Age range: 13–16

POWELL, Anton

ATLAS OF ANCIENT GREECE

Facts on File, 1989, Hdbk, 0–8160–1972–X
Series: Cultural Atlases for Young People
Bibliography, contents list, glossary, index, maps, table of dates, gazetteer, black and white and colour line drawings and photographs

The first part of this book deals with the history of Greece, from the late Bronze Age to the time of the Roman conquest (c.1600–100 BC) and tells the story of the Greeks' rise to power, maps being used mainly to illustrate specific topics in the text, often supported by date charts.

The second part deals with Greek culture and society and the effect on the lands the Greeks occupied. In this section, maps play a larger part and show the many 'city states' of the Greek empire.

By clear text and superb illustrations (not just the maps!) this 'cultural atlas' provides an attractive portrait of a great civilization.

JW

Age range: 9–16

POWELL, Anton

THE GREEK WORLD

Kingfisher, 1987, Hdbk, 0–86272–284–5
Series: History Library
Bibliography, contents list, index, black and white and colour line drawings and photographs

The achievements of classical Greece live on through history, in our language and ways of thinking, in our culture. This known assumption is no use at all to start a book for young people, and Powell knows this. So he rightly emphasizes how the Greeks lived their daily lives, how they dressed and what they ate, what their soldiers and buildings looked like, and how they buried their dead. He brings an ancient people to life, using carefully selected extracts from writers like Herodotus, scenes from pots and friezes, and archaeological evidence (photographic). He is a story-teller rather than a dry instructor, establishing a friendly persona for the reader, putting people (rather than scholarship, which, however, does not suffer) first. Even abstract ideas, like the city state and religion, are mediated intelligibly, though some, like the role of Socrates, will elude this age group of readers, no matter what writers try to do.

SH

Age range: 10–13

BRITISH HISTORY

DURES, Alan

THE ENGLISH CIVIL WAR

Dryad, 1987, Hdbk, 0–85219–665–2
Series: Weighing up the Evidence
Bibliography, contents list, glossary, index, date
list, black and white line drawings and
photographs

The theme of this book could be the excitement of the Civil War and the tragic death of Charles I. Instead, Dures draws on his experience as a history teacher to present historical evidence on what led up to the war and how historians have interpreted those events. The 'how and why' approach emphasizes the causes of the war – the social change, the religious disagreements and political turmoil. Using evidence from contemporary and later sources, Dures presents an imaginative workbook full of opportunities for evaluation: how the king tried to rule without Parliament, what he did to the Scots, the effect of the General Remonstrance. The momentum of past events led irresistibly to conflict. Well chosen and glossed questions invite readers to weigh up the evidence, and creative writing tasks are based on the facts and opinions of history. Many leads are provided to further material and discovery in this very useful and planned study.

SH

Age range: 13–16

ELLENBY, Jean

THE ANGLO-SAXON HOUSEHOLD

CUP, 1986, Pbk, 0–521–31676–6
Colour line drawings

This is a methodical summary of the main features of Anglo-Saxon domestic life. Unpretentious and straightforward, it describes village life, house construction and furniture, clothes, and food and drink in an accessible way for young readers. Imaginative use is made of Sutton Hoo in sections on jewellery and burial, and of the epic about Beowulf in accounts of tale-telling in the great hall, aspects of the book which may well encourage young readers to investigate further in books and museum lore. The format and illustrations have the simple directness of Dinosaur books, and it is indeed they who own the illustration copyright. The period is not romanticized: there were bugs and rats in the buildings, and trial by ordeal was common. It is nearly patronized for being pagan. This is a useful book for library and classroom, and for personal ownership, particularly if the family likes visiting archaeological sites.

SH

Age range: 8–12

GOODALL, John S.

THE STORY OF A HIGH STREET

André Deutsch, 1987, Hdbk, 0–233–98070–9
Contents list, colour line drawings

We begin in an open air market with thatched dwellings, a medieval scene; flip over a half-page and the image is transformed, timber-framed houses under construction. Turn again, there is an Elizabethan town centre, the half-page in more detail, then the interior of a clothing shop. Next, alterations in Restoration and Georgian times. By now the road is cobbled, interiors of a coffee shop and a coaching inn. Victorian and Edwardian views of the street and interiors down to the present. Throughout, the church and the market cross preserve the basic form of the street through changing fashions of building.

A beautiful evocation of the development of a high street which I have browsed many times. I find it very appealing. Just a lingering doubt, whether it stands on its own with children. Will they be able to interpret it? There is no text.

SS

Age range: 8–12

HARRIS, Nathaniel

THE ARMADA: THE DECISIVE BATTLE

Dryad, 1987, Hdbk, 0–85219–686–5
Series: A Day that Made History
Bibliography, contents list, index, black and white line drawings

The first part of the book – the Events – presents a detailed account of the action of the Battle of Gravelines and the subsequent scattering of the Armada and its fate as the wind blew it around Britain to its destruction. A gripping narrative including elements of reported comments of some participants. After a thorough account of what happened we have – the Investigation – a consideration of why the war came about, laying out the historical context, examining the plan and whether the Armada could have succeeded.

I found it extremely readable and the arguments clear. The legends are stripped away; Drake and his bowls, the fast little English ships outmanoevring the great Spanish galleons, but the story loses no drama and excitement for it. It is a pity the conditions and experience of the ordinary seamen and soldiers are not more prominent and some of the illustrations not of reproductive quality.

SS

Age range: 11–16

McDOWALL, David

THE SPANISH ARMADA

Batsford, 1988, Hdbk, 0–7134–5671–X

Series: Living Through History
Bibliography, contents list, index, black and white line drawings

The Armada seems to have carried the seeds of the failure from the first, but what a catalogue of horror on both sides, especially for the poor Spaniards. I found it a fascinating read but painful and distressing as to the actual battle and aftermath. The presentation is a series of biographies of the leading figures involved, the commentary interspersed with contemporary extracts. First the planning; then the action from Spanish, then English viewpoints; finally sections about the conditions of the soldiers and sailors and their fates. The text is complemented with a variety of interpretative illustrations. What a pity the reproduction is so very poor.

SS

Age range: 11–16

MENDES, Linda

THE ENGLISH CIVIL WAR

Batsford, 1987, Hdbk, 0–7134–5569–1
Series: Living Through History
Bibliography, contents list, glossary, index, biographical notes, black and white line drawings and photographs

People live through history, and their lives, as they and other people describe them, are used as a way of unfolding the period of the English Civil War of the 1640s. Drawing on a wide range of resources (all carefully listed), Mendes weaves vivid and well selected quotations with highly organized accounts of a dozen such people, five for the king, five for Parliament and Cromwell, and two simply (and tragically) caught up in the struggle. Some are heroes (Prince Rupert, John Hampden, Montrose), while others are pragmatists or idealists. One is an ordinary soldier in the New Army, another (Brilliana Harvey) a noblewoman distrusted by both sides. The pathos and contingency of war comes powerfully through these stories. Its way of telling is informative (Mendes is a practising teacher), for G.C.S.E. students will find its use of sources as useful as what the sources say.

SH

Age range: 12–15

PLACE, Robin

MEDIEVAL BRITAIN

Wayland, 1989, Hdbk, 1–85210–578–X
Series: History as Evidence
Bibliography, contents list, glossary, index, places to visit, black and white and colour line drawings and photographs

The years from 1300 to 1485 are known as the Middle Ages. There are three main ways of finding out about life in Medieval Britain. First, there are writings and pictures that tell us what people did. Second, we can visit buildings still standing (e.g. castles and churches). Third, archeologists study the remains of buildings that have largely disappeared and dig up artefacts. This book shows how, through such evidence, it is possible to reconstruct the way people lived and died in the Middle Ages.

There is an interesting section on the Princes in the Tower. From recent scientific studies, it now seems likely that the bones dug up there (in 1674) were, as suspected, the remains of the little princes murdered in 1483, though we still do not know who murdered them.

JW

Age range: 7–11

RAWCLIFFE, Michael

VICTORIAN PUBLIC HEALTH AND HOUSING

Batsford, 1987, Hdbk, 0–7134–5050–9
Series: Finding out About . . .
Bibliography, contents list, index, black and white line drawings and photographs

It might be thought that public health and housing are not topics to interest many school children, but the well chosen quotations, documents and photographs used in this book make what could be a dull subject quite interesting. The book first describes the overcrowded conditions and the high incidence of diseases in the slums of industrial cities, the poor quality of their water supplies and their inadequate sanitation, at the beginning of Victoria's reign. Although many reforms occurred in her reign, and great improvements were made, many of the standards of health and housing that we take for granted nowadays were not achieved until this century.

The book has been designed with project work in mind, with plenty of questions and suggestions for further study. Although it is primarily about the problems of cities, sufficient ideas and sources of information are given to encourage any child, city-dweller or not, to make a local study of public health and housing.

JW

Age range: 11–16

REGAN, Geoffrey

ELIZABETHAN ENGLAND

Batsford, 1990, Hdbk, 0–7134–6094–6
Series: Living Through History
Bibliography, contents list, glossary, index, biographical notes, date list, black and white line drawings and photographs

History is said to come to life through its personalities. This series looks at a period through a dozen or so people, unfolding their lives and evaluating how it affected and was influenced by its context. The rich tapestry of Elizabethan England can be oversimplified, but Regan is alert to this. Four divisions enable him to show key cross-currents and viewpoints of the time, using ample quotation from contemporary sources. In government were Cecil, Dudley, Howard, and

Devereux, some for Elizabeth, some against, all worth knowing about. In religion were men like Cartwright and Campion, who disputed Elizabeth's royal supremacy, or Whitgift who had to deal with the famous Marprelate Tracts. Literary figures like Sidney and explorers like Frobisher and Hakluyt complete the gallery. Regan gets behind myths about Raleigh, and in clear, always readable discussions, remains interesting even about heavily covered figures like Mary Queen of Scots. Apt facsimiles and portraits brings things further to life.

SH

Age range: 13–16

SANCHA, Sheila

THE LUTTRELL VILLAGE

Collins, 1982, Hdbk, 0–00–195838–0
Glossary, black and white line drawings

Inspired by the beautiful Luttrell psalter, Sheila Sancha has reconstructed the lives of the people who lived in Gerneham – one of Sir Geoffrey Luttrell's villages in the fourteenth century. The book depicts a year in the village, the farming cycle, and how independent and self-sufficient people had to be. The clear, simple text complements the delightfully detailed drawings, which really bring the story to life. Unusually for these days, the drawings – apart from the cover design – are not in colour, but they show great artistry, expert draughtsmanship and shading. They give a fascinating picture of early village life. An exquisite book.

JW

Age range: 9–13

SANCHA, Sheila

WALTER DRAGUN'S TOWN: TRADE IN STAMFORD IN THE 13TH CENTURY

Collins, 1987, Hdbk, 0–00–195874–7
Black and white line drawings

Mixtures of fact and fiction can work well in the historical field. Sheila Sancha's portrait of this medieval town (now Stamford in Lincolnshire) uses the framework of story (Walter is a tyrannical steward who treats local people unfairly) in order to unfold a wealth of interesting and authentic detail about trade and traders at the time. The visit of an Italian merchant forms the climax as Hugh bargains with him over the sale of silks and fabrics. Sancha's line drawings capture the intricate and engrossing detail of workshops and dye-houses, weavers' sheds and market place, spread as they are across double-page openings with text neatly slotted in between. The pictures hold a rather meandering text together. Using archaeological and documentary resources, and using them lightly, this book, with its personalities and street scenes, will serve personal reading and classroom research well.

SH

Age range: 9–12

SARAGA, Jessica

CROMWELL

Batsford, 1990, Hdbk, 0–7134–6033–4
Series: Reputations
Bibliography, contents list, index, Cromwell's
contemporaries, black and white line drawings
and photographs

Legends sediment around historical characters like Oliver Cromwell, not least of all because of his piety, his involvement with Roundheads, and the regicide of Charles I. Opinion about him was mixed at the time, and has been since, as Saraga shows, leaving the teenage reader to make up his or her own mind. Plenty of thoughtful background is provided, on the political and religious upheaval in which Cromwell came to prominence. External events, like the army and Parliament, are told as they exemplify cross-currents of ideology and convictions at the time (e.g. what power could Parliament have? Did Cromwell ever see himself as a monarch?) Was he a repressive opportunist or a chosen instrument of God trying to do an impossible task? Evidence from his own letters and from contemporaries show him as a complex figure easy to caricature. Saraga expects prior knowledge of the period in this demanding and rewardingly scholarly study, eclectically decorated with engravings and marginal notes.

SH

Age range: 13–16

SOMERSET FRY, Fiona

A SOLDIER IN WELLINGTON'S ARMY

Wayland, 1987, Hdbk, 0–85078–801–3
Series: How They Lived
Bibliography, contents list, glossary, index, black and white and colour line drawings and photographs

Life for a soldier in Wellington's army was often far from congenial and this book certainly does not glorify war. It tells how the soldiers lived, describes their training, their uniforms, their life at camp and how they spent their time in winter quarters. Both the infantry and cavalry were rigorously trained and discipline was harsh for those who made mistakes.

The clear text and coloured illustrations make it an attractive book, very suitable for project work (e.g. on the Peninsular War).

JW

Age range: 9–13

SPEED, Peter and Mary

FARMERS AND TOWNSFOLK

OUP, 1987, Pbk, 0–19–917114–9
Series: History Source Books – The Elizabethan Age
Contents list, notes on money, black and white and colour line drawings and photographs

The Elizabethan Age series looks at

nobles, farmers and townsfolk, the poor, and seamen, and aims to recreate the atmosphere of circa 1600 by letting contemporary documents speak for themselves. Accordingly, content and method of presentation aim to be innovative and have impact on the young reader. Each of five sections begins with an interview, rather like a TV programme (e.g. the mayor of Elizabethan Leicester). The authors use original but adapted dialogues to represent lessons in school or conversation at the dinner table. Facsimiles of documents, photographs of everyday objects, engravings and action drawings all work to bring the period to life. The organization of data is encouraged through displaying an inventory and then information about plague deaths. These methods help to hold a rather diverse array of topics together (farming, houses, education, food and drink). Continual use of documentary evidence with questions will make this a useful classroom and research resource book, but it's rather earnest for spontaneous personal reading.

SH

Age range: 10–13

SPEED, Peter and Mary

THE SEAMEN

OUP, 1987, Pbk, 0–19–917116–5
Series: History Source Books: The Elizabethan Age
Contents list, black and white and colour photographs

This topic-based history text book explains, through an interpretative approach in keeping with G.C.S.E. requirements, how Elizabethan England became a great seafaring nation. The initial chapters investigate the daring exploits of men like Hawkins and Drake who harried the Spanish in the New World. Further chapters explain how the Armada was dealt with and how afterwards English privateers carried on the war of attrition with Spain. The book traces its topic and presents interpretation work through a variety of historical source materials, such as letters, memoirs, court proceedings, pictures, accounts and maps. Frequently these documents are used to give pupils the conflicting Spanish and English viewpoints of an event. The related questions and activities which accompany the evidence encourage pupils to practise the historical skills of analysis, exposition and the detection of bias. The linking explanatory text which the authors provide is clear and straightforward.

RG

Age range: 14–16

STEEL, Barry

MEDIEVAL MARKETS

Wayland, 1989, Hdbk, 1–85210–814–2
Series: Beginning History
Colour line drawings and photographs

School children, particularly those in a market town, would find this an interesting social history book. It describes how medieval markets grew from simple trading to elaborate fairs, with an entertainment as well as a commercial role.

It is an attractive book, full of interest. Its many coloured illustrations capture the lively mood of medieval markets.

JW

Age range: 7–9

TRIGG, Tony D.

VIKING BRITAIN

Wayland, 1989, Hdbk, 1–85210–577–1
Series: History in Evidence
Bibliography, contents list, glossary, index, list of
places to visit, colour line drawings and
photographs

A pleasant change from the usual books about the Vikings, this book has no longships, raids or pillaging. Instead, you are shown archaeological evidence that has been used to deduce how the Vikings lived and worked during their years in Britain. It starts with a clear map of Danelaw (Viking Britain), showing where the Vikings came from, and the sites and towns mentioned in the book.

Throughout, photographs of digs and the artefacts found are used to show how the Vikings lived in the towns and in the country. Photographs of the beautiful Lewis chessmen and the silver jewellery found in the River Ribble contrast well with those of the coprolite and toilet reconstruction at the Jarvik Centre in York. It is fascinating to read how finding small wooden shapes led to the discovery of the remains of a Viking cupmaker's shop in a street in York, which probably owes its name, Coppergate, to the work done there.

This is an excellent book for juniors.

JW

Age range: 7–11

MODERN BRITISH HISTORY

HILL, Maureen

GROWING UP AT WAR

Armada, 1989, Pbk, 0–00–693547–8
Black and white and colour line drawings and
black and white photographs

World War II was a time of large events
and international danger, but it was also a
time when ordinary people's lives were
turned upside-down. How it affected
them is the theme of this book. Using
photo-montage techniques and varied
window and caption layouts, Hill
powerfully builds up a feel for the period.
Blackout and conscription, gas masks and
ration books: bringing it home to the
reader is her aim, and the numerous
things to do help this along well. Work
out how to feed a family from rationed
food, make a war poster, make a list of
what you would take if disturbed in the
night and told to go to a shelter.
Research, too, is covered, like
interviewing old people about the war.
The spread is general but presentation, in
clear, generally unbiased prose (a bit
contentious about how good we all
were), exciting and atmospheric. Good
for home and classroom use.

SH

Age range: 10–14

HURST, Alison

FAMILY IN THE FIFTIES

Black, 1987, Hdbk, 0–7136–2703–4
Series: Family in the . . .
Bibliography, contents list, index, black and white
line drawings and photographs

The 1950s saw postwar austerity turn into
a new affluence. It was also a time of
change a long time ago for today's
children. So the what and how of
selection are crucial. Hurst takes an
imaginary family and allows them to
comment on the changes as they take
place: Eileen's view of new supermarkets
or women going out to work, Valerie's
feelings when rock and roll came in,
John's memories about school dinners.
She also works, without nostalgia getting
in the way (for it is irrelevant here),
through themes like travel and fashion
and cars, using period photos to show
what she means. Clear description and
the personal touch, and a general
freedom from bias (except on schools),
make this a dependable sourcebook for
the decade. There is a feel about new
discoveries there, something which
young readers know well. Comparisons
with the present day can be made all the
time with a book like this, and not always
to the detriment of the past.

SH

Age range: 9–12

HURST, Alison

FAMILY IN THE SIXTIES

Black, 1987, Hdbk, 0–7136–2704–2
Series: Family in the . . .
Bibliography, contents list, index, facts and
figures, black and white line drawings and
photographs

For many readers the 1960s were their
parents' generation, dim and perhaps
odd images refracted by nostalgia and the
passage of time. Alison Hurst uses black
and white photos of the period to give a
cinematic portrait of the decade. Looking
through the eyes of the Turners, an
imaginary family whose children were
born then, and hearing their thoughts and
memories, we get an idea of what
happened and what it felt like to be there.
Much is now taken for granted – TV,
comprehensive schools, foreign travel,
fashion for the young, and much of it

started then. People saw *The Sound of Music* at the cinema, drove Mini cars, and watched Kennedy being shot. This is modern social history told without self-consciousness or apology, in a tone which can be adopted by readers in coursework and essays, backed up with other reading, helping to make sense of the last 30 years. Teachers will need to supply much more on the broader political context.

SH

Age range: 11–14

KELSALL, Freda

HOW WE USED TO LIVE, 1954–1970

Black, 1987, Hdbk, 0–7136–2925–8
Series: How we Used to Live
Contents list, index, things to do, who was who, some important events, black and white and colour line drawings and photographs

The years from 1954 to 1970 will go down in history as a period of rapid change. This was attributable not only to ex-servicemen anxious to build a new world, but also to younger people, scarcely out of their teens, who as children had known only the austerity of wartime and the immediate postwar years: they, on completing their National Service (strangely, not mentioned in this book!) suddenly enjoyed a new affluence and fewer constraints, and could try to implement their ideas.

They confidently sought to change the world in which they grew up. It was a time when young people influenced, not only fashions in politics and pop music, but all aspects of everyday life in a consumer society.

The author of this interesting book, wrote the award-winning Yorkshire TV series, *How we Used to Live*: this book not only serves as an invaluable background reader for the TV programmes but is, in its own right, a well

written and carefully illustrated account of those years.

WFW

Age range: 9–14

MITCHELL, Graham

THE ROARING TWENTIES: BRITAIN IN THE 1920s

Batsford, 1986, Hdbk, 0–7134–5201–3
Series: Living Through History
Bibliography, contents list, index, date list, black and white line drawings and photographs

Graham Mitchell's way of dealing with the cliché of the 1920s is to face it head on. If it was a time of frivolity and excess, who lived like that? The answer is high society, particularly the aesthete Brian Howard and socialite Nancy Cunard. More thoughtful were the misunderstood Prince of Wales and the witty Noel Coward. Through these the myth of the 1920s is explored and evaluated. Four traditional literary portraits (Huxley, Wyndham Lewis, Edith Sitwell and Arlen) are used to consider preoccupations of the period. Most provocative of all were lives like Stopes and Russell. Historical and critical works, memoirs and journals are used to investigate them, revealing much of value, and showing how such sources may be used in the readers' own projects and essays. Heavily trodden aspects of the period are avoided by this approach, and students have a dozen 'life and times' vignettes to ponder and develop.

SH

Age range: 12–15

RAWCLIFFE, Michael

THE WELFARE STATE

Dryad, 1990, Hdbk, 0–85219–806–X
Series: Weighing up the Evidence
Bibliography, contents list, glossary, index, sources, chronology, black and white line drawings and photographs

Nothing comes into being simply: there is often disagreement and delay. The evolution of the welfare state demonstrates this. Rawcliffe shows how, from the start of the nineteenth century to the years after World War II, ideas about how to deal with the poor went to and fro. They were implicated with health, housing and employment, influenced by political and philanthropic causes, and upset by major events like war and economic depression. The approach is to structure these events, without partisan commentary, within a clear timeline (the series name indicating an emphasis on the process of change), and let quotations from speeches and newspapers, cartoons and oral evidence, speak to the reader. The concept of the welfare state takes a lot for granted, and this unemotional and readably detailed historical analysis will open many young readers' eyes. Others in the series, on housing and public health, will prove useful companion volumes.

SH

Age range: 13–16

THOMSON, Neil

WORLD WAR II

Franklin Watts, 1989, Hdbk, 0–86313–873–X
Series: When I was Young
Contents list, glossary, index, 'Timeline', black and white line drawings and photographs

What a very good idea: introduce young people to history through the experiences of someone who was young at the time. And it is fascinating to see the war through the eyes of a young person – family life, evacuation, bombing and shelters, gas masks and blackouts, school, rationing, cadets, victory, and postwar apprenticeship to make the return to normality. Rationing, for example, meant in practice not merely that people had less but, in some cases, that people had more: I hadn't realized that though butter was rationed, it was the first time that many people had had butter: 'it was the first time a lot of people in Stoke Newington had ever had butter. . . Before the war they had margarine or dripping'.

Using the interviewee's words as far as possible lifts history away from the dryness of impersonal books on the subject, and occasions the aside, titbit or oddity which makes for interest. There is structure here, and range, and the individual's story is complemented by various historical documents, newspaper excerpts, photographs, maps and cartoons to make the book visually dynamic. This is rounded off by suggestions of projects and activities on which readers can embark.

PSG

Age range: 10–14

THOMSON, Ruth

EARLY 20TH CENTURY

Franklin Watts, 1989, Hdbk, 0–86313–872–1
Series: When I was Young
Contents list, glossary, index, black and white and colour line drawings and photographs

Each picture book in this series offers a fascinating view of modern history through the memories of a living person. In this book, the writer, Ruth Thomson, meets Nancy Emery (née Gillah), who was born in 1906 in Yorkshire. She was the seventh of nine sisters and tells of her childhood. Snapshots from her family album and other contemporary photographs and materials have been used to illustrate this book (together with several newly commissioned photographs of places remembered by her) to demonstrate both change and continuity. In the 'Things to do' section, the author suggests how children can research their own family history.

WFW

Age range: 8–13

GERMAN HISTORY

BERWICK, Michael

THE THIRD REICH

Wayland, 1987, Hdbk, 1–85210–280–2
Series: Documentary History
Bibliography, contents list, glossary, index, black and white photographs

Tracing the rise and fall of the Third Reich – created to last for a thousand years, but surviving for only twelve disastrous ones – is not a pleasant enterprise, but it is an instructive one. Extracts from newspapers, diaries, novels and other sources combine to recreate the conditions of life for the German middle classes, the rich, the poor and the non-Aryan minorities of the time. The S.S., the citizenship laws of the Reich, the idea of *Lebensraum*, the impact of war on German society and the final reckoning of the leaders of the Reich at the Nuremberg war trials are all presented here through text, photographs, cartoons and other graphic material.

PMR

Age range: 12–16

BRADLEY, Catherine

HITLER AND THE THIRD REICH

Franklin Watts, 1990, Hdbk, 0–7496–0117–5
Series: World War II Biographies
Bibliography, contents list, glossary, index, maps, chronology, colour line drawings and black and white and colour photographs

This book looks at the career of Adolf Hitler, the man responsible for engulfing Europe in war in 1939 – a war that drew in countries around the globe, and affected both civilians and the armed forces.

During the course of World War II some 50 million died, many millions of others suffered physical and psychological injuries, while new and horrifying weapons caused devastation on an unprecedented scale.

Over half a century later, we still live with many of the consequences of that war, yet many, particularly the young, do not know why and how it was fought.

This biography of Hitler seeks to explain how he was able to cause so much destruction.

WFW

Age range: 11–16

HARRIS, Nathaniel

HITLER

Batsford, 1989, Hdbk, 0–7134–5961–1
Series: Reputations
Bibliography, contents list, index, time chart (dates), dramatis personae (Hitler's contemporaries), black and white line drawings and photographs

Nathaniel Harris is an experienced author, with more than 40 books to his name, including two of the seven in this series (of which he is series consultant). Each book in this series is on a famous (or, in this case, infamous!) character, and written in four sections (Reputation, Background, Interpretation, Conclusion), and intended for project work and background reading.

This one deals with Hitler's appalling reputation as leader of the Nazi Party; his remarkable rise to power; the skill with which he transformed the Weimar Republic into the Third Reich; his striking personality and leadership; his policies that led eventually to World War II and his downfall.

The book is attractively presented with primary source material, e.g. quotations both from Hitler's own words and his contemporaries; and illustrations such as cartoons, paintings and photographs. The helpful way the wide margins have been

RUSSIAN HISTORY

ROSS, Stewart

THE RUSSIAN REVOLUTION

Wayland, 1988, Hdbk, 0–85210–322–1
Series: Witness History
Bibliography, contents list, glossary, index,
leading figures, biographies, black and white and
colour line drawings and black and white
photographs

Stewart Ross concentrates on the period just before the Russian Revolution of 1917 and when, in the 1920s, the new state and order came into being, galvanized by the energy of Lenin and the Bolsheviks. It is easy to see the transition from Tsarist Russia as quick and simple, but Ross makes clear it was complex (economic decline, defeat at the hands of Germany, top-heavy bureaucracy). At the heart of the book is the period of change, motivated by many things, embodied in many conflicting ideas and parties. Ross invites readers to consider contradictory evidence, from historians and contemporary documents. He uses posters as discussion points, and supplies many excellent questions which will encourage readers to evaluate events in the manner of criteria suggested by modern curricula. The achievements of the Tsar, of Trotsky, of 'state capitalism' are presented for review. Helpful summaries focus on key issues, and important biographical sketches and an excellent structured reading list are provided at the end.

SH

Age range: 12–15

HUNGARIAN HISTORY

BLACKWOOD, Alan

THE HUNGARIAN UPRISING

Wayland, 1986, Hdbk, 0–85078–729–7
Series: Flashpoints
Bibliography, contents list, glossary, index,
'Timeline', black and white line drawings and
photographs

Before the present vogue for *perestroika* changed the Eastern bloc, there were other well known attempts on the part of these peoples to guide their own destinies. East Germany in 1953; Poland, 1956; Czechoslovakia, 1968; Poland again, 1983. But none of them came as close to shaking the foundations of Soviet power as the Hungarian uprising of 1956. The infuriating details of that story are here retailed calmly and unemotionally – the misjudgement by the Hungarians themselves about how far and how fast they should go, irresponsible broadcasting by Radio Free Europe, the timidity of the West which feared a war more than it respected the democratically expressed wishes of the people, the inexcusable delay of the United Nations in responding to the appeal of the Hungarian government for assistance, the bloodthirsty savagery of Soviet troops (some of whom thought they were in Berlin fighting capitalists and landlords). There are sad parallels with Czechoslovakia 1968, when the populace fought tanks with nothing more than their bare hands and their ingenuity, and there are many obvious lessons for the Baltics, and for Central and Eastern Europe today.

PSG

Age range: 11+

JAPANESE HISTORY

TAMES, Richard

Batsford, 1989, Hdbk, 0–7134–5930–1
Series: The Post-war World
Bibliography, contents list, index, 'Timeline',
'Sketches of important figures', black and white
line drawings and photographs

As usual with Tames, he has turned out yet another book which is well written and seen whole. A brief glance at previous history enables him to see the war defeat from both the Western and the Japanese points of view. He looks at the occupation of Japan, and its psychological and political consequences on the country. The apparent miracle of Japanese resurgence from 1965 to 1972 is explained, going back to the country's emergence from the economic opportunity provided by the Korean War, the political will which rebuilt the country's infrastructure and laid the foundations of manufacturing resurgence and export-led growth, the manpower planning and resourcing through the universities and technical training, the encouragement of backward regions so that they did not suffer in comparison with regions which were prospering. He documents the seven-year period of uncertainty following the oil shock in 1973. He then explores what was happening in the 1980s, and what the future holds. What emerges from the book as a whole is a sense of the Japanese, with their strengths and weaknesses.

PSG

Age range: 13–16

MIDDLE EAST HISTORY

EVANS, Michael

THE GULF CRISIS

Franklin Watts, 1988, Hdbk, 0–86313–727–X
Series: Issues
Contents list, index, colour line drawings and
black and white and colour photographs

This is a photo-journalistic history and analysis of the Gulf crisis during the decade leading up to 1988. The series aim is to identify problems and who and what caused them, and this work does just that. Iran under Ayatollah Khomeini (now dead) and Iraq under President Hussein went to war in 1980. Religion, politics and economics merge in an intricate way: Islamic fundamentalism inspired Iran, imperialistic ambitions Iraq, and the fact of oil gave them both power over other nations. Michael Evans, defence correspondent of *The Times*, gives his informed opinions: it is not a neutral position, challenging readers to ask who can afford to be neutral about such an issue. Superpower diplomacy is full of hypocrisy and self-interest. Vivid photography with superimposed images of key participants blend well with a forceful commentary in a variety of typefaces and occasional fact windows to make a thought-provoking research source explaining what young people will have seen on television.

SH

Age range: 10–13

HARPER, Paul

THE ARAB–ISRAELI ISSUE

Wayland, 1986, Hdbk, 1–85210–657–3
Series: Flashpoints
Bibliography, contents list, glossary, index, black
and white line drawings and photographs

In *The Arab–Israeli Issue*, Paul Harper deals with this protracted, highly complex conflict in an unbiased, straightforward way. He charts the history of Palestine, explaining how it is the Holy Land of three of the world's main religions and how Biblical promises and prophecies played an important part in engaging Western support for the establishment of the Jewish state. The book deals sympathetically with the Palestinians, who had their homeland invaded and confiscated, and with understanding for the Jews, who after centuries of oppression felt justified in their actions, led as they were by their religious belief that Palestine was their 'promised land'. The final chapters bring the conflict up to date, as far as 1985. This bitter struggle is reported in great detail, with the aid of many first-class black and white photographs and useful sketch maps, and provides excellent informative reading for G.C.S.E. students and young adults alike.

RG

Age range: 14–adult

HARPER, Paul

THE SUEZ CRISIS

Wayland, 1986, Hdbk, 0–85078–776–9
Series: Flashpoints
Bibliography, contents list, glossary, index, maps,
black and white line drawings and photographs

More than a dozen thought-provoking, well illustrated books have appeared in this series, each of which focuses upon a crisis in postwar history. This book gives an informative account of the Suez Crisis. The factual details are correct: but the way they are presented expresses a viewpoint – one with which, inevitably, not everyone will agree. For instance, was the Middle East policy of the United States as very even-handed as suggested here? It is easy, too, in hindsight, to dismiss the collusion of Britain, France and Israel in the invasion of Egypt as an act of aggression that was sheer folly, leading to the humiliation (nemesis) of Britain and France, the diversion of attention from the invasion of Hungary by Russia and a great fillip to Arab nationalism. It must be remembered that Nasser was regarded as a threat in 1956, just as Saddam Hussein is at present. Eden is deemed to have had poor judgement, without any mention of his poor health or the precarious political position of the UK, so dependent upon oil supplies from the Middle East.

The book ends appropriately with President Eisenhower's words spoken in the aftermath of the Suez Crisis: 'Should a nation which attacks and occupies foreign territory in the face of United Nations disapproval be allowed to impose conditions on its withdrawal?' (They have a new significance in view of the Gulf Crisis.)

WFW

Age range: 13–16

MESSENGER, Charles

THE MIDDLE EAST

Franklin Watts, 1987, Hdbk, 0–86313–606–0
Series: Conflict in the 20th Century

Bibliography, contents list, index, chronology, colour line drawings and black and white and colour photographs

For the peoples of the Middle East, war and violence have become a way of life. This is how defence writer Messenger concludes this meticulous analysis of politics and military action in the area. The imperialist legacy over Israel, and later superpower involvement, complicated an already volatile mix of nationalism, religious conflict, and terrorism. He sets current discussion in the news in a historical context for young people, making clear what all the groups and factions stand for and what motivates them, and how wars like Suez, Yom Kippur, and the Gulf War came about and what little they settled. Detailed military maps provide clear information about troop movements, and dramatic pictures of fighting provide atmosphere. No wonder the plight of Beirut is impossible to sort out. In a clear expository style, the history of this troubled area unfolds: it is difficult to see how young people can regard the Middle East as 'merely out there' after reading this book.

SH

Age range: 12–14

AFRICAN HISTORY

HARRIS, Sarah

SOUTH AFRICA

Dryad, 1988, Hdbk, 0–85219–724–1
Series: Timeline
Bibliography, contents list, glossary, index,
'Timeline', black and white line drawings and
photographs

Though this book has been somewhat overtaken by events, it remains excellent, because it provides a variety of historical evidence, linked by narrative, and poses questions which encourage the reader to think through the complex and subtle nature of historical evidence and its sources.

Essentially, Harris traces the development of South Africa from before the arrival of Europeans (a valuable corrective to many accounts of southern Africa which ignore the pre-white period) to 1986.

PSG

Age range: 13–16

ROWELL, Trevor

THE SCRAMBLE FOR AFRICA
(1870–1914)

Batsford, 1986, Hdbk, 0–7134–5200–5
Series: Living Through History
Bibliography, contents list, index, date list, maps,
black and white line drawings and photographs

In 1870, Europe controlled only 10 per cent of the African continent but, by 1900, over 90 per cent of it was carved up, with little regard for the African peoples. This book is a collection of biographies of people who lived through this period. The infamous scramble is told from the point of view of explorers, missionaries, empire builders, exploiters and the victims and survivors of many races.

There are many quotations from original sources and the illustrations, especially the rather faded photographs, are equally authentic. It is a useful and interesting sourcebook for project work, but its appeal is not immediate, for the absence of colour printing makes it seem, at first, rather drab.

JW

Age range: 11–16

AMERICAN HISTORY

EDWARDS, Richard

THE KOREAN WAR

Wayland, 1987, Hdbk, 1–85210–022–2
Series: Flashpoints
Bibliography, contents list, glossary, index, maps,
black and white line drawings and photographs

Each of the information books in this excellent series focuses on a crisis that has occurred since World War II. This book gives an account of the Korean War (1950–3), how the war began, and describes its aftermath. Korea was divided temporarily at the 38th parallel by the Great Powers after VJ-day but any nationalistic aspirations receded as the country became a battleground, and eventually two separate states, with opposing ideologies, were created from the one nation. The war-torn economy of South Korea was revived, chiefly by investment from Japan, so that once again that country exercises power in the land – power that is economic rather than imperial. Once again, Japan looks to Korea to provide cheap labour, to grow food, and as a market for its consumer goods.

WFW

Age range: 13–16

MACAULAY, David

MILL

Collins, 1984, Hdbk, 0–00–195545–4
Glossary, black and white line drawings

Though the title of this book is *Mill*, it is the story of several American cotton mills in the nineteenth century. American capital and British expertise joined together to build a whole succession of mills in Providence, Rhode Island – starting with a wooden building and water power, progressing to stone and brick buildings and culminating with one of the first textile mills to use steam power. With Macaulay's architectural drawings – meticulous as ever – of the constructions, there are background details of the lives of the people involved, and of contemporary events. Also, there are excerpts from letters and diaries belonging to families of the people mentioned. This human interest brings the story very much to life, and we are reminded how dangerous life was in the new industrial society. This is a book which will fascinate young historians.

JW

Age range: 9–16

VIKING HISTORY

RICHARD, Terence

THE VIKINGS

Wayland, 1986, Hdbk, 0–85078–708–4
Series: Living History
Bibliography, contents list, glossary, index,
'Things to do', colour line drawings and
photographs

This small colourful book gives a simple account of the Vikings which is suitable for young children. It tells of their voyages and longships, their raids and battles. The map showing the wide extent of their travels would be more useful if the countries were named. Much is made of the beautiful longships and there are instructions for making a simple model of one and collages, in the 'Things to do' pages. However, the Vikings are shown not only as warriors, but also as farmers with a full family life. There is a photograph of some fine jewellery and a brief mention of Valhalla and their Gods.

JW

Age range: 5–7

BIBLIOGRAPHY

◆

Bacon, Betty, 'The art of non-fiction', *Children's literature in education*, vol. 12, no. 1, Spring 1981, pp.3–14.

Dakin, Robert and Pain-Lewins, Helen, 'Non-fiction books and primary school logic work', *Education 3–13*, vol. 17, no. 1, March 1989, pp.49–55.

Fisher, Margery, *Matters of fact*, Brockhampton Press, 1972.

Glastonbury, Marion, 'What do you know?' *Books for keeps*, no. 36, January 1986, pp.6–7.

Griffiths, Anne, 'Needing to know – now' *Books for keeps*, no. 13, March 1982, pp.20–21.

Heeks, Peggy, *Ways of knowing*, Thimble Press, 1982.

Hull, Robert, 'Some fictions of non-fiction', *Books for keeps*, no. 60, January 1990, pp.16–19.

Paice, Shirley, 'Reading to learn', *English in education*, vol. 18, no. 1, Spring, 1984 pp.3–8.

Quicke, John, 'Information books and special needs awareness', *Books for keeps*, no. 64, September 1990, pp.20–21.

Stones, Rosemary, 'How the other two thirds live', *Books for keeps*, no. 30, January 1985, pp.4–6.

Triggs, Pat, 'Where do information books come from?' *Books for keeps*, no. 36, January 1986, pp.4–5.

Tucker, Nicholas, 'In praise of encyclopedias', *Books for your children*, vol. 23, no. 3, Autumn/Winter 1988, p.23.

Von Schweinitz, Eleanor 'Facing the facts', *Books for keeps*, no. 55, March 1989, pp.4–8.

Von Schweinitz, Eleanor, 'Information '89 and curriculum '90', *Books for keeps*, no. 61, March 1990, pp.20–21.

Von Schweinitz, Eleanor, 'Information books for four to six year olds', *Books for keeps*, no. 57, July 1989, pp.4–6.

Wilson, Jennifer 'Choosing information books', *Signal*, no. 39, September 1982, pp.163–168.

Wilson, Jennifer, 'Information books 1983: weeds or flowers? *Signal*, no. 44, May 1984, pp.112–119.

Wilson, Jennifer, ' "This is a good book!": choosing information books' in Griffiths, Vivien (ed.), *Buying books,* Youth Libraries Group, 1983, pp.21–28.

ANNUAL SELECTIONS

There are two regular annual selections which also include information books:

Children's Books of the Year, most recently selected by Julia Eccleshare and published by Andersen Press in conjunction with Book Trust. In 1990 the selection covered 87 information book titles.

Signal Selection of Children's Books, edited by Nancy Chambers and published by Thimble Press. In 1990 the selection covered 184 information book titles.

REVIEWING JOURNALS

There are three main reviewing journals for children's books and designed for professionals:

Books for Keeps is published six times per year. Details from 6 Brightfield Road, Lee, London SE12 8QF. In 1990 the number of information book titles reviewed was 84.

The Junior Bookshelf is published six times per year. Details from Marsh Hall, Thurstonland, Huddersfield HD4 6XB. In 1990 the number of information book titles reviewed was 124.

The School Librarian is published four times per year. Details from School Library Association, Liden Library, Barrington Close, Liden, Swindon, Wiltshire SN3 6HF. In 1990 the number of information book titles reviewed was 295.

AUTHOR AND PHOTOGRAPHER PROFILES

◆

The editor has chosen outstanding authors and photographers for inclusion in this section.

AUTHOR AND PHOTOGRAPHER PROFILES

ALTHEA BRAITHWAITE

Althea Braithwaite is one of the most experienced and prolific of children's information book writers. She began by publishing her own books (which she had also printed and bound, having taught herself to do this) when she had small children of her own and discovered that there did not appear to be available information material which was simple without being simplistic. Her Dinosaur titles now sell in great quantities and have won several book prizes. She begins by thoroughly researching a topic (quite often one of which she has little previous knowledge). She also believes in not being partisan; for example, when she won the Other Award for her book on trade unions, she shocked the selection panel when she informed them she was researching a book on the Stock Exchange! Her books, she feels, are intended to be 'useful'.

HEATHER COUPER

Heather Couper is a well known figure in the field of astronomy and is the past president of the British Astronomical Association (in succession to Patrick Moore). Having gained a degree in Astronomy and Physics, she went on to Oxford University to do research. In 1987 she won the *Times Educational Supplement* Senior Information Book Award. She appears regularly on TV and her direct style and personality have made an enormous contribution in making astronomy accessible to more young people, a feature which is also apparent in her books.

DAVID MACAULAY

David Macaulay was born in Burton upon Trent but when he was eleven, his family moved to the United States. He was helped to feel less of an outsider when he showed his drawing talents. This developed into a keen interest in architecture which he studied at Rhode Island School of Design. However, he did not want to practise architecture on graduating and friends suggested he tried illustration. He did freelance illustration for a while and then submitted a book about gargoyles. His editor felt that the cathedral which he had illustrated as a background for these gargoyles was of far more interest and this book on cathedrals was the first of his fascinatingly accurate guides to how buildings have been constructed which help to make history alive for so many young people.

RUTH THOMSON

Ruth Thomson was born in Birmingham and educated in England and France where she gained a degree in sociology. She began her career in children's books with the Macdonald *Starters* series. She has also worked with ILEA. She is the winner of several book awards, including the Other Award and the *Times Educational Supplement* junior information book award. She has always had a keen interest in research but she also feels that a vital and exciting part of her work is in meeting and observing people and in being allowed access to places not generally available to the public. She feels her aim is to produce books which will encourage children to want to look further and to question and discover the world for themselves.

CHRIS FAIRCLOUGH

By the age of 25, Chris Fairclough had had 49 jobs! For the next three years, however, he was on a course at the West Surrey College of Art and Design where he determined to become a photo-journalist. His first assignments were for Mary Glasgow educational publications and it was from this that he decided to work exclusively in children's books. He believes strongly that the photographer should be involved in the design and layout of the finished book, an attention to detail which has helped him earn several book awards. He has now started his own picture library which includes his own and others' photographs.

BARRIE WATTS

Barrie Watts is renowned for his nature photography. He originally worked as an auditor but decided at the age of 27 to concentrate on photography. He feels that education of young people on conservation and nature is vital for the survival of natural heritage. He believes nature photography can play a vital role in this by informing in a factual, interesting and visually stimulating way.

AUTHOR INDEX

♦

TITLE INDEX

♦

SUBJECT INDEX

◆